Deaf and Hard of Hearing Learners With Disabilities

This volume offers foundational information and research-based strategies for meeting the needs of deaf and hard of hearing learners with disabilities. The disabilities covered in this volume include developmental delays, autism spectrum disorder, intellectual and learning disabilities, deafblindness, emotional and behavioral disorders, attention deficit hyperactivity disorder, and a variety of high incidence syndromes. Contributors examine the literature within each disability category, share best practices, and consider demographics/characteristics, intervention/identification, placement, communication/language, psychosocial issues, assistive technologies/accommodations, assessments, and transition/post-secondary outcomes.

Each chapter begins with learning objectives and concludes with discussion questions and a resource list. *Deaf and Hard of Hearing Learners with Disabilities* is an essential book for courses at the undergraduate and graduate level, and in workshops and webinars for in-service teachers, professionals, and families.

Caroline Guardino is a Professor of Exceptional and Deaf Education at the University of North Florida in Jacksonville, Florida.

Joanna E. Cannon is an Associate Professor in the Department of Educational and Counselling Psychology, and Special Education, and is coordinator of the Education of the Deaf and Hard of Hearing graduate program at the University of British Columbia in Vancouver, Canada.

Peter V. Paul is a Professor of Special Education, emphasis on d/Deaf Education, at the Ohio State University. Paul is the current editor of the *American Annals of the Deaf.*

Deaf and Hard of Hearing Learners With Disabilities

Foundations, Strategies, and Resources

Edited by Caroline Guardino,
Joanna E. Cannon, and Peter V. Paul

Routledge
Taylor & Francis Group

NEW YORK AND LONDON

Cover Image: Getty Images/DrAfter123

First published 2022
by Routledge
605 Third Avenue, New York, NY 10158

and by Routledge
4 Park Square, Milton Park, Abingdon, Oxon, OX14 4RN

Routledge is an imprint of the Taylor & Francis Group, an informa business

Library of Congress Cataloging-in-Publication Data
A catalog record for this book has been requested

ISBN: 978-1-032-17162-3 (hbk)
ISBN: 978-1-032-15564-7 (pbk)
ISBN: 978-1-003-25205-4 (ebk)

DOI: 10.4324/9781003252054

Typeset in Garamond Pro
by Apex CoVantage, LLC

For support material please visit: www.routledge.com/9781032155647

This book is dedicated to my mother, Dolores A. Guardino
(January 23, 1942–August 7, 2020), who unequivocally supported
every effort in which I set my mind.
I love and miss you Mom.

Contents

Contents

Preface

Peter V. Paul

We the editors (Guardino, Cannon, & Paul) believe that this is a user-friendly timely book that synthesizes existing research and provides instructional strategies and resources for addressing the needs of d/Deaf and hard of hearing learners with disabilities and their families. Covering this broad diverse cohort adequately is a "tall order;" however, we are fortunate to have had the opportunity to work and consult with a number of experts, particularly the contributors for this volume. With this level of expertise, we hope that our readers will consider this book to be well-balanced, meticulous, thorough, and, of course, useful.

We the editors have extensive professional experiences in working with individuals who are d/Deaf and hard of hearing, ranging from teaching in PreK-12 settings to coordinating teacher-education/deaf education university programs. I (Paul) have this experience personally, or you might say "as a insider", given my bilateral profound hearing loss, now ameliorated by bilateral cochlear implants. In addition, the information in this book touches another personal aspect: I am the father of a son who has Down syndrome and autism (autism spectrum disorders), and our co-editor (Cannon), is a parent of a son who is deaf with disabilities.

This long overdue book is an elaboration of a special issue that was published in the American Annals of the Deaf (see, for example, Guardino & Cannon, 2015). As mentioned previously, the focus is on d/Deaf and hard of hearing students who have one or more disabilities. In the introductory chapter (Chapter 1), the authors state that it has been a challenge to estimate the incidence and prevalence of various cohorts. Estimates of the entire group of individuals who are DWD range from about 35% to more than 50%. Whatever the incidence or prevalence figure, this commands detailed attention to the various subgroups of this unique population with complex intense needs—and we believe that the contributors have accomplished this task.

Professionals and families desire, at least, strategies—whether evidence-based, creative, or facilitative—for addressing the needs of individuals who are DWD. There are eight chapters covering diverse cohorts with developmental delays (Chapter 2), autism spectrum disorders (Chapter 3), disabilities due to genetic causes (Chapter 4), intellectual disabilities (Chapter 5), deafblindness (Chapter 6), learning disabilities (Chapter 7), emotional and behavioral challenges (Chapter 8), and those with attention deficit hyperactivity disorders (Chapter 9). The introductory chapter (Chapter 1) and the final chapter (Chapter 10) might be viewed as "book ends"—so to speak.

Defining or describing formally what it means to be, for example, d/Deaf and hard of hearing with a learning disability or d/Deaf and hard of hearing with attention deficit hyperactivity disorder or, even the general cohort of DWD, is, without a doubt, challenging, given the meager research and available valid and reliable data and procedures. Nevertheless, to best serve children and adolescents, it is important to understand the characteristics and challenges of a specific DWD cohort. Thus, the contributors to this volume provide valuable insights on an impressive array of constructs such as demography, identification, placement, language/communication, psychosocial development, intervention, technology, assessment, and transition to postsecondary domains. Readers should appreciate the discussions of, for example, familycentered practices, and adaptations and accommodations to develop what can be labeled as a strengths-based curriculum and optimal individualized educational plans.

The introductory chapter (Chapter 1) sets the tone for the rest of the book. The authors discuss constructs such as an asset-based approach, The Radical Middle (TRM), and critical educational frameworks that can be applied to the education of students who are DWD. The authors state that the two major purposes of the book are to present an overview of existing literature and to delineate effective strategies and practices. Specifically, this chapter argues that the focus should be on the strengths of individuals—which is the essence of an asset-based approach. This approach should not only be the foundation for the development of instructional practices, but also should be the basis for scaffolding instruction. The assetbased approach leads to the application of important instructional frameworks such as the Universal Design for Learning (UDL) and tiered systems of support such as Response to Intervention (RtI). Undergirding this approach (and others) is TRM construct, which encourages professionals to be creative and to work together to solve problems, rather than to debate the merits of specific instructional approaches.

The final chapter (Chapter 10) reiterates salient points covered throughout the book, particularly in the eight chapters on cohorts of individuals who are DWD. Despite challenges with, for example, instruction, assessment, and planning, this chapter highlights common themes related to the overall asset-based approach. This provides the foundation for the authors' construct titled "Nested Cycle of Support," which elaborates the issues associated with identification, assessment, planning and placement, and instruction. Educators are encouraged to collaborate and engage in a continuous self-examination of strategies and ideas to improve their practices and, thus, to better meet the complex needs of individuals who are DWD. The final chapter also circles back to the concepts of UDL, TRM, and RtI (or tiers of support) as salient tenets for the development and application of effective practices. The last sections of the chapter provide recommendations for stakeholders such as practitioners, parents, and researchers/scholars.

What makes this book even more attractive and useful is the list of learning objectives at the beginning of each chapter, which should focus and guide the attention of the reader. At the end of each chapter is a list of resources (e.g., organizations, websites, etc.) that can be consulted for additional information and insights. For those of us in professional preparation programs there are discussion questions, activities, quiz banks, and chapter presentations (see also, the separate instructor's manual) to inflame the intellect of students—hopefully, to inspire these individuals to become advocates and, of course, proficient professionals.

This book is an attempt to develop an up-to-date single comprehensive resource for working with individuals who are DWD. We the editors believe that this is a good start for assisting families and professionals. Our hope is that the information in the book can be a springboard for producing significant improvements in the educational and social lives of individuals who are d/Deaf and hard of hearing with disabilities.

REFERENCE

Guardino, C., & Cannon, J. E. (2015). Theory, research, and practice for students who are deaf and hard of hearing with disabilities: Addressing the challenges from birth to postsecondary education. *American Annals of the Deaf, 160*(4), 347-355.

Acknowledgments

We are humbled and honored to have worked with 21 experts regarding learners who are d/Deaf or hard of hearing with disabilities (DWD). With your dedication and commitment, we have helped shape the future for students who are DWD and their families.

This text would not be as thorough, well-balanced, and complete without the review and edits from our external reviewers: Drs. Jennifer Beal, Jessica Bergeron, Vicki Knight, Christina Rivera, Jessica Trussell, and Jenna Voss. We appreciate your time and careful analysis of each chapter, which helped to ensure this book acknowledges and respects the spectrum of professionals and students who constitute the field of d/Deaf and hard of hearing (d/Dhh) education.

Furthermore, we had the great fortune to have assistance from stellar graduate researchers: Eun Young Kwon from the University of British Columbia, as well as Arien Peppers, Emily Lopes, Kaela Raper, and Morgan Green from the University of North Florida. Your contribution to the review of every manuscript, including APA formatting, assisting with discussion questions, and editing content within the instructor's manual, greatly contributed to the final version of the text. A special thanks to Dr. Bonita Squires, postdoctoral fellow at the University of British Columbia for her contribution to the index. From this experience and all others in your graduate studies, we know you will continue to blaze a path of leadership with compassion, particularly for those with disabilities. Thank you for approaching each assigned task with the thirst to learn, understand, improve, and succeed. And thank you for allowing us to be part of your professional journey!

A special thank you to Sara Schley from the Rochester Institute of Technology who spearheaded a project involving professional development using Universal Design for Learning. Dr. Caroline Guardino has worked closely with Sara and her team, which helped to inform the introduction chapter of this text. In addition, Sara's work highlighted the various data sets from which we were able to gather prevalence rates of students who are d/Dhh.

I, Caroline, would like to recognize my family. I am grateful to my children, Avalon and Roman, who have been incredibly flexible and supportive during this process. Thank you for supporting me when I worked through dinnertime and gave you goodnight hugs from my computer. I love you both very much. And to my husband and eternal partner, Gerard Reyes, I am grateful for your unconditional support and never-ending love. Thank you!

Finally, we want to thank all the professionals working with students who are DWD, their families, and the students who are DWD themselves. *To the professionals*: You have been resourceful in your practice and patient in your professionalism. We encourage you to engage in action-based research, so collaboratively we can move the field forward with data-based decisions supported with your professional insight. *To the parents*: You are an essential piece of the puzzle that helps the field of deaf education become better and stronger at serving students who are DWD. As you believe in your child, please continue to believe in us. We are eager to work with you and understand your daily challenges and successes. Without your contribution, the puzzle will remain unfinished. And last but not least, *to the students who are DWD*: This textbook is inspired by the fact that you can and will find success, as defined by you. We are committed to understanding what is best for your overall development: big or small . . . we realize your potential!

Contributors

Sarah B. Ammerman
Harriet and J. David
  Oppenheimer Endowed
  Associate Professor in Deaf
  Education and Hearing Science
University of Texas Health Science
  Center
San Antonio, TX

Brooke A. Barnhill
Doctoral Candidate
University of Utah
Salt Lake City, UT

Stacey Jones Bock
Professor
Illinois State University
Normal, IL

Christy M. Borders
Professor
Illinois State University
Director
Cecilia J. Lauby Teacher
  Education Center
Normal, IL

Susan M. Bruce
Professor and Chairperson
  of Teacher Education
Boston College
Boston, MA

Joanna E. Cannon
Associate Professor
University of British Columbia
Vancouver, BC, Canada

Stephanie W. Cawthon
Professor and Director
Deaf and Hard of Hearing Institute
Meadows Center for Preventing
  Educational Risk
University of Texas at Austin
Austin, TX

Ivette Cejas
Director
Family Support Services
Associate Professor
University of Miami
Miami, FL

Amanda Clements
Teacher of Deaf/Hard of Hearing
Cobb County School District
Marietta, GA

Caroline Guardino
Professor
University of North Florida
Jacksonville, FL

Rebecca L. W. Jackson
Project Coordinator
Preparation About Collaborative
   Teaching (PACT) Grant
University of Minnesota
Minneapolis, MN

John Luckner
Professor
University of Northern Colorado
Greeley, CO

Pamela Luft
Professor
Kent State University
Kent, OH

Alex Mestres
Educational Specialist
University of Miami
Miami, FL

Catherine Nelson
Associate Professor
University of Utah
Salt Lake City, UT

Jenna A. Nelson
Outbreak Epidemiologist
Nicklaus Children's Hospital
   Research Institute
Miami, FL

Nancy Norman
Professor
Vancouver Island University
Nanaimo, BC, Canada

Peter V. Paul
Professor
Ohio State University
Columbus, OH

Kristi M. Probst
Initiative Lead, Interveners and
   Qualified Personnel
National Center on
   Deaf-Blindness
Hortonville, WI

Alexandra L. Quittner
Senior Scientist
Nicklaus Children's Hospital
   Research Institute
Miami, FL

Natalia Rohatyn-Martin
Assistant Professor
MacEwan University
Edmonton, AB, Canada

Christina M. Sarangoulis
Clinical Research Coordinator
University of Miami
Miami, FL

Brent Stutzman
Learning Behavior Specialist
Chicago Home Tutor
Chicago, IL

Blane A. Trautwein
Professor
University of Texas Health Science
   Center
Houston, TX

1

Approaches and Frameworks That Support Students Who Are d/Deaf or Hard of Hearing With Disabilities

Caroline Guardino and Joanna E. Cannon

Learning Objectives

Readers will:

- Recognize several sources that report prevalence rates of students who are d/Deaf or hard of hearing (d/Dhh) with a disability or disabilities (DWD).
- Gain information regarding the history of publications on students who are DWD, which have led to the current text.
- Define an asset-based approach and discuss how that perspective can benefit students who are DWD, their family members, as well as professionals working with these individuals.
- Understand The Radical Middle (TRM) perspective that encourages professionals to possess an open-minded perspective when working with one another, individuals who are DWD, and their families.
- Examine educational frameworks and explain how these systems can be applied when educating students who are DWD.

DOI: 10.4324/9781003252054-1

An individual who is d/Deaf or hard of hearing (d/Dhh) with a disability or disabilities (DWD) is defined within this book as a student who is d/Dhh and has one or more disabilities (e.g., learning disability, autism, attention deficit hyperactivity disorder [ADHD]). Deafness is viewed by some as a disability but not by others (Padden & Humphries, 2005). We respect both opinions and recognize the unique academic, social, emotional, and/or behavioral needs across both deafness and all disability areas. Therefore, we use the overarching term "DWD" throughout the text and within individual chapters (e.g., d/Dhh-ADHD) to remind readers that each d/Dhh learner requires unique assessment and instructional planning to maximize their potential.

The authors and editors have collaboratively strived to use inclusive, asset-based terminology with consideration of multiple perspectives across the vast field of educating students who are d/Dhh. Examples throughout the chapters in this book include using both "deaf" and "Deaf" in the abbreviation "d/Dhh" to include all identities. The use of "loss" is utilized to describe audiological/medical terms within some chapters, and "hearing levels" are used in place of "loss" in others. "Identification" is used in place of "diagnosis" (when applicable); "received a cochlear implant" in place of "implanted"; and "strategies" or "practices" in place of "intervention" (when applicable). Terminology commonly used in other areas of special education is used intermittently (e.g., visual impairment, disability), with the chapter context guiding the varying use of terms (e.g., the chapter on syndromes contains more medical jargon).

The purpose of this introductory chapter is to (a) discuss national data sets used to determine prevalence rates of learners who are DWD; (b) review select comprehensive, historical publications regarding students who are DWD; (c) call for professionals and parents/guardians to use an asset-based approach when working with learners who are DWD; and (d) examine promising frameworks utilized in education to address the diverse needs of learners.

National Data Set Reports

Individuals who are DWD constitute approximately 40%–50% of the general population of learners who are d/Dhh (Gallaudet Research Institute [GRI], 1999–2011). This statistic is consistent with parent-reported data from the National Longitudinal Transition Study-2 (NLTS2). Using the NLTS2 data set, Leppo et al. (2014) noted that half of the parents (310/620) who completed the survey reported that their children were d/Dhh with a disability or disabilities. The Special Education Elementary Longitudinal Study (SEELS; Marder, 2009) also shows that school personnel reported at least half of the students who were d/Dhh in their classrooms had at least one disability (Marder, 2009).

Reports From Teachers of d/Dhh Students

A national survey of nonresidential schools and programs with students who are d/Dhh was conducted to identify more students in mainstream and inclusive settings (Schley et al., 2013). Of the 469 schools that completed the survey, 45.7% reported a range of 1–5 d/Dhh students in each setting. Approximately 51.4% of the school programs reported that at least one of their d/Dhh students had a disability or multiple disabilities. More specifically, 38% of the programs reported that their d/Dhh students had a specific learning disability (SLD), 27% had emotional disturbances, 23% had orthopedic disabilities (e.g., cerebral palsy), and 46% of the learners had ADHD.

Guardino (2015) conducted another national survey of 264 teachers and other professionals, with more than half of the respondents (53.1%) reporting working with students who are DWD. Further analysis revealed that teachers reported a much higher incidence rate than in the data collected by the GRI. For example, the GRI (2013) data reported that 7.2% of school-aged d/Dhh children have a learning disability (LD). Whereas, the teachers in Guardino's (2015) survey suspected that 28.8% of their d/Dhh students had LDs, a stark 21.6% greater than the incidence rate reported by the GRI. This is consistent across every disability category, with teachers suspecting a greater number of students having disabilities than the statistics captured by the GRI data (see Figure 3 in Guardino, 2015, for a breakdown of contrasting data for each disability area). Although teachers recognize that students who are DWD have needs beyond deafness, the education system often labels the student as qualifying for special education services based upon their "primary" disability label, namely, "deaf/hard of hearing" or "hearing impaired," yet not necessarily their "secondary" disability.

The challenge for parents and professionals lies in the special education system because most schools require a disability label for the student to receive services from educational professionals who have expertise in that disability. Wagner and Blackorby (2002) summarize that parents and educators recognize that a disability(ies) (i.e., LD, ADHD, or emotional and behavioral disorders [EBD]) often causes a greater impact on the learners' ability to make gains across one or more developmental domains (e.g., academic, social-emotional). Yet, the system may not recognize that "secondary" disability. Wagner and Blackorby (2002) state:

> Even low-incidence conditions, such as hearing and vision impairments and autism, were reported for students in every primary disability category. This prevalence of additional disabilities clearly reveals a complexity in the concept of disability that the primary disability category label cannot help but mask. (p. 5)

In essence, students who are DWD need services that meet all their needs regardless of the label(s) the system may or may not provide.

Multiple national reports and surveys completed by parents, teachers, and other professionals serving learners who are DWD reveal that at least half of the population of d/Dhh students have a disability(ies). This demands a continued need to conduct research and compile resources to better serve this population. First, we examine the historical context of the education of learners who are DWD over the past 4 decades.

A JOURNEY TO . . . THE PRESENT

Nearly 40 years ago, a federally funded project by the U.S. Department of Education, Office of Special Education, issued a report that became the first comprehensive publication with a focus on DWD students (Nowell, 1980). Written by a variety of authors specializing in working with students who are DWD, the eight chapters reviewed service delivery models, psychosocial and audiological assessment, structured curriculum, communication modes, language board (similar to the more current picture exchange communication system [PECS]; Bondy & Frost, 1994;

Frost & Bondy, 2002), family involvement, and an evaluation of programs for students who are DWD.

Two years later, in 1982, Tweedie and Shroyer coedited and helped write a textbook titled *The Multihandicapped Hearing Impaired: Identification and Instruction*. This text contains 20 chapters across four topic areas: (a) understanding the population, (b) providing comprehensive programming, (c) developing curriculum, and (d) developing language and communication strategies. The chapters were written by a wide range of professionals, all with expertise in working with students who are DWD.

In 1988, Prickett and Duncan wrote the book *Coping With the Multi-Handicapped Hearing Impaired: A Practical Approach*. The authors urge professionals in the field of deaf education to be "creative" with their educational approach to teaching students who are DWD. The text spans six chapters on the following topics: (a) an education program for students with EBD, (b) classroom management, (c) home and school support for deaf physically "handicapped" children, (d) building the language of infants and toddlers who are deafblind (DB), (e) a case study of a deaf boy with autism, and (f) vocational training for "multihandicapped" deaf secondary students. The chapters were written by teachers and directors of various deaf education programs across the United States.

Following a 20-year gap, Guardino (2008) wrote a comprehensive literature review, discussing the identification and placement of students who are DWD. The review was written across the following disability areas: (a) autism spectrum disorder (ASD), (b) EBD, (c) ADHD, and (d) "mental retardation" (which is now referred to as "intellectual disabilities" [ID]). The review also revealed the need for both better access to information and solutions to challenges that professionals and families face regularly.

Most recently, in 2015, Guardino and Cannon coedited a special issue of the *American Annals of the Deaf*, with an emphasis on the theoretical models, research, and practices employed with children and adolescents who are DWD (Guardino & Cannon, 2015). The special issue examined students who are DWD across the span of their educational progression. The six articles begin with an analysis of early intervention services and then address the major issues of communication and language, assessment, transition, and teacher preparation. The special issue provided up-to-date, comprehensive information to address the long-standing lack of literature and resources that focus on this unique population of learners. The editors and authors of this textbook elaborate upon the special issue with the intent to increase the dissemination of information specific to students who are DWD.

The purpose of the present work is to provide a resource for professionals and families working with these individuals. The goal of this book is twofold. First, to present an overview of the existing literature in the field of deaf education specific to students who have a disability or disabilities. Second, and most importantly, to provide valuable strategies that can be easily implemented when working with these individuals.

Within this text, eight chapters cover the following disabilities: at-risk/developmental delay, ASD, syndromes, ID, DB, LD, EBD, and ADHD. High-ability learners (Lo et al., 2018) or those who are gifted and are d/Dhh are not included in this textbook because of the dearth of research (Belcastro, 2004; Blough et al., 1999; Buisson & Salgo, 2012; Pollard & Howze, 1981; Whiting et al., 1980). These eligibility areas were chosen because they coincide with the definitions/criteria a student must meet to receive special education services. Thus, this text is an educational resource for pre- and in-service teachers, parents, and other professionals working with students who are DWD in early intervention to postsecondary school settings.

The editors and authors note that the terminology used in the definitions/criteria of the Individuals With Disabilities Education Act (IDEA) is not necessarily culturally affirmative. Members of the Deaf community may see deafness as part of their identity rather than a medical diagnosis (Padden & Humphries, 2005). This may be particularly important when considering how individuals who are DWD identify themselves.

The authors of each chapter first examine literature within the field of deaf education, and in most cases, because of the dearth of research within this field, they extend their investigation into the broader field of special education. Research from special education provides helpful strategies to use with students who are DWD; however, investigations specific to this population are imperative to accurately understand what is most effective for these learners. The authors cautiously extrapolate from the special education literature, embedding their expertise regarding d/Dhh learners throughout each chapter, noting the unique language and cognitive aspects these learners may experience. Each chapter examines demographics, characteristics, practices, identification, placement, communication, language, psychosocial issues, assistive technologies, accommodations, assessments, and transitions to postsecondary settings for students who are d/Dhh and their respective disabilities. Each chapter concludes with a list of resources such as organizations, websites, and additional literature that may be beneficial to the readership. Discussion questions are then provided for those utilizing this resource as a textbook in professional preparation programs at colleges and universities or in workshops for in-service teachers or families.

PROMISING APPROACHES

Professionals working with students who are DWD should utilize an asset-based approach, focusing on what the individual can do as the foundation for instruction and using these strengths to scaffold instruction. Also, an asset-based approach enables professionals to create accessible educational learning environments through the use of frameworks such as the Universal Design for Learning (UDL; Center for Applied Special Technology [CAST], 2011; Rose & Gravel, 2010) and tiered systems of support (Fuchs et al., 2008; Hoover et al., 2018).

An Asset-Based Approach

When we believe an individual can learn, they will. An asset-based approach examines a learner from the perspective of what they can accomplish, emphasizing the individual's strengths and assets. This requires open-mindedness to the needs of the learner over the bias that professionals and caregivers may experience. Acknowledging our biases (e.g., cultural, educational, communication modality/language) allows us to more objectively offer advice in the best interests of the individual learner and their family.

It is imperative that professionals use an open-minded and asset-based approach when working with students who are DWD, as these learners have complex needs that may not be supported with traditional methods used with d/Dhh learners without disabilities. The editors suggest merging the asset-based approach with The Radical Middle (TRM; Easterbrooks &

Maiorana-Basas, 2015) perspective. TRM perspective calls for professionals to work together to meet individual student needs, rather than convoluting what is best by debating communication choices and educational options. Simply stated, this merger will result in a "try everything" approach, wherein assessment, identification, placement, and instruction are a result of unbiased intervention based upon the assets and potential of the learner.

By capitalizing on learners' strengths and interests, professionals assist students who are DWD in realizing their abilities and building their self-confidence to help them approach and master new skills. Professionals implementing the asset-based approach do not assume a learner's needs based upon prescribed standards or models of achievement. Instead, professionals use this approach to harness the aptitudes of the student, scaffold learning, and foster positive and continual growth.

An asset-based approach aligns with Vygotsky's zone of proximal development (ZPD) described within his sociocultural theory (1978; for further information on Vygotsky's sociocultural theory and DWD learners, refer to Guardino & Cannon, 2015) as well as the cultural model of deafness (Padden & Humphries 2005). Professionals, or the "more knowledgeable other," use the learner's ZPD to determine developmental strengths across all domains (social, emotional, behavioral, and academic) and utilize this information to incrementally teach new skills by scaffolding the task. The ZPD also provides subjectivity, which allows the learner and "more knowledgeable other" to come to an agreed-upon understanding of a concept through scaffolding. The ZPD targets the difference between the learner's development level and their level of potential to increase socialization and cognition (Easterbrooks & Baker, 2002; Vygotsky, 1978). The foundation of the cultural model of deafness is also asset-based as individuals do not view deafness as a disability and have their own language, American Sign Language, and are therefore bilingual (Padden & Humphries, 2005).

Researchers and theorists such as Lev Vygotsky have adopted frameworks that align with the principles of UDL (discussed in the next section). The fundamental aspects of ZPD and UDL, while considering the facets of Deaf culture, guide professionals to implement evidence-based strategies to account for the variation of different learning styles inevitable in all classrooms, especially those with students who are d/Dhh. We invited the authors of each chapter in this book to write from an asset-based perspective.

Educational Frameworks

The field of education offers frameworks to guide professionals and parents when working with students who are DWD: UDL, Response to Intervention (RTI), and Multitiered Systems of Support (MTSS). These frameworks offer a systematic approach to planning interventions and instruction to meet the diverse needs of *all* learners, not only those with exceptionalities.

Universal Design for Learning

UDL is a framework that promotes an asset-based approach to meet the needs of all learners through accessible environments. This framework is built on the foundation that all students have individualized learning styles and capabilities, navigating their learning environment through a variety of means. UDL provides a promising framework for strengthening the accessibility of learning environments by utilizing differentiated instruction techniques. These techniques encourage flexibility and innovation to meet the needs of diverse learners, which is particularly important for students who are DWD.

More specifically, research shows that integrating a UDL framework creates more supportive and accessible learning environments for those with disabilities to increase their participation, engagement, and learning success (Coyne et al., 2012). The three principles of UDL include providing: (a) multiple means of representation, (b) multiple means of action and expression, and (c) multiple means of engagement (see Table 1.1; CAST, 2011; Rose & Gravel, 2010). These principles ensure that educational goals, materials, methods, and assessments are differentiated to meet the individualized needs of learners (Hartmann, 2011; Rose & Gravel, 2010).

TABLE 1.1 UDL Principles and Guidelines With Examples

Principle 1: Provide multiple means of representation *How is the information presented to the learner? Have you customized the display of information? Did you use alternative formats for auditory and visual information in examples? Did you provide content at varying levels of challenge and relevance?*	
Guidelines	Examples
1. Provide options for perception	• Alternating size for text, images, graphs, and tables • Contrast of background and text • Color coding for emphasis • Utilizing digital formats, graphic organizers, color coding • Adjusting volume and rate of speech • Providing info through multiple sensory inputs • Adjusting speed and timing of video, sounds, or simulations • Adjusting layout of material • Adjusting type of font
2. Provide options for language models	• Preteach concepts and connect to background knowledge • Use alternative visual formats with text descriptions • Highlight root words • Embed hyperlinks or footnotes to further explanations of concepts • Provide explanations of unfamiliar concepts in a text • Provide multiple examples of cultural and language models • Provide explicit connections between print concepts and visual representations

(Continued)

TABLE 1.1 (*Continued*)

Guidelines	Examples
3. Provide options for comprehension	• Use visual imagery, concept anchoring, or concept mastery routines • Use advanced organizers such as KWL (Know, Want-to-Know, Learned) or concept maps • Preteach via modeling • Design lessons to increase information processing skills • Connect concepts through analogies/metaphors • Provide explicit cross-curricular connections

Principle 2: Provide multiple means of action and expression
How does the learner express what they know?
What is your plan for accepting varied response formats?
How will learners access tools and assistive technology
to provide flexibility in expression?

Guidelines	Examples
4. Provide options for physical action	• Nonpen/pencil response formats • Switches, joysticks, keyboards, etc. • Alternative keyboards • Customized overlays for touch screen or keyboard • Accessible software
5. Provide options for expressive skills and fluency	• Formats include text, speech, drawing, illustration, design, film, music, dance/movement, visual art, sculpture, or video • Virtual or physical manipulatives such as blocks, 3D models, or base-10 blocks • Social media and online tools, such as discussion forums, chats, website design, annotation tools, storyboards, comic strips, animated presentations

(*Continued*)

TABLE 1.1 (*Continued*)

Guidelines	Examples
	• Spellcheckers, grammar checkers, word prediction software • Text-to-speech software (voice recognition), human dictation, recording • Calculators, graphing calculators, geometric sketchpads, or preformatted graph paper • Sentence starters or sentence strips • Story webs, outlining, or concept mapping tools • Computer-aided design, music notation (writing) software, or mathematical notation software
6. Provide options for executive function	• Scaffold lower-level skills to reduce executive processing • Scaffold higher-level skills to enhance development • Embed prompts for categorizing • Provide checklists and guides for note-taking • Provide questions to guide self-monitoring and reflection • Document progress through before/after photos, graphs, or charts showing progress over time, process portfolios • Provide self-reflection templates • Provide differentiated models of self-assessment strategies, including role-playing, video reviews, peer feedback • Provide assessments, checklists, rubrics, and student work/performance examples

(*Continued*)

TABLE 1.1 *(Continued)*

Principle 3: Provide multiple means of engagement
Why is the learner engaged in the topic?
Have you provided a variety of avenues to comprehension?
Have you provided opportunities for choice and goal setting?

Guidelines	Examples
7. Provide options for recruiting interest	• Provide choice in challenge level, rewards, context, content, information-gathering tools, graphics, and design of layouts, sequence/timing for tasks • Plan for participation, exploration, and experimentation of learners in all classroom activities and tasks • Initiate learners to set academic and behavioral goals • Connect activities and information to learners' lives, use imagination to solve problems, and make sense of complex ideas through creative means • Ensure that tasks are culturally and linguistically responsive, are age and ability appropriate, contain authentic and clear learning outcomes, and invite self-reflection • Establish an asset-based classroom climate • Increase predictability of activities and transitions by using charts, calendars, schedules, visible timers, cues, class routines, alerts, and previews to prepare for changes • Maximize the unexpected by varying the following in daily routines: the level of sensory stimulation, background noise, visual stimulation, noise buffers, number of items presented, pace, length, breaks, or sequence • Include all participants in all class discussions

(Continued)

TABLE 1.1 (*Continued*)

Guidelines	Examples
8. Provide options for sustaining effort and persistence	• Direct learners to develop goals and monitor progress in multiple ways • Use technology scheduling and reminder tools • Visually represent outcomes • Differentiate instruction and assessment to focus on process, effort, and improvement • Create cooperative learning groups with clear roles and expectations • Implement school-wide positive behavior support programs • Establish peer tutors and a community of learners • Provide timely, specific, substantive, and informative feedback that models how to incorporate evaluation
9. Provide options for self-regulation	• Explicitly address self-regulation techniques in the classroom • Provide prompts, reminders, guides, rubrics, checklists, coaches, and mentors to aid in goal setting • Provide differentiated instruction that includes modeling, scaffolding, and feedback to manage frustration, seek emotional support, develop coping skills, handle phobias, and use an asset-based mindset • Use role-play or real-life situations to develop coping skills • Teach academic and behavioral progress-monitoring skills in accessible formats such as charts, tables, and templates

Note. For details, see the following references: CAST (2011); Coyne et al. (2012); Hartmann (2011); Rose and Gravel (2010). UDL = Universal Design for Learning.

The three principles of UDL were developed because of their common theoretical and research bases in education, psychology, cognitive science, and neuroscience. In the most simplistic form, scientists divide the brain into three learning regions: (1) the posterior cortex is responsible for pattern recognition; (2) the frontal cortex manages motor and executive functioning; and (3) the medial region of the nervous system regulates motor and executive capabilities (Rose & Gravel, 2010). UDL principles align with these learning regions wherein the means of representation are managed by the posterior region, the means of action and expression are controlled by the frontal region, and the means of engagement are regulated by the medial region; thus, the framework addresses the overall needs of every learner.

The UDL principles, guidelines, and examples (see Table 1.1) can be differentiated for learners' academic, social, or behavioral levels. The guidelines of the UDL framework match effective pedagogy and are examples of long-standing best practices in the field of educating learners who are d/Dhh and those who are acquiring English as an additional language. The guidelines to implement UDL include (a) comprehension, (b) executive function, and (c) self-regulation, encompassing the optimal goals for all learners. In essence, effective comprehension skills allow learners to use and apply strategies across concepts to continue to build their cognition. Moreover, the UDL guidelines of executive function and self-regulation assist learners in planning and monitoring progress on tasks and allow them autonomy in selecting tasks that match their areas of interest (self-regulation is discussed further in Chapter 8 by Cejas et al., 2022; and Chapter 9 by Norman et al., 2022).

The building blocks of UDL emphasize scaffolding instruction, using technology, and implementing evidence-based and best practices. Coyne et al. (2012) noted, "Scaffolding is a balance between obtaining and maintaining a child's engagement, simplifying the task when needed, providing confidence for risk-taking, marking relevant information, and demonstrating potential solutions" (p. 164). The use of technology is one potential building block to achieve accessibility and differentiation of instruction based on learning needs. For learners who are DWD, technology may provide multiple means of representation and expression, thus promoting creativity, engagement, and motivation. Both scaffolding and technology must be matched with evidence-based practices supported by sound research to increase the efficiency and effectiveness across differentiated instruction. For example, Norman et al. (2022, see Chapter 9) describe how the UDL framework encompasses a differentiated instructional approach, thus allowing educators to curtail their instruction based upon a student's capabilities and assets.

UDL promotes inclusive practices and benefits all learners, especially those who are DWD. The widespread implementation of UDL is a promising change in the mindsets of professionals across the education field. When professionals follow the UDL guidelines, learners who are DWD have the potential to thrive in any educational placement as learners who are (a) resourceful and knowledgeable, (b) strategic and goal-directed, and (c) purposeful and motivated (CAST, 2011).

Tiered Systems of Support

Response to Intervention. Since the No Child Left Behind Act of 2001, RTI began to be used throughout the United States to assess students' needs through a multitiered approach. RTI allows professionals to monitor students' progress in a systematic, research-based manner. The process of RTI requires professionals working with students to gather data to determine the level of intervention that individual students need to achieve continued academic, social, and emotional growth, with the goal of long-term success.

The three tiers of RTI differentiate between the levels of intervention that a student needs to be included in the general education setting. Tier 1 interventions typically address the quality of instruction and implementation at the whole-class level, with the RTI team (consisting of teachers, administrators, school psychologists, specialized service providers, educational assistants, etc.) meeting three or more times a year to review data and adjust instruction as needed. When reinforced, 80%–90% of students will respond positively to Tier 1 interventions. When students do not respond to Tier 1 interventions, professionals must target Tier 2 interventions. Tier 2 interventions consist of small-group instruction, and data are collected more often, approximately every 2 weeks. And finally, Tier 3 interventions are for students who need the highest level of intervention, a possible referral for special education services and the development of an Individualized Education Plan (IEP).

Moores (2008) noted that d/Dhh students typically already have an IEP; therefore, where are they placed within the RTI multitiered model? Moores advocates that a version of the RTI model should be implemented in conjunction with a student's IEP because the current IEP system does not provide sufficient support for d/Dhh students who continually struggle to make gains year after year. This is an interesting and plausible suggestion, especially when considering the ramifications for students who are DWD. Essentially, students who are DWD are likely to benefit from Tier 1 and 2 supports and interventions, in conjunction with the accommodations set-forth by the IEP, for maximum success.

The RTI framework ensures that educators consider IEP goals and objectives as well as plan targeted instruction based upon progress-monitoring data. Luckner and Bowen (2010) support Moore's suggestion by stating that RTI is another way for teachers to continually monitor the progress of students who are not making adequate academic, social, emotional, and/or behavioral gains. Because students who are DWD tend to fall behind their d/Dhh peers, a modified version of the RTI framework, posited by Moores (2008), should be utilized.

Luckner and Pierce (2013) analyzed the use of RTI with students who are d/Dhh. They concluded that the framework is beneficial and should be supported and used by teachers of the d/Dhh, yet important factors may be impeding this process. First, teacher preparation programs should teach educators about the RTI framework so that they are prepared to integrate these concepts into their instructional activities. Secondly, RTI requires knowledge of various interventions, time to implement, and a team of trained members to ensure the success of the intervention.

Luckner and Pierce (2013) describe an alternative approach to the application of RTI with students who are d/Dhh because the interventions may differ from those typically implemented with general education students. For example, Tier I interventions would include accommodations such as preferential seating, use of visuals, and minimizing background noise. Tier 2 interventions would include more intense individualized interventions such as the introduction of visual phonics, tutoring, or explicit vocabulary instruction. This is especially important for students who are DWD because their needs may vary from their d/Dhh peers based upon their disability(ies). And finally, Tier 3 interventions would include specialized curricula such as community-based instruction or life-skills training. Tier 3 is particularly important for students who are DWD with more severe challenges. In addition, RTI requires the professionals working with DWD students to monitor progress more frequently. Students receiving Tier 2 support would be assessed every 2 weeks to determine the efficacy of the intervention and whether additional supports are needed. Tier 3 interventions should be evaluated weekly. See Figure 1 in Luckner and Pierce (2013) for a detailed presentation of various tiered interventions for students who are d/Dhh.

A Multitiered System of Support. MTSS is a collaborative asset-based approach that supports teachers in scaffolding instruction and monitoring progress in general education settings (Hoover et al., 2018). The MTSS approach is similar to RTI in that it provides tiered support while implementing progress-monitoring tools to document student strengths and needs and provide supplemental instruction to increase skills as needed. However, MTSS also incorporates behavioral and social considerations when identifying learners who require extra assistance. Similar to the RTI framework, MTSS also documents student progress through a collaborative decision-making model (Hoover et al., 2018). Findings from the MTSS team can be used to guide IEP development. Supports that focus on the whole learner may be especially important for DWD students who experience difficulty with self-regulation of their emotional and behavioral challenges.

Conclusion

Professionals and families must be prepared to address the unique needs of students who are d/Dhh with one or more disabilities, as they constitute approximately half of the population of d/Dhh learners. There is an ongoing need for up-to-date strategies and resources to effectively meet the needs of these students. Sharing best practices regarding identification, assessment, placement, and instruction will aid in this endeavor.

Publications have been limited, and best practices are not regularly shared or easily accessible.

This text provides a collective source of strategies and resources using an open-minded, asset-based approach. As suggested by TRM, professionals need to ensure that their own biases (i.e., communication modality, use of hearing technology) do not influence their perception of what learners who are DWD need. Biases are generalizations that can become blinders to clearly understanding and effectively meeting the needs of these learners. UDL, RTI, and MTSS frameworks are also highlighted as recommended practices to use when working with *all* students and are particularly important for students who are DWD.

Deaf and Hard of Hearing Learners With Disabilities: Foundations, Strategies, and Resources provides extensive information on the varying disabilities that co-occur with deafness, making many learners twice exceptional. These disabilities include LDs, ASD, developmental delays, ADHD, IDs, DB, EBDs, and a variety of syndromes. Each chapter examines the existing literature within each disability category, as well as information on demographics/characteristics, intervention/identification, placement, communication/language, psychosocial, assistive technology/ accommodations, assessment, and transition/postsecondary settings. Knowledge mobilization and dissemination of valuable strategies that are easy to implement should provide professionals and families working with learners who are DWD the support required to address their diverse needs.

This book addresses a 30-year gap as a comprehensive resource solely focused on students who are DWD. The authors address the challenges that children and their families may face with early intervention services, specialized assessment, educational placement options, and specific transition considerations. The best way to mitigate this challenge is for researchers to further study this population of students. Most importantly, the editors pose a call to action for these studies to be conducted across communication modalities, hearing levels, disabilities, or other defining characteristics of students who are DWD. Further research is imperative to address the gaps in the literature and understand how to better provide supports for these learners.

Discussion Questions

1. How is the prevalence of students who are DWD represented across multiple sources?
2. How did the history of publications about students who are DWD influence the current text?
3. What is an asset-based approach, and how can it benefit DWD students?
4. What frameworks are used in education, and how can these systems be applied when educating students who are DWD?

Resources

- **ASHA Wire**
  - https://leader.pubs.asha.org/article.aspx?articleid=2289769
  - "Red Flags for Disabilities in Children who are Deaf/Hard of Hearing" by Wiley and Moeller reviews characteristics to look for when you suspect your child is not only deaf but may be twice exceptional.
- **Boys Town National Research Hospital**
  - https://www.boystownhospital.org/KnowledgeCenter/Pages/default.aspx
  - Boys Town is a national research center that researches syndromes related to Deafness, among other things. The website provides information about various syndromes and the research studies conducted by Boys Town.
- **CAST**
  - http://udlguidelines.cast.org/
  - http://www.cast.org/
- **Hands & Voices**
  - http://www.handsandvoices.org/comcon/articles/deafplus.htm
  - Hands & Voices is an organization for families of the d/Dhh community. Their website provides information on deaf advocacy, deaf education, and resource guides specific to those who are d/Dhh-DD.
- **IRIS Center**
  - https://iris.peabody.vanderbilt.edu/

- **National Association of Special Education Teachers**
  - https://www.naset.org/index.php?id=hearingimpairments2
- **National Deaf Children's Society**
  - http://www.ndcs.org.uk/family_support/childhood_deafness/causes_of_deafness/genetic_conditions.html
- **Supporting Success for Children With Hearing Loss**
  - https://successforkidswithhearingloss.com/for-professionals/hearing-loss-plus-additional-disabilityies/
- **The Radical Middle Project**
  - https://radicalmiddledhh.org/
- **Understanding Deafness and Diversity**
  - http://understandingdad.net/

REFERENCES

Belcastro, F. P. (2004). Rural gifted students who are deaf or hard of hearing: How electronic technology can help. *American Annals of the Deaf, 149*(4), 309–313.

Blough, L. K., Rittenhouse, R. K., & Dancer, J. (1999). Identification of gifted deaf children: A complex but critical educational process. *Perceptual and Motor Skills, 89,* 219–221.

Bondy, A., & Frost, L. (1994). *The picture exchange communication system: Training manual.* Pyramid Educational Consultants.

Buisson, G. J., & Salgo, J. (2012). College collaboration with gifted programs: Deaf studies unit (Part 2). *American Annals of the Deaf, 157*(2), 87–91.

Cejas, I., Sarangoulis, C. M., Mestres, A., Nelson, J. A., & Quittner, A. L. (2022). Assessment and intervention with learners who are d/Deaf or hard of hearing with emotional and behavioral challenges. In C. Guardino, J. E. Cannon, & P. V. Paul (Eds.), *Deaf and hard of hearing learners with disabilities: Foundations, strategies, and resources* (pp. 230–261). Routledge.

Center for Applied Special Technology (CAST). (2011). *Universal design for learning (UDL) guidelines: Version 2.0.* https://udlguidelines.cast.org/

Coyne, P., Pisha, B., Dalton, B., Zeph, L., & Smith, N. (2012). Literacy by design: A universal design for learning approach for students with significant intellectual disabilities. *Remedial and Special Education, 33*(3), 162–172.

Easterbrooks, S., & Baker, S. B. (2002). *Language learning in children who are deaf and hard of hearing: Multiple pathways.* Allyn & Bacon.

Easterbrooks, S. R., & Maiorana-Basas, M. (2015). Literacy and deaf and hard of hearing students. In H. Knoors & M. Marschark (Eds.), *Educating deaf learners: Creating a global evidence base* (pp. 149–172). Oxford University Press.

Frost, L., & Bondy, A. (2002). *Picture exchange communication system training manual* (2nd ed.). Pyramid Education Products.

Fuchs, D., Fuchs, L. S., & Vaughn, S. (Eds.). (2008). *Response to intervention.* International Reading Association.

Gallaudet Research Institute (GRI). (2013). *Regional and national summary report of data from the 2011–2012 Annual Survey of Deaf and Hard of Hearing Children and Youth.* https://www.gallaudet.edu/documents/Research-Support-and-International-Affairs/Intl%20Affairs/Demographics/AS12_RegNat.pdf

Guardino, C. A. (2008). Identification and placement for deaf students with multiple disabilities: Choosing the path less followed. *American Annals of the Deaf, 153*(1), 55–64. http://doi.org/10.1353/aad.0.0004

Guardino, C. (2015). Evaluating teachers' preparedness to work with students who are deaf and hard of hearing with disabilities. *American Annals of the Deaf, 160*(4), 415–426. http://doi.org/10.1353/aad.2015.0030

Guardino, C., & Cannon, J. E. (2015). Theory, research, and practice for students who are deaf and hard of hearing with disabilities: Addressing the challenges from birth to postsecondary education. *American Annals of the Deaf, 160*(4), 347–355. http://doi.org/10.1353/aad.2015.0033

Hartmann, E. (2011). Universal design for learning. *Practice Perspectives, 8,* 1–4. https://files.eric.ed.gov/fulltext/ED531767.pdf

Hoover, J. J., Erickson, J. R., Herron, S. R., & Smith, C. E. (2018). Implementing culturally and linguistically responsive special education eligibility assessment in rural county elementary schools: Pilot project. *Rural Special Education Quarterly, 37*(2), 90–102.

Leppo, R. H. T., Cawthon, S. W., & Bond, M. P. (2014). Including deaf and hard of hearing students with co-occurring disabilities in the accommodations discussion. *Journal of Deaf Studies & Deaf Education, 19*(2), 189–202. http://doi.org/10.1093/deafed/ent029

Lo, C. O., Porath, M., Yu, H. P., Chen, C. M., Tsai, K. F., & Wu, I. C. (2018). Giftedness in the making: A transactional perspective. *Gifted Child Quarterly, 63*(3), 172–184. http://doi.org/10.1177/0016986218812474

Luckner, J. L., & Bowen, S. K. (2010). Teachers' use and perceptions of progress monitoring. *American Annals of the Deaf, 155*(4), 397–406.

Luckner, J. L., & Pierce, C. (2013). Response to intervention and students who are deaf or hard of hearing. *Deafness & Education International, 15*(4), 222–240. https://doi.org/10.1179/1557069X13Y.0000000027

Marder, C. (2009). *Facts from the Special Education Elementary Longitudinal Study (SEELS)*. http://www.seels.net/info_reports/DisabilityClassif1.9.09.pdf

Moores, D. F. (2008). Improving academic achievement: Can a response-to-intervention (RTI) model help? *American Annals of the Deaf, 153*(4), 347–348.

No Child Left Behind Act of 2001, 20 U.S.C. § 6319 (2002).

Norman, N., Rohatyn-Martin, N., & Luckner, J. (2022). Supporting students who are Deaf and hard of hearing and have Attention Deficit Hyperactivity Disorder: Strategies for success. In C. Guardino, J. E. Cannon, & P. V. Paul (Eds.), *Deaf and hard of hearing learners with disabilities: Foundations, strategies, and resources* (pp. 262–287). Routledge.

Nowell, R. C. (1980). *A handbook on the education of multiply handicapped, hearing impaired children* (Contract No. 300-77-0240). Report for U.S. Department of Education, Office of Special Education. Pennsylvania State University, PA.

Pollard, G., & Howze, J. (1981). School-wide talented and gifted program for the deaf. *American Annals of the Deaf, 126*(6), 600–606.

Prickett, H. T., & Duncan, E. (1988). *Coping with the multi-handicapped hearing impaired: A practical approach.* Charles C. Thomas.

Rose, D. H., & Gravel, J. W. (2010). Universal design for learning. In E. Baker, P. Peterson, & B. McGaw (Eds.), *International encyclopedia of education* (3rd ed., pp. 119–124). Elsevier. http://www.udlcenter.org/resource_library/articles/udl

Schley, S., Lane-Outlaw, S., & Foster, S. (2013, February). *Secondary disabilities and the landscape of deaf-plus education in the U.S.* [Paper presentation]. ACE-DHH Annual Conference, Santa Fe, NM.

Stinson, M., Leannah, C., MacDonald, J., & Powers, C. (2014, June). *Using technology to improve communication in small groups with deaf and hearing students* [Paper presentation]. Effective Access Technology Conference, Rochester, NY.

Tweedie, D., & Shroyer, E. H. (Eds.). (1982). *The multihandicapped hearing impaired: Identification and instruction.* Gallaudet College Press.

Vygotsky, L. S. (1978). *Mind in society: The development of higher psychological processes.* Harvard University Press.

Wagner, M., & Blackorby, J. (2002). Disability profiles of elementary and middle school students with disabilities. *Special Education Elementary Longitudinal Study (SEELS).* http://seels.net/designdocs/SEELS_disability_profile.pdf

Whiting, S. A., Anderson, L., & Ward, J. (1980). Identification of the mentally gifted minor deaf child in the public school system. *American Annals of the Deaf, 125*(1), 27–33.

2

Infants and Toddlers Who Are d/Deaf or Hard of Hearing With a Developmental Delay or Are At Risk for Developmental Delays

Rebecca L. W. Jackson, Sarah B. Ammerman, and Blane A. Trautwein

Learning Objectives

Readers will:

- Identify aspects of demographics that have changed for infants and toddlers who are d/Deaf and hard of hearing (d/ Dhh) with a developmental delay (DD; d/Dhh-DD).
- Discuss the impact of Newborn Hearing Screening and Early Hearing Detection and Intervention on identification, service provision, and outcomes for infants and toddlers who are d/Dhh-DD and their families.
- Describe the requirements for receiving early intervention services under the DD category in IDEA, and understand how these requirements might differ across states.
- Review the current assessment tools available for early intervention teams working with infants and toddlers who are d/Dhh-DD.
- Recognize the benefits of family-centered practices in early intervention services.
- Compare the transdisciplinary approach to early intervention services with other models discussed in the chapter.

DOI: 10.4324/9781003252054-2

Programs such as Early Hearing Detection and Intervention (EHDI) and Newborn Hearing Screening (NBHS) have led to earlier identification of infants with varying hearing levels in recent decades (Schmeltz, 2014). Consequently, the number of infants and toddlers who are d/Deaf or hard of hearing (d/Dhh) qualifying for annual early intervention (EI) services has increased dramatically (Sininger et al., 2009). A significant portion of these children have a disability other than deafness (d/Dhh with a disability; DWD), have a developmental delay (DD; d/Dhh-DD), or are considered at risk for developmental delays. A label of DD is often used for young children, rather than a more specific categorical label, due to age minimums required by identification assessments. The Individuals With Disabilities Education Act (IDEA) defines DD as diagnosed delays or risks for delays in cognitive, physical, communication, social-emotional, or adaptive development (Individuals With Disabilities Education Act of 2004, 2015).

To best serve children who are d/Dhh-DD, the professionals with whom they work should understand the demographics, identification, assessment, and strategies associated with this population. In some of these areas, a dearth of information exists regarding children who are d/Dhh-DD. In addition, there are challenges (e.g., family adjustment, collaboration) associated with providing EI services for infants and toddlers who are d/Dhh-DD. Families of infants and toddlers who are d/Dhh-DD may face logistical and emotional complexities related to the needs of their child. The low incidence of d/Dhh-DD may also result in service providers having few opportunities for collaboration with colleagues focusing on similar caseloads (Jones & Jones, 2003). Being familiar with best practices related to children with DD will help refine methods used with children who are d/Dhh-DD.

This chapter will discuss the population of children who are d/Dhh-DD as well as issues related to infants and toddlers who are d/Dhh and at risk for DDs. The state and federal laws and policies that impact eligibility for EI services in the United States will be examined. These laws and policies can be complex and often differ across states. Moreover, the differentiation between infants and toddlers who have identified DDs and those who are at risk for DDs can be subtle and is not always clear. Identification and assessment practices and resources that may be helpful for EI teams as well as service models and strategies that have potential benefits for infants and toddlers who are d/Dhh-DD and their families will be explained. Given the high level of recent changes in the field, the notable shifts in the demographics of the population of children who are d/Dhh, and the increasingly positive outcomes for students who are d/Dhh, it is a compelling time to be involved in EI activities with infants and toddlers who are d/Dhh.

Demographics

The rate of newborns being screened for hearing loss was 98% in 2016 (Centers for Disease Control [CDC], 2018), compared with 3% in 1999, only 17 years earlier (National Center for Hearing Assessment and Management [NCHAM], 2014; White, 2006). In many areas of the United States, NBHS and EHDI have contributed to the identification of hearing levels at <6 months of age, compared to a historical average age of 2.5–5 years (Schmeltz, 2014). Nearly 40%–50% of children who are d/Dhh have a disability (Cupples et al., 2014). In the 2013/2014 school year, children <3 years old were reported as 4.3% of the total d/Dhh student population (Gallaudet Office of Research Support and International Affairs [RSIA], 2014), an almost 3% increase from 1.4% in 2011–2012 (Gallaudet Research Institute [GRI], 2013). Furthermore, the RSIA (2014) demographic survey reflected that 6.1% of young children who were d/Dhh were reported as having a DD. These children may be eligible for additional EI services.

Infants and Toddlers Who Are Deaf or Hard of Hearing With DDs

In the United States, the 1991 and 1997 amendments to IDEA designated the category of DD for eligibility for special education services. Identifying specific characteristics of disabilities in young children can be difficult, and this challenge may be greater in infants and toddlers who are d/Dhh. Many disabilities, including attention deficit hyperactivity disorder (ADHD), emotional and behavioral disorders, and learning disabilities, are typically not identified until age 3 or older. Even for developmental differences, which may be identified from birth to 3 years, children who are d/Dhh are likely to be identified later than their peers with typical hearing levels. For example, autism spectrum disorder (ASD) is identified at a median age of 66.5 months for children who are d/Dhh (Meinzen-Derr et al., 2013; Roper et al., 2003), which is more than a year later than the average age for identification in children who are not d/Dhh (Baio et al., 2018).

The assignment of a specific categorical disability label may result in miscategorization or premature labeling for young children (Division for Early Childhood of the Council for Exceptional Children, 2009). The DD category under IDEA allows children to receive services without the assignment of a specific categorical disability label. In addition, the flexibility afforded by the DD label may mitigate doubts related to the validity of some assessment instruments for very young children (Division for Early Childhood of the Council for Exceptional Children, 2009).

Learning needs for infants and toddlers who are d/Dhh-DD vary widely. While a specific critical window for EI has not been identified (Spencer & Marschark, 2010), significant positive effects of age at intervention on language outcomes for children who are d/Dhh exist (Leigh et al., 2010; Moeller, 2000). Research has demonstrated that children who receive EI have language development levels considered to be in the low-to-average range, compared with peers who have typical hearing levels (Yoshinaga-Itano, 2003).

Several years ago, a national grassroots campaign called Language Equality and Acquisition for Deaf Kids (LEAD-K) began in the United States to promote kindergarten readiness and language acquisition for children who are d/Dhh from birth to 5 years of age. The LEAD-K movement is led by professionals across the field, along with advocates for legislation and policy at the state level, to address the language needs of young children who are d/Dhh (LEAD-K, n.d.). LEAD-K activities are intended to (a) raise awareness of the impact of language deprivation for young children who are d/Dhh, (b) advocate for full access to language, (c) compile literacy resources relevant to the needs of children who are d/Dhh, and (d) grow a network of Deaf mentors to work with young children who are d/Dhh and their families (Fahrina et al., 2017). In October 2018, leaders from the Alexander Graham Bell Association for the Deaf and Hard of Hearing (AG

Bell) and LEAD-K collaboratively met and agreed that the LEAD-K model bill would be revised to include the following principles:

> parent choice for language and communication mode; creation of a parent resource that contains fair, balanced, and comprehensive information about language, communication, and available services and programs; and a balanced advisory committee in which representatives of language and communication modes would be included and where the majority of committee members would be deaf or hard of hearing (some of whom likely will be professionals). (AG Bell, para. 7)

INFANTS AND TODDLERS WHO ARE AT RISK FOR DDS

Forty percent of all children from 4 months to 5 years of age are considered "at risk" for a DD, with 11% considered at "high risk," 15% considered "moderate risk," and the remaining 14% considered "low risk" (Health Resources and Service Administration [HRSA], 2014). IDEA (2004) defines an infant or toddler who is at risk as "an individual under three years of age who would be at risk of experiencing a substantial developmental delay if EI services were not provided to the individual" (§ 1432 [1]). Although nonverbal cognitive levels are similar for children with typical hearing and those with varying hearing levels (Akamatsu et al., 2008), the presence of hearing loss may put an infant or toddler at risk for language, social, and academic challenges (Spencer & Marschark, 2010).

Risk factors for a DD, many of which are preventable, affect children very early in life and, for some, before birth (Walker et al., 2011). Risk factors can be grouped into two broad categories: genetic and environmental. Genetic factors may include gender (with a higher prevalence in males than in females; Stevens et al., 2011; Werling & Geschwind, 2013) and syndromes. Evidence regarding the role of ethnicity as a risk factor is inconsistent (Hillemeier et al., 2009; Morgan et al., 2015). Infectious viruses, exposure to lead, iron deficiency, maternal depression, inadequate cognitive stimulation, low birth weight, and low socioeconomic status are environmental factors. An additional risk factor, prematurity, can result from both genetic and environmental causes associated with DDs. Medical advances have increased the survival rates of premature infants. These infants, however, are more likely to be d/Dhh (Roizen, 2003) and are at risk for intellectual disabilities, vision loss, and cerebral palsy (Vernon, 1982). These factors put children at risk of not achieving their developmental potential (CDC, 2016; Hillemeier et al., 2009; HRSA, 2014; Walker et al., 2011).

Protective factors that mitigate these negative effects have been identified, including breastfeeding, maternal education, and access to education and health care. Higher levels of maternal education are associated with less maternal depression, better child nutrition, increased parenting quality, and better access to and implementation of interventions (CDC, 2016; Walker et al., 2011). Programs that increase access to health care, including maternal mental health supports, positively impact all child developmental outcomes (CDC, 2016).

EI programs can increase protective factors and ameliorate risk factors (Walker et al., 2011); however, under IDEA, states are given the discretion to decide whether to provide special education service to infants and toddlers (birth through 2 years of age) and children (ages 3–9 years) who are at risk for DDs (IDEA, 2015). In some states, this discretion may result in EI services not being made available to infants and toddlers who are at risk for DD.

IDENTIFICATION AND ASSESSMENT

This section will explore the five domains (communication, physical, social-emotional, cognitive, and adaptive) in which DDs may occur, as well as recommended practices for assessing infants and toddlers who are d/Dhh-DD or at risk for DDs. Table 2.1 provides an overview of relevant assessment tools categorized by the developmental domain to assist in detecting DDs. The EI services provided in the United States under IDEA will be explained, along with variations in laws and policies related to the disability category of DDs across states.

The precise incidence of DDs in the general population is difficult to determine. Fewer than 15% of all children <5 years old are diagnosed with a DD (Boyle et al., 2011; Rosenberg et al., 2008). However, approximately

65% of developmental disabilities are not diagnosed prior to school age, suggesting that DDs are underdiagnosed in the birth to 5-year-old population (Perna & Loughan, 2013). Only about one-third of children aged 9–35 months in the United States received a developmental screening in 2016 (Hirai et al., 2018). Similarly, only 30% of caregivers recall their child being screened for DD through the use of a standardized tool (Perna & Loughan, 2013). This is concerning, given the risk for negative long-term outcomes for children who exhibit early delays and do not receive EI services (Perna & Loughan, 2013).

Developmental progress must be assessed on an ongoing basis to inform any necessary modifications to placement and service decisions (Moeller et al., 2013; Spencer & Marschark, 2010). The speech, language, and cognitive skills of children who are d/Dhh between birth and age 3 should be evaluated in 6-month intervals (Joint Committee on Infant Hearing [JCIH], 2007) so that skills can be targeted for instruction in a timely manner (Jackson, Ammerman, & Trautwein, 2015). Additional assessment recommendations for infants and toddlers who are d/Dhh-DD include the following:

- Adults who are d/Dhh should be on the assessment team as they can bring important perspectives concerning the design of the assessment environment and activities (Hafer & Stredler-Brown, 2003).
- Assessments should be conducted in a child's dominant language (Division for Early Childhood [DEC], 2014).
- Preferred language and communication mode of family members should be used when communicating assessment results (Jackson et al., 2015).
- Assessment results should be shared with families in a way that is useful and understandable (DEC, 2014).
- Arena- or play-based assessments should be prioritized, which generally have one professional interacting with the child, while other relevant transdisciplinary team members observe (Wolery & Dyk, 1984) using developmental checklists specific to their area of expertise, working together to determine whether a delay is present (Myers et al., 1996).

Assessment Across the Five Domains of DD

Ascertaining the prevalence of a delay within the five domains of development (communication, physical, social-emotional, cognitive, and adaptive) for a child who is d/Dhh can be challenging. Determining whether issues other than varying hearing levels are contributing to a delay is not an easy task, particularly in communication. Regardless of the domain, if a delay is suspected, the child must be assessed so that proper services can be identified and implemented.

Communication Domain

Young children who are d/Dhh may exhibit delays in communication. In a study, among children ages 3–6 years in the general population, 11% were diagnosed with a voice, speech, language, or swallowing disorder; when examining language alone, the prevalence was between 2.3% and 19% (McLaughlin, 2011). Few instruments exist that assess speech and language in very young children (see Table 2.1 for further description of available standardized communication assessments with age ranges and targeted skills).

Physical Domain

Many children with gross motor delays will eventually attain milestones; however, some children may have permanent motor delays due to conditions such as cerebral palsy and developmental coordination disorder, which affect 0.003% and 6% of the population, respectively (Noritz & Murphy, 2013). Motor delay may be the most obvious sign of a global DD, as characterized by delays in two or more of the five domains. Given this, the American Academy of Pediatrics (AAP) recommends that pediatricians screen children's motor development three times before their third birthday (AAP, 2006), and some experts recommend screening for motor development at four points in time: the 9-, 18-, 30-, and 48-month well-child visits with the pediatrician (Noritz & Murphy, 2013). Screenings may indicate that a more extensive standardized assessment, like the Peabody Developmental Motor Scales (Folio & Fewell, 2000), is warranted.

TABLE 2.1 Assessments Useful for Detecting Developmental Delays

Developmental Area(s)	Assessment	Age Range (Years:Months)	Skills Targeted
Communication	Clinical Evaluation of Language Fundamentals-Preschool 2 (CELF-P2) (Semel et al., 2004)	3:0–6:11	Receptive and expressive spoken language
Communication	Oral and Written Language Scales, Second Edition (OWLS-II) (Carrow-Woolfolk, 2004)	3:0–21:11	Oral language, written language, receptive processing, expressive processing, and overall language processing
Communication	Comprehensive Assessment of Spoken Language, Second Edition (CASL-2) (Carrow-Woolfolk, 2017)	3:0–21:11	Receptive and expressive spoken language
Communication	Preschool Language Scales, Fifth Edition (PLS-5) (Zimmerman et al., 2011)	Birth–7:11	Receptive and expressive language
Communication	Goldman-Fristoe Test of Articulation 3 (GFTA-3) (Goldman & Fristoe, 2015)	2:0–21:11	Articulation

(Continued)

TABLE 2.1 (*Continued*)

Developmental Area(s)	Assessment	Age Range (Years:Months)	Skills Targeted
Communication	The MacArthur Communicative Development Inventory for American Sign Language (ASL-CDI) (Anderson & Reilly, 2002)	0:8–3:0	ASL vocabulary
Communication	Visual Communication and Sign Language (VCSL) Checklist for Signing Children (Simms et al., 2013)	Birth–5:0	ASL milestones
Physical	Peabody Developmental Motor Scales-Second Edition (PDMS-2) (Folio & Fewell, 2000)	Birth–5:0	Gross and fine motor skills
Social-emotional	Ages and Stages, Social and Emotional (ASQ:SE2) (Squires et al., 2017)	0:6–3:0	Self-regulation, communication, autonomy, compliance, adaptive functioning, affect, and interaction with people

Developmental Area(s)	Assessment	Age Range (Years:Months)	Skills Targeted
Social-emotional/ adaptive behavior	Vineland Adaptive Behavior Scales, Second Edition (Sparrow et al., 2005)	Birth–90	Communication, daily living skills, and socialization
Cognition	Kaufman Assessment Battery for Children-Second Edition (KABC-II) (Kaufman & Kaufman, 2018)	2:6–18:0	Short-term memory, visual processing, long-term storage and retrieval, fluid reasoning, and crystallized ability (verbal ability can be excluded)
Cognition	Kaufman Infant and Preschool Scale (KIPS) (Kaufman, 1979)	1:4–4:0	General reasoning, storage, and verbal communication
Cognition	Stanford-Binet Intelligence Scales, Fifth Edition (SB-5) (Roid, 2003)	2:0–adult	Fluid reasoning, quantitative, visual-spatial, and working memory
Cognition	Wechsler Preschool and Primary Scale of Intelligence, Third Edition (WPPSI-III) (Wechsler, 2012)	2:6–7:3	Fluid reasoning, receptive and expressive vocabulary, and processing speed

(*Continued*)

TABLE 2.1 (*Continued*)

Developmental Area(s)	Assessment	Age Range (Years:Months)	Skills Targeted
Adaptive	Adaptive Behavior Assessment System, Second Edition (ABAS II) (Harrison & Oakland, 2003)	Birth–89:0	Self-care, social, functional academics, health and safety, and self-direction
Global	Batelle Developmental Inventory (Newborg et al., 2004)	Birth–8:0	Personal-social, adaptive, motor, communication, and cognitive skills
Global	Bayley Scales of Infant and Toddler Development, Third Edition (Bayley-III) (Bayley, 2005)	0:1–3:6	Cognitive, language, motor, social-emotional, and adaptive behavior
Global	Developmental Profile III (DP-III) (Alpern, 2007)	Birth–12:11	Physical, adaptive behavior, social-emotional, cognitive, and communication

Social-Emotional Domain

Between 12% and 16% of all 2-year-olds will manifest some area of social-emotional variation in development (Briggs-Gowan et al., 2001). Children who are d/Dhh have a higher risk of attention and behavioral difficulties than their hearing peers (Edwards & Crocker, 2008; Edwards et al., 2006). Early assessments and screening of infants and toddlers can provide predictive information regarding future social-emotional differences. For example, 50% of 12- to 36-month-olds who were evaluated and found to have social-emotional differences, such as extreme difficulty with transitions and limited enjoyment of people (as described by their parents), were later characterized by teachers as having social-emotional challenges (Briggs-Gowan & Carter, 2008). Fortunately, assessments exist that can be used with very young children, including the Vineland Adaptive Behavior Scales, which measures communication, socialization, daily living skills, and motor development (Sparrow et al., 2005).

Cognitive Domain

Approximately 8% of children have a cognitive DD; these children have difficulty obtaining and retaining knowledge. Risk factors for cognitive delays are similar to other delays and include gender (being male), prematurity, low birth weight, and being a member of multiple births. Children whose mothers are <18 years old and/or have attained low levels of education are also at increased risk for a cognitive delay (Tervo, 2003). Norm-referenced assessments that examine cognitive ability generally require a cognitive or educational psychologist to administer. For example, the Wechsler Preschool and Primary Scale of Intelligence (2012), which measures intellectual functioning in verbal and performance domains, must be administered by a trained professional. However, early interventionists, teachers, and parents can monitor intellectual development by noting the attainment of cognitive milestones, such as obtaining object permanence by 12 months of age and sorting objects by category between 2 and 3 years of age.

Adaptive Domain

Adaptive behaviors are the skills necessary for children to function safely and appropriately in daily life and, eventually, to live independently. Adaptive behaviors include life skills such as self-grooming, dressing, safety, following rules, working, money management, cleaning, making friends, social skills, and the personal responsibility expected at various ages. Because adaptive behavior encompasses skills from several other domains, it is rarely assessed or discussed in isolation. Instead, communication, social/emotional, physical, and/or cognitive skills are almost always parts of the equation. Two assessments that largely focus on adaptive skills are the Vineland Adaptive Behavior Scales (Sparrow et al., 2005) and the Adaptive Behavior Assessment System (Harrison & Oakland, 2003). Many assessments focus on skills in one developmental area, while others measure multiple areas of development (e.g., global development), including the Developmental Profile III (Alpern, 2007) and the Bayley Scales of Infant and Toddler Development (Bayley, 2005). Table 2.1 delineates assessments discussed earlier, as well as additional instruments.

While parents and caregivers should be vigilant about monitoring development in young children, initial evaluation results should be interpreted with caution. Many skills, including those in the motor and communication domains, are incredibly variable in typically developing young children (Darrah et al., 2003; Rydz et al., 2006). A time-lapse of only 3 months can result in a score that no longer indicates a delay. Consequently, screening/assessment protocols should involve multiple evaluations over time (AAP, 2006; Rydz et al., 2006) by a variety of team members.

INDIVIDUALIZED FAMILY SERVICES PLAN/ INDIVIDUALIZED EDUCATION PROGRAM

In the United States, children who are d/Dhh-DD may be eligible for services under IDEA. IDEA is composed of four sections: Parts A, B, C, and D. IDEA Part A delineates the general provisions of the law, while Part B is specific to children aged 3–21 years. Part C pertains to infants and toddlers from birth through age 2, and Part D is related to national activities to improve education for students with disabilities. Children who are d/Dhh-DD may receive EI services under IDEA Part C until their third birthday. They may qualify for services under the category of DD as well as the category of Deafness. States are allowed to define DD for infants, toddlers, and children within the following parameters:

- Each state must describe the evaluation and assessment procedures that are used to measure a child's development in each domain (communication, physical, social-emotional, cognitive, or adaptive).
- Each state must specify the level of functioning or other comparable criteria that constitute a DD in one or more developmental areas, thus requiring special education or related services.
- States may determine the age range to which DD applies.

Differences in development do not have to be correlated to a specific disability to qualify for services under IDEA (2015). The National Early Childhood Technical Assistance Center (NECTAC) provides information pertaining to how IDEA is implemented in each state. For example, in Texas, a child with at least a 25% delay, which affects functioning in one or more areas of development, qualifies for services, while a child in Tennessee qualifies for services with a 25% delay in *two* developmental areas or a 40% delay in one area (NECTAC, 2015). Because criteria vary across states, practitioners should be aware of differences that are relevant if they or the children and families with whom they work move from one state to another.

The first step in accessing EI services is a referral made to a service provider. IDEA mandates that providers assess and, if needed, create an Individual Family Service Plan (IFSP) within 45 days of receiving a referral. The components of an IFSP are included in Table 2.2. A critical element of creating and implementing an IFSP is a formal meeting to approve, review, and update the document. IDEA specifies that these meetings must comprise the following:

- parent(s)
- service coordinator
- at least one evaluator who worked with the child
- professionals providing services, as appropriate
- other family members, advocates, or professionals as invited by parents

TABLE 2.2 The Components Required to Be Included in an IFSP

Statement of the present level of infant/toddler's cognitive, communication, social or emotional, or adaptive development. This statement must be based upon evaluations and assessments identified for usage by the state in which the child resides.
Family information, including a statement regarding resources, priorities, and concerns related to enhancing the development of the child. This information is gathered via a family assessment.
Results or outcomes with a timeline expected for the child to achieve. Must also include the criteria to be used to determine growth. These criteria will also be utilized to determine whether any modifications or revisions are needed to be made to the IFSP.
EI services to be received. This must include a statement regarding the length, duration, frequency, intensity, and method of delivery. A statement must also be made regarding the environment from which services will be received (natural environment of child mandated).
A listing of other services provided either not required or funded in Part C.
A listing of the coordinator for all services.

Note. IFSP = Individual Family Service Plan; EI = early intervention.

Parents may approve the IFSP in its entirety or refuse individual services. Once established, the IFSP must be reviewed every 6 months and updated annually (IDEA, 2015). Most of the individuals included in the IFSP meeting will constitute the EI team for the infant or toddler and their family.

TRANSITION FOR STUDENTS WHO HAVE DDS OR ARE AT RISK

Approximately 6 months before a child's third birthday, the EI team will begin working with the family to plan for the transition from Part C to Part B services. Once children turn 3 years old, they are likely to transition to special education services covered under IDEA Part B, and the IFSP will evolve into an IEP. However, states in the United States have the flexibility to continue to provide services under Part C until a student's kindergarten year. Once a student is eligible for Part B services, the label of DD can continue until their ninth birthday (IDEA, 2015), allowing special education services to continue without having to meet the initial eligibility criteria for a new categorical disability.

STRATEGIES

This section will discuss strategies that may be beneficial to infants and toddlers who are d/Dhh-DD and their families. General practices that EI teams may use, such as a family-centered focus, will be discussed first, followed by an examination of more specific strategies. Strategies beneficial to infants and toddlers who are d/Dhh-DD and their families, namely, utilizing the transdisciplinary approach to collaboration in a culturally competent manner, have positive effects. Lastly, understanding the nuances among various EI settings and applying different practices in each further enhance outcomes for children who are d/Dhh-DD.

General Practices

When working with infants and toddlers who are d/Dhh-DD, early identification alone is not sufficient, and it must be followed immediately by evidence-based EI practices that focus on both the child and the family (Spencer & Marschark, 2010). Early interventionists working with infants and toddlers who are d/Dhh-DD should utilize information and research related to various disabilities to help inform practice while focusing on the particular strengths and needs of the child receiving services (Ewing & Jones, 2003; Marschark et al., 2011; Spencer & Marschark, 2010). Closely monitoring progress and carefully considering language development are vital to success as well.

To encourage family participation in EI services, providers should consider supporting the family as a key component of their work (Jackson et al., 2015; Meadow-Orlans et al., 2003; Sass-Lehrer et al., 2016). Utilizing a family-centered planning approach helps ensure that the needs and interests of the child and family are prioritized and allows families to be thoroughly involved in EI services (Moeller et al., 2013). In *Best Practices in Family-Centered Early Intervention for Children Who Are Deaf or Hard of Hearing*, Moeller et al. (2013) emphasize that partnerships between service providers and families need to include "reciprocity, mutual trust, response, honesty, shared tasks, and open communication" (p. 432). Incorporating the distance services model of EI (discussed below) may be another way to encourage active participation by family members.

Research has demonstrated several features of parent–child interaction that promote communication development, including (a) joint attention, (b) responsiveness, (c) child-directed communication, (d) language quantity, and (e) everyday life experiences (Brown & Nott, 2006). While the majority of this research was specific to communication development in children who have typical hearing levels, the findings have implications that are relevant to infants and toddlers who are d/Dhh-DD. EI service providers should incorporate the features mentioned above into their work with the children and their families to encourage their use on a daily basis.

Making choices related to communication mode(s) and language approaches can be one of the most challenging aspects of EI for families of infants and toddlers who are d/Dhh-DD. While a variety of approaches support the language development of children who are d/Dhh, "Research has indicated each [approach to supporting language development] to be effective in some cases, but no one approach is appropriate for all" (Spencer & Marschark, 2010, p. 188). One point of agreement, however, is that focusing on infants' and toddlers' receptive and expressive English and/or American Sign Language skills is critical during EI, as 0–36 months of age is the crucial period for language development (Ewing & Jones, 2003).

Collaboration Through a Transdisciplinary Approach

The continuum of collaborative models in the provision of EI services includes multidisciplinary, interdisciplinary, and transdisciplinary (Orelove & Sobsey, 1996). The multidisciplinary approach involves individual team members working separately with the infant or toddler toward progress on their goals and objectives (Cloninger, 2004). This approach to service delivery may result in fragmented services and conflicting recommendations (Ewing & Jones, 2003). In contrast, the interdisciplinary approach requires that professionals make decisions by consensus; assessments and service provisions tend to be conducted individually, resulting in multiple professionals providing services directly to the child and family (Cloninger, 2004).

The Division for Early Childhood's *Recommended Practices in Early Intervention/Early Childhood Special Education* includes a discussion of the importance of teaming and collaboration. Luckner and Carter's (2001) list of essential competencies for teachers of d/Dhh students with disabilities includes the importance of teachers being both knowledgeable of and skilled in collaboration. Models of providing EI services that include a high level of collaboration, such as routines-based transdisciplinary models, have been identified as evidence-based practices (Cole et al., 2011). Moeller et al. (2013) specifically recommended a transdisciplinary model of collaboration for EI services for children who are d/Dhh.

The transdisciplinary approach utilizes an indirect service model in which only one or two members of the team provide services directly to the child and their family, while the other professionals on the team act as consultants. Unique features to this approach, also known as the primary provider model, include the use of arena- or play-based assessment (discussed earlier in the chapter), frequent interaction among team members, and the use of planned role release when working with infants and toddlers and their families (King et al., 2009). Role release occurs when roles and responsibilities are shared and exchanged among team members (Giangreco et al., 2000). In a transdisciplinary approach, planned role release is used when the direct service provider(s) put techniques and strategies from another discipline into practice, with the guidance of the professional from that discipline. For example, after consultation and training from an orientation and mobility specialist, a teacher of the d/Dhh may incorporate techniques to help the child who is deafblind navigate their learning environment.

The use of the transdisciplinary approach to EI helps avoid duplication and fragmentation of services, allows the knowledge and skills of team members to be utilized in complementary ways, provides opportunities for professionals to develop new knowledge and skills, reduces conflicting communication, and increases service efficiency (Carpenter, 2005; King et al., 2009; Pletcher, 2012). EI services include teams composed of multiple professionals. Infants and toddlers who are d/Dhh-DD may require a range of practitioners to effectively meet their unique and diverse needs. EI service providers on the interdisciplinary team for infants and toddlers who are d/Dhh may include teachers of the d/Dhh, speech-language pathologists, audiologists, physical and occupational therapists, social workers or counselors, orientation and mobility specialists, adaptive physical education teachers, and assistive technology specialists. The providers included on a team will vary, depending on the specific needs of each infant or toddler and their family.

Members of a transdisciplinary team work to blend their skills with those of their colleagues, with a focus on outcomes for the children and families with whom they work (Pletcher & Younggren, 2013). The intense communication and consultation among members of a transdisciplinary team increase the level of collaboration among the team members, which allows for a more coordinated approach to programming and a greater level of strategy alignment (Pletcher, 2012). This method of team functioning reinforces the importance of one or two professionals acting as the primary service providers (Cloninger, 2004). This streamlines services and increases the familiarity of the professionals working with the child, which is how infants and toddlers learn best (Pletcher & Younggren, 2013). To ensure that there is a primary service provider, the individual who will most frequently work with the team should be identified when the transdisciplinary team is formed and documented in the IFSP (Pletcher, 2012). Background knowledge and expertise in language and communication should be key considerations when selecting the professional(s) to act as the primary provider(s) on the transdisciplinary team for infants and toddlers who are d/Dhh-DD. Some tools that may be helpful when using the transdisciplinary approach are listed in Table 2.3.

Cultural Competency

EI professionals working with infants, toddlers, and their families must be aware of the influence that cultural and linguistic diversity may have on the perspectives, expectations, and practices of family members (Georgetown University Center for Child Development, 2011). This is especially critical in the field of educating students who are d/Dhh, in which deafness itself can be a cultural difference. In addition, there are higher percentages of

TABLE 2.3 Transdisciplinary Approach Resources

Resource	Purpose	Organization
Worksheet for Selecting the Most Likely Primary Provider https://des.az.gov/search/node/sites%20default%20files%2021%20Selecting%20Most%20Likely%20Team%20Lead%20pdf	Teams can use the worksheet and companion documents to help determine the team member(s) that are most appropriate to act as the direct service provider(s) and to identify any role gaps that exist.	The Center for Advanced Study of Excellence in Early Childhood and Family Support Practices
Joint Visit Planning Tool https://fipp.org/static/media/uploads/casetools/casetool_vol6_no2.pdf	Teams can use this document to plan for family visits during which the direct service provider(s) requires support or assistance from other members of the team.	The Center for Advanced Study of Excellence in Early Childhood and Family Support Practices
Checklists for Implementing a Primary-Coach Approach to Teaming https://fipp.org/static/media/uploads/casetools/casetool_vol5_no1.pdf	The checklists can be used by programs, team leads, supervisors, and service providers to assess the extent to which the program implements the Primary-Coach Approach.	The Center for Advanced Study of Excellence in Early Childhood and Family Support Practices

ethnic minorities among samples of individuals who are d/Dhh (Calderon et al., 1998; Cannon & Luckner, 2016; Guardino & Cannon, 2015, 2016), and the number of young children who are d/Dhh from diverse racial, ethnic, cultural, and socioeconomic backgrounds is increasing (Wu & Grant, 2013). These factors should be taken into consideration when assessing an infant or toddler as well as during programming, planning, and service provision.

The JCIH (2007) recommends that children and adults from d/Dhh communities be involved as mentors and role models during EI for infants and toddlers who are d/Dhh. Similarly, the National Consensus Conference on Effective Educational and Health Care Interventions for Infants and Young Children With Hearing Loss (Marge & Marge, 2005) recommends that families of young children who are d/Dhh have opportunities to meet and interact with adults and children who are d/Dhh. Regular contact with individuals from the d/Dhh community has been shown to improve communication, increase social support and social-emotional learning, as well as increase parental acceptance (Calderon & Greenberg, 2003; Hintermair, 2006; Meadow-Orlans et al., 2003; Watkins et al., 1998).

Families of infants and toddlers who are d/Dhh-DD should be involved in the process of forming the transdisciplinary team and should be given the option of including individuals who are d/Dhh if they are not already a part of the team (Jackson et al., 2015). This will allow families to interact with adults who are d/Dhh and will also provide a role model for their young child. Research related to the Deaf Mentor Experimental Project conducted at Utah State University showed that children with a d/Dhh mentor had better language outcomes than those who did not have a d/Dhh mentor (Watkins et al., 1998). In addition, children who are d/Dhh-DD or at risk may be less likely to be considered a part of the Deaf community than those who are d/Dhh, which may result in these children and their parents having fewer opportunities to interact with adults who are d/Dhh (Jones & Jones, 2003). Given this, the involvement of adults who are d/Dhh in EI services may be even more important for infants and toddlers who are d/Dhh-DD and their families (Jackson et al., 2015). This demonstrates the potential benefit of including a d/Dhh adult on trans-disciplinary teams for infants and toddlers who are d/Dhh-DD (Jackson et al., 2015).

Similarly, the participation of cultural brokers on teams planning special education services has been discussed in the literature as a way to meet the needs of increasingly diverse populations (Cannon & Luckner, 2016; Correa-Torres & Durando, 2011). Cultural brokers can provide relevant cultural background information that may help to bridge cultural gaps, improve communication, and reduce conflict among members of a special education team (Correa-Torres & Durando, 2011). While teachers or family members may be able to fulfill the function of a cultural broker (Cooper et al., 1999), individuals serving in this role should be bicultural themselves and able to navigate both cultures well (Gentemann & Whitehead, 1983). For students who are d/Dhh, these cultures will likely be Deaf culture and the culture of the school but may also include a student's home culture. A bicultural individual may also be able to act as a role model for students and help them acquire the skills necessary to succeed in school and beyond (Cooper et al., 1999). In light of the high level of diversity of students who are d/Dhh today, the participation of a cultural broker who represents a student's home culture may be particularly beneficial, particularly given the lack of diversity among professionals providing services to children who are d/Dhh (Wu & Grant, 2013).

Service Delivery Options

EI services can occur in a variety of settings: (a) the home, (b) a center, (c) within the community (e.g., a daycare), or (d) via distance technology. Regardless of the setting in which services are provided, high levels of family involvement are critical (Brown & Nott, 2006). While the setting dictates changes in some practices, many essential EI tenets remain the same, regardless of the environment. This section will look at the various service delivery settings that EI teams may utilize when providing services to infants and toddlers who are d/Dhh-DD and their families.

Service Delivery Settings

Home-Based Services. IDEA includes the section *Early Intervention Services in Natural Environments* (2004, § 303.126), which requires that services be provided in the child's home and community settings to the maximum extent possible. In the 2007 guidelines for EHDI programs, the JCIH emphasized the importance of offering families both home-based and center-based options. The provision of services in a child's home has many benefits; however, some families may feel more comfortable in a community setting or traveling to a center to receive EI services. For young children who are d/Dhh-DD, these types of settings may provide an opportunity for children and their families to meet and interact with other families and children who are d/Dhh (Gallegos et al., 2016; Marschark, 2007; Sass-Lehrer, 2003; Sass-Lehrer & Bodner-Johnson, 2003).

Distance Services. Traveling to center-based EI services for infants and toddlers who are d/Dhh-DD may be challenging for families due to scheduling and travel constraints. In some areas, the provision of services in the child's home or community may be equally difficult. In these situations, EI teams may consider providing services via distance technology, sometimes referred to as "telepractice." The American Speech and Hearing Association defines telepractice as "the application of telecommunications technology at a distance by linking clinician to client, or clinician to clinician for assessment, intervention, and/or consultation" (n.d.). While this method of service delivery is still relatively new and requires more research to explore its efficacy (Houston & Stredler-Brown, 2012), the use of telepractice has been associated with positive outcomes for children (Blaiser et al., 2013; Houston, 2011; McCarthy et al., 2010). One benefit of providing services through distance technology is that it supports a more family-centered approach than in-person services. During in-person EI sessions, the provider often takes an active role, while the family member(s) observe the interactions between the provider and the infant or toddler, whereas with telepractice, the lack of the physical presence of a service provider necessitates that family members become more active in the EI sessions. Telepractice also requires the service provider to become a "coach" to the family members who are in the room with the infant or toddler, thus providing an opportunity for the family member(s) to become more comfortable utilizing and replicating the strategies used during EI sessions (Houston & Stredler-Brown, 2012).

While the benefits of providing services via distance technology include increased access to qualified providers and interpreters, and a reduction in cancellations and travel challenges (NCHAM, 2014), EI teams must consider the potential issues in this method of service delivery (Jackson et al., 2015). Privacy must be a factor whenever service providers are using technology while working with children and their families. Access to technology must also be considered. Families and Part C service providers in some areas may not have reliable internet access or the hardware or software needed to provide services via distance technology. The EI team should also work to ensure that both professionals and families are comfortable with the technology being used.

Finally, principles of Universal Design for Learning (UDL; Rose & Gravel, 2010) should be included in all services provided via distance technology to ensure accessibility for the infants and toddlers and their family members, as well as for the professionals providing the service. Utilizing UDL components to ensure accessible services via distance technology includes providing multiple means of (a) engagement (e.g., optimize options and minimize distractions); (b) representation (e.g., offer alternatives to visual and auditory information, and clarify language and symbols); and (c) action and expression (e.g., vary the methods for response and use multiple media for communication).

CONCLUSION

Although children who are d/Dhh and have disabilities are an increasing percentage of the population of students who are d/Dhh (Spencer & Marschark, 2010), research and evidence-based practices specific to this population remain scarce. For infants and toddlers who are d/Dhh-DD, research related to young children who are d/Dhh and studies that focus on DD should be referred to for potential strategies to meet the unique needs of these young children. However, given the high level of heterogeneity in the d/Dhh-DD population, generalizations from the literature should be made cautiously.

Assessment, programming, and planning for infants and toddlers who are d/Dhh-DD should be family-centered and, given the critical window for language development in early childhood, should focus heavily on language. Having an adult who is d/Dhh involved with the EI team may be beneficial for both families and young children. The transdisciplinary approach to EI services is a promising strategy to meet the individual needs of young children who are d/Dhh-DD and to ensure that practices remain collaborative and family-centered. Although providing services via distance technology is still relatively new, the practice has the potential to ameliorate some of the common logistical challenges associated with EI services and may help to make services more family-centered. These distance technologies could also be used as a platform to facilitate transdisciplinary collaboration (Jackson et al., 2015).

The implementation of NBHS and EHDI programs has increased the number of infants and toddlers receiving EI services under the Deafness category (Sininger et al., 2009). Simultaneously, these programs have decreased the average age at identification, which has laid the foundation for increasingly positive outcomes for infants and toddlers who are d/Dhh. The population of young children who are d/Dhh-DD will continue to evolve and diversify, which will require an ongoing effort on the part of EI service providers to become proficient in evidence-based practices for the infants and toddlers they serve. Given the recent shifts in demographics and the increased positive outcomes for children who are d/Dhh, it is an exciting time for the field of EI in deaf education.

DISCUSSION QUESTIONS

1. What are the complications with identifying disabilities in children who are d/Dhh-DD?
2. What assessment recommendations do the authors provide? Describe one additional strategy that professionals might use when assessing this unique population.
3. What are some potentially negative impacts of assigning a special education categorical label to an infant or toddler?
4. Criteria for DD in infants, toddlers, and children are allowed to be defined by each state. What impact does this have on families? How could the state's criteria impact long-term educational and psychosocial outcomes for the child?
5. Who is required to attend the IFSP meetings? What other individuals could be added to enhance an IFSP team?

RESOURCES

- **American Association on Intellectual and Developmental Disabilities (AAIDD)**
  - https://www.aaidd.org/
  - This organization provides relevant news and policy affecting those with DD.
- **The Division for Early Childhood of the Council for Exceptional Children (DEC)**
  - https://www.dec-sped.org/
  - DEC is a membership organization that promotes policies and evidence-based practices that support young children who have or are at risk for developmental delays and disabilities and their families. The DEC website includes a range of resources for EI professionals and families.
- **Early Beginnings for Children Who Are Deaf or Hard of Hearing: Guidelines for Effective Services**
  - https://www3.gallaudet.edu/clerc-center/info-to-go/early-intervention/family-and-professional-resources/early-beginnings.html
  - This document provides guidelines for the development of EI services specific to the needs of young children who are deaf or hard of hearing.
- **Early Childhood Technical Assistance Center (ECTA)**
  - https://ectacenter.org/contact/ptccoord.asp
  - The ECTA Center supports Part C programs and offers resources on a range of topics related to EI and preschool services with a focus on positive outcomes for young children receiving special education services and their families.
- **Eligibility and Service Delivery Policies: Differences Between IDEA Part C and IDEA Part B**
  - https://www.infanthearing.org/earlyintervention/docs/aspect-idea-part-c-and-idea-part-b.pdf
  - This document compares IDEA Part C and Part B policies in the following areas: eligibility criteria, eligibility determination, types of services, service settings, service recipients, parental rights, and system of payments.

- **High Scope Curriculum**
  - https://highscope.org/our-practice/curriculum/
  - The High Scope Curriculum is research-based and child-focused, and it addresses all areas of development through multiple content areas and key developmental indicators. There are curricula for Infant-Toddler, Preschool, and Family Child Care.
- **National Association for the Education of Young Children (NAEYC)**
  - https://www.naeyc.org/
  - NAEYC is a professional membership organization that connects early childhood practice, policy, and research to promote high-quality early learning for all young children.
- **National Center for Hearing Assessment and Management (NCHAM)**
  - http://www.infanthearing.org/resources_home/
  - NCHAM's resource center includes a range of materials related to Early Hearing Detection and Intervention (EHDI) and Universal Newborn Hearing Screening programs.
- **PACER Center**
  - https://www.pacer.org/
  - PACER Center's mission is to expand opportunities and enhance the quality of life of children and young adults with disabilities and provide family programs. The PACER website provides links to resources, workshops, news, and events to support children receiving special education services and their families.
- **Wrights Law**
  - https://www.wrightslaw.com/
  - Wrights Law is a website about special education law and advocacy that includes free resources about a range of special education topics.
- **Zero to Three**
  - https://www.zerotothree.org/
  - Zero to Three (ZTT) is a professional membership organization that focuses on the well-being and development of babies and toddlers. The ZTT website includes a range of resources and services for professionals and families.

References

Akamatsu, C. T., Mayer, C., & Hardy-Braz, S. (2008). Why considerations of verbal aptitude are important in educating deaf and hard-of-hearing students. In M. Marschark & P. C. Hauser (Eds.), *Deaf cognition: Foundations and outcomes* (pp. 131–169). Oxford University Press.

Alpern, G. D. (2007). *Developmental Profile 3 (DP-3)* [Assessment instrument]. WPS Publishing.

American Academy of Pediatrics, Council on Children With Disabilities, Section on Developmental Behavioral Pediatrics, Bright Futures Steering Committee and Medical Home Initiatives for Children With Special Needs Project Advisory Committee. (2006). Identifying infants and young children with developmental disorders in the medical home: An algorithm for developmental surveillance and screening. *Pediatrics, 118*(1), 405–420.

American Speech and Hearing Association. (n.d.). *Telepractice: Overview.* http://www.asha.org/Practice-Portal/Professional-Issues/Telepractice/

Anderson, D., & Reilly, J. (2002). The MacArthur Communicative Development Inventory: Normative data for American Sign Language. *Journal of Deaf Studies and Deaf Education, 7*(2), 83–119. https://doi.org/10.1093/deafed/7.2.83

Baio, J., Wiggins, L., Christensen, D. L., Maenner, M. J., Daniels, J., Warren, Z., & Dowling, N. F. (2018). Prevalence of autism spectrum disorder among children aged 8 years: Autism and developmental disabilities monitoring network, 11 sites, United States, 2014. *Morbidity and Mortality Weekly Report, 67*(6), 1–23.

Bayley, N. (2005). *Bayley Scales of Infant and Toddler Development* (3rd ed., Bayley-III) [Assessment instrument]. Pearson.

Blaiser, K. M., Behl, D., Callow-Heusser, C., & White, K. R. (2013). Measuring costs and outcomes of tele-intervention when serving families of children who are deaf/hard-of-hearing. *International Journal of Telerehabilitation, 5*(2), 3–10. https://doi.org/10.5195/ijt.2013.6129

Boyle, C. A., Boulet, S., Schieve, L. A., Cohen, R. A., Blumberg, S. J., Yeargin-Allsopp, M., Visser, S., & Kogan, M. D. (2011). Trends in the prevalence of developmental disabilities in US children, 1997–2008. *Pediatrics, 127*(6), 1034–1042.

Briggs-Gowan, M. J., & Carter, A. S. (2008). Social-emotional screening status in early childhood predicts elementary school outcomes. *Pediatrics, 121*(5), 957–962.

Briggs-Gowan, M. J., Carter, A. S., Skuban, E. M., & Horwitz, S. M. (2001). Prevalence of social-emotional and behavioral problems in a community sample of 1- and 2-year-old children. *Journal of the American Academy of Child and Adolescent Psychiatry, 40*(7), 811–819.

Brown, P. M., & Nott, P. (2006). Family-centered practice in early intervention for oral language development: Philosophy, methods, and results. In P. E. Spencer & M. Marschark (Eds.), *Advances in the spoken language development of deaf and hard-of-hearing children* (pp. 136–165). Oxford University Press.

Calderon, R., Bargones, J., & Sidman, S. (1998). Characteristics of hearing families and their young deaf and hard of hearing children: Early intervention follow-up. *American Annals of the Deaf, 143*(4), 347–362.

Calderon, R., & Greenberg, M. (2003). Social and emotional development of deaf children: Family, school, and program effects. In M. Marschark & P. Spencer (Eds.), *Oxford handbook of deaf studies, language, and education* (Vol. 1, pp. 177–189). Oxford University Press.

Cannon, J. E., & Luckner, J. L. (2016). Increasing cultural and linguistic diversity in deaf education teacher preparation programs. *American Annals of the Deaf, 161*(1), 89–103.

Carpenter, B. (2005). Early childhood intervention: Possibilities and prospects for professionals, families and children. *British Journal of Special Education, 32*(4), 176–183.

Carrow-Woolfolk, E. (2004). *Oral and Written Language Scales* (2nd ed., OWLS-II) [Assessment instrument]. Pearson.

Carrow-Woolfolk, E. (2017). *Comprehensive Assessment of Spoken Language* (2nd ed., CASL-2) [Assessment instrument]. Pearson.

Centers for Disease Control (CDC). (2016). Health care, family, and community factors associated with mental, behavioral, and developmental disorders in early childhood—United States, 2011–2012. *Morbidity and Mortality Weekly Report (MMWR), 65*(9), 221–226.

Centers for Disease Control (CDC). (2018). Summary of 2016 national CDC EHDI data. *2016 CDC EHDI Hearing Screening & Follow-up Survey*, 1–4. https://www.cdc.gov/ncbddd/hearingloss/2016-data/01-2016-HSFS-Data-Summary-h.pdf

Cloninger, C. J. (2004). Designing collaborative educational services. In F. P. Orelove, D. Sobsey, & R. K. Silberman (Eds.), *Educating children with multiple disabilities: A collaborative approach* (4th ed., pp. 1–29). Brookes.

Cole, P., Oser, C., & Walsh, S. (2011). Building on the foundations of Part C legislation: Beginning the conversation for reauthorization. *Zero to Three, 31*(4), 52–60.

Cooper, C. R., Denner, J., & Lopez, E. M. (1999). Cultural brokers: Helping Latino children on pathways toward success. *Future of Children, 9*(2), 51–57.

Correa-Torres, S. M., & Durando, J. (2011). Perceived training needs of teachers of students with visual impairments who work with students from culturally and linguistically diverse backgrounds. *Journal of Visual Impairment & Blindness, 105*(9), 521–532.

Cupples, L., Ching, T., Crowe, K., Seeto, M., Leigh, G., Street, L., & Thomson, J. (2014). Outcomes of 3-year-old children with hearing loss and different types of additional disabilities. *Journal of Deaf Studies and Deaf Education, 19*(1), 20–39. https://doi.org/10.1097/AUD.0b013e3182857718

Darrah, J., Hodge, M., Magill-Evans, J., & Kembhavi, G. (2003). Stability of serial assessments of motor and communication abilities in typically developing infants—Implications for screening. *Early Human Development, 72*(2), 97–110.

Division for Early Childhood (DEC). (2009). *Developmental delay as an eligibility category.* https://www.decdocs.org/concept-paper-developmental-delay

Division for Early Childhood (DEC). (2014). *DEC recommended practices in early intervention/early childhood special education 2014.* https://www.dec-sped.org/recommendedpractices

Edwards, L., & Crocker, S. (2008). *Psychological processes in deaf children with complex needs.* Jessica Kingsley.

Edwards, L. C., Frost, R., & Witham, R. (2006). Developmental delay and outcomes in pediatric cochlear implantation: Implications for candidacy. *International Journal of Pediatric Otorhinolaryngology, 70,* 1593–1600. https://doi.org/10.1016/j.ijporl.2006.04.008

Ewing, K. M., & Jones, T. W. (2003). An educational rationale for deaf students with multiple disabilities. *American Annals of the Deaf, 148*(3), 267–271. https://doi.org/10.1353/aad.2003.0019

Fahrina, S. A., Rems-Smario, J., & Dickeson, C. (2017, February). *LEAK-K: What it means and why it complements EHDI efforts* [Paper presentation]. 16th Annual Early Hearing Detection & Intervention Meeting, Atlanta, GA.

Folio, M. R., & Fewell, R. R. (2000). *Peabody Developmental Motor Scales* [Assessment instrument]. Pearson.

Gallaudet Office of Research Support and International Affairs (RSIA). (2014). *Regional and national summary report of data from the 2013– 2014 Annual Survey of Deaf and Hard of Hearing Children and Youth.* https://www.gallaudet.edu/documents/Research-Support-and-International-Affairs/Intl%20Affairs/Demographics/AS14_RegNat.pdf

Gallaudet Research Institute (GRI). (2013). *Regional and national summary report of data from the 2011–2012 Annual Survey of Deaf and Hard of Hearing Children and Youth.* https://www.gallaudet.edu/documents/Research-Support-and-International-Affairs/Intl%20Affairs/Demographics/AS12_RegNat.pdf

Gallegos, R., Halus, K., & Crace, J. (2016). Individualized family service plans and programming. In M. Sass-Lehrer (Ed.), *Early intervention for deaf and hard-of-hearing infants, toddlers and their families* (pp. 275–303). Oxford University Press.

Gentemann, K. M., & Whitehead, T. L. (1983). The cultural broker concept in bicultural education. *Journal of Negro Education, 52*(2), 118–129.

Georgetown University Center for Child and Human Development. (2011). *Contemporary practices in early intervention: Developmental delay and IDEA primer.* https://www.teachingei.org/disabilities/primers/Developmental_Delay.pdf

Giangreco, M. F., Prelock, P. A., Reid, R. R., Dennis, R. E., & Edleman, S. W. (2000). Role of related service personnel in inclusive schools. In R. A. Villa & J. S. Thousand (Eds.), *Restructuring for caring and effective education: Piecing the puzzle together* (2nd ed., pp. 360–388). Brookes.

Goldman, R., & Fristoe, M. (2015). *Goldman Fristoe Test of Articulation 3* (GFTA-3) [Assessment instrument]. Pearson.

Guardino, C., & Cannon, J. E. (2015). Theory, research, and practice for students who are deaf and hard of hearing with disabilities: Addressing the challenges from birth to postsecondary education. *American Annals of the Deaf, 160*(4), 347–355.

Guardino, C., & Cannon, J. E. (2016). Deafness and diversity: Reflections and directions. *American Annals of the Deaf, 161*(1), 104–112.

Hafer, J. C., & Stredler-Brown, A. (2003). Family-centered developmental assessment. In B. Bodner-Johnson & M. Sass-Lehrer (Eds.), *The young deaf or hard of hearing child: A family-centered approach to early intervention* (pp. 127–149). Brookes.

Harrison, P. L., & Oakland, T. (2003). *Adaptive Behavior Assessment System* (2nd ed.) [Assessment instrument]. Harcourt.

Health Resources and Service Administration. (2014). *The health and well-being of children: A portrait of states and the nation 2011–2012.* U.S. Department of Health and Human Services. https://mchb.hrsa.gov/nsch/2011-12/health/

Hillemeier, M. M., Farkas, G., Morgan, P. L., & Maczuga, S. (2009). Disparities in the prevalence of cognitive delay: How early do they appear? *Pediatric and Perinatal Epidemiology, 23*, 186–198.

Hintermair, M. (2006). Parental resources, parental stress, and socio-emotional development of deaf and hard-of-hearing children. *Journal of Deaf Studies and Deaf Education, 11*(4), 493–513.

Hirai, A. H., Kogan, M. D., Kandasamy, V., Reuland, C., & Bethell, C. (2018). Prevalence and variation of developmental screening and surveillance in early childhood. *JAMA Pediatrics. 172*(9), 857–866.

Houston, K. T. (2011). Teleintervention: Improving service delivery to young children with hearing loss and their families through telepractice. *SIG 9 Perspectives on Hearing and Hearing Disorders in Childhood, 21*(2), 66–72.

Houston, K. T., & Stredler-Brown, A. (2012). A model of early intervention for children with hearing loss provided through telepractice. *Volta Review, 112*(3), 283–296.

Individuals With Disabilities Education Act (IDEA) of 2004, 20 U.S.C. §§ 1400–1482 (2004 & rev. 2015).

Jackson, R. L., Ammerman, S. B., & Trautwein, B. A. (2015). Deafness and diversity: Early intervention. *American Annals of the Deaf, 160*(4), 356–367.

Joint Committee on Infant Hearing (JCIH). (2007). Year 2007 position statement: Principles and guidelines for early hearing detection and intervention programs. *Pediatrics, 120*(4), 897–921. https://doi.org/10.1542/peds.2007-2333

Jones, T. W., & Jones, J. K. (2003). Educating young deaf children with multiple disabilities. In B. Bodner-Johnson & M. Sass-Lehrer (Eds.), *The young deaf or hard of hearing child: A family-centered approach to early education* (pp. 291–329). Brookes.

Kaufman, H. (1979). *Kaufman Infant and Preschool Scale* [Assessment instrument]. Stoelting.

Kaufman, A. S., & Kaufman, N. L. (2018). *Kaufman Assessment Battery for Children* (2nd ed.) [Assessment instrument]. Pearson.

King, G., Strachan, D., Tucker, M., Duwyn, B., Desserud, S., & Shillington, M. (2009). The application of a transdisciplinary model for early intervention services. *Infants & Young Children, 22*(3), 211–223.

LEAD-K. (n.d.). *FAQ*. http://www.lead-k.org/leadkfaq/

Leigh, G., Newall, J. P., & Newall, T. (2010). Newborn screening and earlier intervention with deaf children: Issues for the developing world. In M. Marschark & P. Spencer (Eds.), *The Oxford handbook of deaf studies, language, and education* (Vol. 2, pp. 345–359). Oxford University Press.

Luckner, J. L., & Carter, K. (2001). Essential competencies for teaching students with hearing loss and additional disabilities. *American Annals of the Deaf, 146*(1), 7–15. https://doi.org/10.1353/aad.2012.0065

Marge, D. K., & Marge, M. (2005). *Beyond newborn hearing screening: Meeting the educational and health care needs of infants and young children with hearing loss in America*. Department of Physical Medicine and Rehabilitation, SUNY Upstate Medical University. https://www.upstate.edu/pmr/pdf/beyond_newborn.pdf

Marschark, M. (2007). *Raising and educating a deaf child: A comprehensive guide to the choices, controversies, and decisions faced by parents and educators*. Oxford University Press.

Marschark, M., Spencer, P. E., Adams, J., & Sapere, P. (2011). Evidence-based practice in educating deaf and hard-of-hearing children: Teaching to their cognitive strengths and needs. *European Journal of Special Needs Education, 26*(1), 3–16.

McCarthy, M., Muñoz, K., & White, K. R. (2010). Teleintervention for infants and young children who are deaf or hard-of-hearing. *Pediatrics, 126*, S52–S58. https://doi.org/10.1542/peds.2010-0354J

McLaughlin, M. R. (2011). Speech and language delay in children. *American Family Physician, 83*(10), 1183–1188.

Meadow-Orlans, K. P., Mertens, D. M., & Sass-Lehrer, M. (2003). *Parents and their deaf children: The early years.* Gallaudet University Press.

Meinzen-Derr, J., Wiley, S., Bishop, S., Manning-Courtney, P., Choo, D., & Murray, D. (2013). Autism spectrum disorders in 24 children who are deaf or hard of hearing. *International Journal of Pediatric Otorhinolaryngology, 78*(1), 112–118. https://doi.org/10.1016/j.ijporl. 2013.10.065

Moeller, M. P. (2000). Early intervention and language development in children who are deaf and hard of hearing. *Pediatrics, 106*(3), 1–9.

Moeller, M. P., Carr, G., Seaver, L., Stredler-Brown, A., & Holzinger, D. (2013). Best practices in family-centered early intervention for children who are deaf or hard of hearing: An international consensus statement. *Journal of Deaf Studies and Deaf Education, 18*(4), 429–445. https://doi.org/10.1093/deafed/ent034

Morgan, P. L., Farkas, G., Hillemeier, M. M., Mattison, R., Maczuga, S., Li, H., & Cook, M. (2015). Minorities are disproportionately underrepresented in special education: Longitudinal evidence across five disability conditions. *Educational Researcher, 44*(5), 278–292.

Myers, C. L., McBride, S. L., & Peterson, C. A. (1996). Transdisciplinary, play-based assessment in early childhood special education: An examination of social validity. *Topics in Early Childhood Special Education, 16*(1), 102–126.

National Center for Hearing Assessment and Management (NCHAM). (2014). *A practical guide to the use of tele-intervention in providing listening and spoken language services to infants and toddlers who are deaf or hard of hearing.* http://www.infanthearing.org/ti-guide/index.html

National Early Childhood Technical Assistance Center (NECTAC). (2015). States' and territories' definition of criteria for IDEA Part C eligibility. http://ectacenter.org/~pdfs/topics/earlyid/partc_elig_table.pdf

Newborg, J., Stock, J. R., Wnek, L., Guidubaldi, J., & Svinicki, J. (2004). *The Battelle Developmental Inventory* [Assessment instrument]. DLM Teaching Resources.

Noritz, G. H., & Murphy, N. A. (2013). Motor delays: Early identification and evaluation. *Pediatrics, 131*(6), e2016–e2027.

Orelove, F. P., & Sobsey, R. (Eds.). (1996). *Educating children with multiple disabilities: A transdisciplinary approach* (3rd ed.). Brookes.

Perna, R., & Loughan, A. R. (2013). Early developmental delays: A cross validation study. *Journal of Psychological Abnormalities, 1*(2), 1–5.

Pletcher, L. (2012). *The transdisciplinary team approach* [Paper presentation]. Family Infants Toddler (FIT) Program Annual Meeting, University of New Mexico's Center for Development and Disability.

Pletcher, L., & Younggren, N. (2013). *The early intervention workbook: Essential practices for quality services.* Brookes.

Roid, G. H. (2003). *Stanford Binet Intelligence Scales* (5th ed.) [Assessment instrument]. Western Psychological Services.

Roizen, N. J. (2003). Nongenetic causes of hearing loss. *Developmental Disabilities Research Reviews, 9*(2), 120–127. https.//doi.org/10.1002/mrdd.10068

Roper, L., Arnold, P., & Monteiro, B. (2003). Co-occurrence of autism and deafness. *Autism, 7*(3), 245–253. https://doi.org/10.1177/1362361303007003002

Rose, D. H., & Gravel, J. W. (2010). Universal design for learning. In E. Baker, P. Peterson, & B. McGaw (Eds.), *International encyclopedia of education* (3rd ed., pp. 119–124). Elsevier.

Rosenberg, S. A., Zhang, D., & Robinson, C. C. (2008). Prevalence of developmental delays and participation in early intervention services for young children. *Pediatrics, 121*(6), e1503–e1509.

Rydz, D., Srour, M., Oskoui, M., Marget, N., Shiller, M., Birnbaum, R., Majnemer, A., & Shevell, M. I. (2006). Screening for developmental delay in the setting of a community pediatric clinic: A prospective assessment of parent-report questionnaires. *Pediatrics, 118*(4), e1178–e1186.

Sass-Lehrer, M. (2003). Programs and services for deaf and hard of hearing children and their families. In B. Bodner-Johnson & M. Sass-Lehrer (Eds.), *The young deaf or hard of hearing child: A family-centered approach to early education* (pp. 153–185). Brookes.

Sass-Lehrer, M., & Bodner-Johnson, B. (2003). Early intervention: Current approaches to family-centered programming. In M. Marschark & P. Spencer (Eds.), *Oxford handbook of deaf studies, language, and education* (Vol. 1, pp. 65–79). Oxford University Press.

Sass-Lehrer, M., Porter, A., & Wu, C. L. (2016). Families: Partnerships in practice. In M. Sass-Lehrer (Ed.), *Early intervention for deaf and hard-of-hearing infants, toddlers, and their families: Interdisciplinary perspectives* (pp. 65–103). Oxford University Press.

Schmeltz, L. R. (2014). Parent counseling in the internet age: The rules and roles have changed. In L. R. Schmeltz (Ed.), *A resource guide for early hearing detection and intervention* (pp. 10.1–10.8). http://www.infanthearing.org/ehdi-ebook/2020_ebook/10%20Chapter10Parent Counseling2020.pdf

Semel, E., Wiig, E. H., & Sicord, W. A. (2004). *Clinical Evaluation of Language Fundamentals: Preschool 2* [Assessment instrument]. Pearson.

Simms, L., Baker, S., & Clark, M. D. (2013). The Standardized Visual Communication and Sign Language Checklist for Signing Children. *Sign Language Studies, 14*(1), 101–124.

Sininger, Y. S., Martinez, A., Eisenberg, L., Christensen, E., Grimes, A., & Hu, J. (2009). Newborn hearing screening speeds diagnosis and access to intervention by 20–25 months. *Journal of the American Academy of Audiology, 20*, 49–57.

Sparrow, S. S., Cicchetti, D. V., & Balla, D. V. (2005). *Vineland Adaptive Behavior Scales* (2nd ed., Vineland II) [Assessment instrument]. Pearson.

Spencer, P. E., & Marschark, M. (2010). *Evidence-based practice in educating deaf and hard-of-hearing students.* Oxford University Press.

Squires, J., Bricker, D., & Twombly, E. (2017). *Ages & Stages Questionnaires: Social-Emotional* (2nd ed., ASQ: SE2) [Assessment instrument]. Brookes.

Stevens, G., Flaxman, S., Brunskill, E., Mascarenhas, M., Mathers, C. D., & Finucane, M. (2011). Global and regional hearing impairment prevalence: An analysis of 42 studies in 29 countries. *European Journal of Public Health, 23*(1), 146–152.

Tervo, R. (2003). Identifying patterns of developmental delay can help diagnose neurodevelopmental disorders. *Pediatric Perspective, 12*(3), 1.

Vernon, M. (1982). Multihandicapped deaf children: Types and causes. In D. Tweedie & E. Shroyer (Eds.), *The multihandicapped hearing impaired: Identification and instruction* (pp. 11–29). Gallaudet College Press.

Walker, S. P., Wachs, T. D., Grantham-McGregor, S., Black, M. M., Nelson, C. A., Huffman, S. L., Baker-Henningham, H., Chang, S. M., Hamadani, J. D., Lozoff, B., Meeks Gardner, J. M., Powell, C. A., Rahman, A., & Gardner, J. M. M. (2011). Inequality in early childhood: Risk and protective factors for early child development. *The Lancet, 378*(9799), 1325–1338.

Watkins, S., Pittman, P., & Walden, B. (1998). The deaf mentor experimental project for young children who are deaf and their families. *American Annals of the Deaf, 143*, 29–34. https://doi.org/10.1353/aad.2012.0098

Wechsler, D. (2012). *Wechsler Preschool and Primary Scale of Intelligence* (WPPSI-IV) [Assessment instrument]. Pearson.

Werling, D. M., & Geschwind, D. H. (2013). Sex differences in autism spectrum disorders. *Current Opinion in Neurology, 26*(2), 146–153.

White, K. R. (2006). Early intervention for children with permanent hearing loss: Finishing the EHDI revolution. *Volta Review, 106*(3), 237–258.

Wolery, M., & Dyk, L. (1984). Arena assessment: Description and preliminary social validity data. *Journal of the Association for Persons With Severe Handicaps, 9*(3), 231–235.

Wu, C. L., & Grant, N. C. (2013). Multicultural deaf children and the hearing families: Working with a constellation of diversities. In C. C. Lee (Ed.), *Multicultural issues in counseling: New approaches to diversity* (4th ed., pp. 235–257). American Counseling Association.

Yoshinaga-Itano, C. (2003). From screening to early identification and intervention: Discovering predictors to successful outcomes for children with significant hearing loss. *Journal of Deaf Studies and Deaf Education, 8*(1), 11–30.

Zimmerman, I. L., Steiner, V. G., & Pond, R. E. (2011). *Preschool Language Scales* (5th ed., PLS-5) [Assessment instrument]. Pearson.

3

Learners Who Are Deaf or Hard of Hearing With Autism Spectrum Disorders

Christy M. Borders, Kristi M. Probst,
and Stacey Jones Bock

LEARNING OBJECTIVES

Readers will:

- Discover overlapping characteristics associated with learners who are d/Deaf and hard of hearing (d/Dhh) and those with autism spectrum disorders (ASD; d/Dhh-ASD).
- Examine the challenges associated with differential diagnosis and the variety of approaches to instruction from the fields of d/Dhh and ASD.
- Understand the demographics of learners who are d/Dhh-ASD and differential identification and assessment practices.
- Review literature on communication/language and psychosocial needs and an overview of practices from the field of ASD.
- Discuss strategies used within the field of ASD designed to address communication, socialization, and behavioral needs.

The 2018 prevalence rates reported by the Centers for Disease Control (CDC, 2018) have indicated that ASD occurs at a similar rate among d/Deaf and hard of hearing (d/Dhh) individuals compared with individuals

DOI: 10.4324/9781003252054-3

with typical hearing. This is a contrast from the past when ASD was found to be more prevalent in d/Dhh children. There are two caveats with these statistics. First, the prevalence rates for d/Dhh students with ASD have not been calculated recently. Second, we have no reason to believe that if rates have increased in the hearing population, they have not also increased in the d/Dhh population.

Demographics of d/Dhh students have consistently included a large percentage of disabilities, including ASD (Borders et al., 2014; Gallaudet Research Institute [GRI], 2013; Guardino & Cannon, 2015). Accurately identifying the number of d/Dhh students with ASD (d/Dhh-ASD) is a difficult task. Multiple studies have indicated higher rates of ASD in individuals who are d/Dhh than in the general population (Cejas et al., 2015; Fitzpatrick et al., 2014; Gordon, 1991; Guardino, 2008; Jure et al., 1991; Rosenhall et al., 1999). Yet most recently, the CDC (2018) has reported that the prevalence rate among the general population rose to 1 in 59 children, the same rate reported by Szymanski et al. (2012) when studying students who are d/Dhh-ASD. Guardino and Cannon (2015) reported statistics from the GRI and the U.S. Department of Education Child Count and surmised that there is likely an underrepresentation of students who are d/Dhh with a disability/disabilities, including students with d/Dhh-ASD. It is also likely that only those students with classic ASD symptoms (i.e., those with severe challenges in social communication and restricted, repetitive behavior) are represented, while those with high-functioning ASD are missing.

The identification of ASD in children who are d/Dhh proves to be a daunting task due to the overlapping symptomology across both populations (Bruce & Borders, 2015; Fitzpatrick et al., 2014; Mood & Shield, 2014; Shield & Meier, 2012; Szymanski et al., 2012). For example, both d/Dhh individuals and those with ASD can experience impacts on language acquisition and development. Furthermore, d/Dhh students who use listening and spoken language (LSL; use assistive hearing devices and LSL techniques) often display atypical responses to auditory stimuli, similar to research findings that have also been reported in children with ASD (Berard, 1993; Rimland & Edelson, 1994; Ring et al., 1999; Rosenhall et al., 1999; Stiegler & Davis, 2010; Tharpe et al., 2006). This overlapping symptomology makes dual diagnosis particularly difficult.

Diagnostic Assessment Practices

Educational and Clinical Diagnostic Criteria

The identification and diagnosis of ASD in a d/Dhh child must be undertaken cautiously and by individuals who are trained in both specialties. Several researchers have suggested strategies for a more thorough assessment of this particular population of learners (Carr et al., 2014; Hoevenaars-van den Boom et al., 2009; Kellogg et al., 2014; Mood & Shield, 2014; Szarkowski et al., 2014). During the assessment process, professionals may further consider educational and/or clinical diagnostic criteria.

In the United States, the Individuals With Disabilities Education Act (IDEA, 2004) defines autism as, "a developmental disability significantly affecting verbal and nonverbal communication and social interaction, generally evident before age three, that adversely affects a child's educational performance."

The American Psychiatric Association (APA) established criteria for the diagnosis of ASD as "persistent deficits in social communication and social interaction across multiple contexts and restricted, repetitive patterns of behavior, interests, or activities" (APA, 2013, p. 50). Currently, the *Diagnostic and Statistical Manual of Mental Disorders* (DSM–5; APA, 2013) describes three levels of severity for ASD. The third level of severity includes individuals "requiring *very substantial* supports"; Level 2 describes an individual who "requires *substantial* supports"; and Level 1 is an individual who "requires support" (APA, 2013). For example, a child classified as needing "very substantial supports" and placed in the Level 3 severity level for social communication could be described thus—the child used very few words that could be understood by others, rarely initiated interaction, used unusual communication methods only to meet needs, and "responded only to very direct social approaches" (APA, 2013; Autism Speaks Organization, 2020).

When planning educational programming for children who are d/Dhh, a medical diagnosis must be made. However, to receive accommodations and modifications to the educational curriculum for ASD, a medical diagnosis is not necessary. If students have a demonstrated need and qualify for educational services, the educational team should provide accommodations and modifications. If a student displays behaviors that are indicative of ASD (e.g., delays in communication and social interaction, insistence on sameness and routine as defined by the DSM-5), professionals use the definition provided by the IDEA (2004) to determine educational eligibility:

> Autism means a developmental disability significantly affecting verbal and nonverbal communication and social interaction, generally evident before age three, that adversely affects a child's educational performance. Other characteristics often associated with autism are engagement in repetitive activities and stereotyped movements, resistance to environmental change or change in daily routines, and unusual responses to sensory experiences. (§ 300.8 [1] [c])

ASD-specific assessments, such as the Autism Diagnostic Observation Scale (Mood & Shield, 2014); the Childhood Autism Rating Scale (CARS; Schopler & Van Bourgondien, 2010); and the Autism Screening Instrument for Educational Planning (Krug et al., 2008), exist and are used by professionals to determine a diagnosis of ASD. A differential diagnosis (i.e., determining a diagnosis between two or more conditions that share similar characteristics) is possible for this population; however, there are difficulties with obtaining a differential diagnosis between learners' needs specifically related to deafness and those related to ASD.

Difficulties Associated With Differential Diagnosis

When seeking to identify ASD in children who are d/Dhh, professionals often rely on ASD assessment tools, with considerable differences in how they utilize them (e.g., types of accommodations provided; Mood & Shield, 2014). Furthermore, one of the most challenging issues with differential diagnosis is the determination of whether behavior issues are due to the child's hearing levels or diagnosis of ASD (Hoevenaars-van den Boom et al., 2009).

When a child is d/Dhh and has disabilities (DWD), the symptomology is not merely additive, but multiplicative. Often, the initial diagnosis of young children with DWD is their hearing level, due to the widespread use of newborn hearing screening. The opposite may be true for a child who has severe disabilities at birth. In this case, the hearing levels may not be identified until later due to complications and irregularities in the neonatal intensive care unit hearing screening (Bruce & Borders, 2015; Jacobs et al., 2010). When more severe disabilities are present, the difficulties with differential diagnosis using the Autism Diagnostic Interview—Revised (ADI-R), CARS, and the Autism Behavior Checklist (ABC) are increased. For example, there is a significant discrepancy in scores of individuals with both visual and hearing losses (Johansson et al., 2010) compared to those with no sensory losses. This is likely because a dual-sensory loss can result in symptomology that resembles ASD, leading to misinterpretation and further confounding diagnostic outcomes (Probst & Borders, 2017). Inconsistency appears in the data presented by researchers noting both over- and underdiagnosis (Johansson et al., 2010) of ASD in children with a variety of severe disabilities.

The time it takes to diagnose ASD in d/Dhh children is also a concern. Researchers agree that there is a delay in diagnosis of ASD in children already identified as d/Dhh, as compared to those with typical hearing (Fitzpatrick et al., 2014; Meinzen-Derr et al., 2014; Mood & Shield, 2014; Myck-Wayne et al., 2011; Roper et al., 2003; Szymanski et al., 2012; Worley et al., 2001). Those investigating this phenomenon hypothesize that delayed diagnosis is based on the difficulty in differentiating the characteristics of individuals who are d/Dhh from those with ASD (e.g., delays in communication, language development, and socialization; Birath et al., 2014; Borders et al., 2017). Researchers also report that, for parents and educators, there are limited resources that provide criteria for the identification and assessment of learners who are d/Dhh-ASD.

Accurate differential diagnosis can occur with a skilled team of trained professionals who know developmental patterns in learners who are d/Dhh-ASD (Bruce & Borders, 2015). The professional team should be compiled to address the individual needs of the student. Team members may include a speech pathologist, audiologist, occupational therapist, a teacher of the d/Deaf and hard of hearing (TODHH), a teacher with special education licensure, or a board-certified behavior analyst. The professional team should include professionals who understand the impact of various hearing levels and are skilled in identifying ASD. Diagnostic tools to identify ASD in a student who is d/Dhh are generally unavailable; however, Mood and Shield (2014) advise using tools created for ASD assessment with modifications to the tasks, scoring, and language (e.g., the conversion of English to American Sign Language [ASL]). Accurate diagnosis is imperative for learners to receive the educational supports necessary for academic progress. For instance, if a student is first identified as being d/Dhh but later receives a diagnosis of ASD, they are initially educated using d/Dhh methodologies (Borders et al., 2017), whereas the opposite is true as well (Guardino, 2008). Roper et al. (2003) confirm that deaf or hard of hearing is more often the initial diagnosis than ASD. Borders et al. (2015) pointed to the link between an educational label and the number, type, and intensity of services received, indicating the critical nature of accurate assessment and diagnosis (see IDEA, 2004) for educational definitions.

COMMUNICATION

Communication and linguistic difficulties for many children who are d/Dhh-ASD are compounded, resulting in significant, unique difficulties (Rosenhall et al., 1999; Trussel & Easterbrooks, 2016; Vernon & Rhodes, 2009). Students need functional communication, which can occur through a variety of modalities (e.g., speech, signed language, pictures, and objects). The process of determining a preferred communication modality is complex for families with children who are d/Dhh; additional considerations that deafness *and* autism bring to the decision-making process are discussed.

Parents/guardians and professionals must consider factors specific to ASD when deciding on communication training methods and modes. Some communication issues related to ASD include the following: engaging in joint attention (Leekam & Ramsden, 2006; Worley et al., 2001), use of eye gaze (Spezio et al., 2007), interpreting facial expressions (Celani et al., 1999; Denmark et al., 2009; Hobson, 1986; Ozonoff et al., 1991), demonstrating emotion (Baron-Cohen et al., 1997), tendency to focus on nonsocial stimuli rather than social stimuli (Dawson et al., 1998; Leekam et al., 2000; Leekam & Ramsden, 2006), and modifying sign language (Shield, 2010, 2014; Shield & Meier, 2012). For example, Shield (2010) studied native d/Dhh learners who use sign language and found marked differences in the signs of those with ASD and those without. Some of those differences included palm reversals and pronoun confusion. Szarkowski et al. (2014) clarify one distinct difference in language development.

> With the exception of difficulty acquiring particular speech sounds, grammatical features/vocabulary, and idioms, deafness is primarily a model of delayed language development, rather than atypical language development. In particular, we do not typically expect hearing loss to interfere with the acquisition of preverbal social communication skills. (p. 246)

Students who are d/Dhh require additional supports to acquire language and communication skills due to their limited access to language. Training programs for the TODHH focus on practices that address language, communication, literacy, and audition delays (Ferrell et al., 2014). However, attention to social, emotional, and behavioral characteristics should also be stressed.

Social/Communication and Ritualistic/Repetitive Behaviors

There is a significant variance among the behavioral characteristics of those with ASD. The APA (2013) describes the range of differences in communication, social-emotional skills, and behavior of individuals with ASD.

- *Social-emotional reciprocity.* For example, learners range from those having an atypical social approach and lacking typical back-and-forth conversation; to those with reduced sharing of interests, emotions, or affect; to those who fail to initiate or respond to social interactions.
- *Nonverbal communicative behaviors used for social interaction.* For example, learners range from having poorly integrated verbal and nonverbal communication; to differences in eye contact and body language or deficits in understanding and use of gestures; to a total lack of facial expressions and nonverbal communication.

- *Developing, maintaining, and understanding relationships.* For example, learners range from having difficulties adjusting behavior to suit various social contexts; to difficulties in sharing imaginative play or in making friends; to an absence of interest in peers.

Individuals with ASD often display rigidity or inflexibility in their behavior, which may impact their lives and result in difficulty with transitions, change, and the unfamiliar. Deficits in social skills tend to increase over time: as children with ASD get older, the gap between their social skills and what is socially acceptable by peers may widen, potentially creating a "friendship disparity" (Lyons et al., 2011). Therefore, focused attention should be placed on social skill development throughout school programming for students with ASD.

When incorporating social skill instruction into programming for students who are d/Dhh and have ASD, it is important to consider the communication modality of peers and professionals in the educational setting. All plans need to include strategies for incorporating communication that can be used by both the child who is d/Dhh-ASD and peers. Creating programming for these students may seem challenging; however, there are many suggested practices that may prove beneficial.

Suggested Strategies From the Field of ASD

There is a lack of guidance regarding best practices or effective strategies for children who are d/Dhh-ASD relative to behavior, social skills, or communication (Bruce & Borders, 2015). It may be beneficial to consider theories based on research from the field of ASD combined with the unique learning needs of students with this dual diagnosis (Bradley et al., 2008; Loveland et al., 2008). Research in the area of ASD includes, but is not limited to, the use of augmentative and alternative communication devices (Davis et al., 2010), Picture Exchange Communication System (PECS; Malandraki & Okalidou, 2007), applied behavior analysis (Easterbrooks & Handley, 2005; Mace et al., 2011; Vernon & Rhodes, 2009), and functional behavioral analysis (Borders et al., 2014; Szymanski et al., 2012; Zane et al., 2014).

In 2014, the National Professional Development Center on Autism Spectrum Disorders (NPDC on ASD) released a report that recognized 27 evidence-based practices (EBPs) to address the communication and behavior needs of individuals from birth to age 22 with ASD. These practices can be adapted to meet the needs of learners who are d/Dhh-ASD, as many of these approaches are visually based, a strategy that TODHHs have found successful for their students (see Table 3.1; Borders et al., 2016).

When reviewing the 27 practices identified by the NPDC, it is clear that many of them are antecedent interventions (e.g., PECS, prompting, reinforcement, functional behavior assessment, modeling, and visual supports). This means that the strategies are proactive, rather than reactive, when working to change behavior. The educational team sets up the environment to anticipate and reduce the challenging behavior (and/or increase desired behavior) before it happens, rather than waiting for the undesired behavior to occur and then planning a reactive strategy. This type of planning is beneficial to all students and can be carried out in any environment. One potential modification to these interventions for students who are d/Dhh-ASD is the communication modality. For example, a picture used in PECS may have a two-dimensional representation with both the sign and the word included on the card. The communication partner can use sign language in addition to or instead of using verbal communication.

Service Provision Planning

Educational Placement

If a student is d/Dhh and is later identified with ASD, they are often educated using methodologies from the field of deafness. The opposite is also true; if identified with ASD initially and as d/Dhh later, they could be educated using ASD methodologies (Guardino, 2008). Students often are bounced back and forth between different educational placements (in d/Dhh or ASD settings). This leads to inconsistency in programming and/or service provision, labeled "the zipper trajectory" (Borders et al., 2017). The zipper trajectory is the alternating of educational placements, which results in a limited amount of academic, language, and behavioral growth

TABLE 3.1 Evidence-Based Interventions for Students With Autism Spectrum Disorders

Evidence-Based Intervention	Level of Evidence	Potential Modifications or Considerations for d/Dhh Students
Antecedent-Based Intervention Arrangement of events or circumstances that come before a problem behavior and are designed to lead to the reduction of the behavior.	0 group design studies and 22 single-case studies	Be sure to account for access to auditory or visual signals used to set up behavior. For example, classroom environmental setup must account for the signal-to-noise ratio.
Cognitive Behavioral Intervention Instruction on management or control of cognitive processes that lead to changes in behavior.	3 group design studies and 1 single-case study	No modifications recommended.
Differential Reinforcement (DRA/DRI/DRO) Delivery of positive/desirable consequences for behaviors or their absence, which reduce the frequency of the negative behavior. Reinforcement is provided: (a) when the learner is engaging in a specific desired behavior (not the inappropriate behavior) (DRA); (b) when the learner is engaging in a behavior that is physically impossible to do while also doing the inappropriate behavior (DRI); or (c) when the learner is not engaging in the inappropriate behavior (DRO).	0 group design studies and 26 single-case studies	Be sure to gain visual or auditory attention (dependent on the student's modality) prior to reinforcement delivery.

Evidence-Based Intervention	Level of Evidence	Potential Modifications or Considerations for d/Dhh Students
Discrete Trial Teaching (DTT) Teaching that usually involves one adult and one student and is designed to teach the appropriate behavior or skills through carefully planned consequences and pausing between trials.	0 group design studies and 13 single-case studies	Consider the addition of visual supports, including signed supports, or the use of pictures to support teacher directions or instructions.
Exercise Increase in physical exertion as a means of reducing problem behaviors or increasing appropriate behavior.	3 group design studies and 3 single-case studies	Consider the limited auditory access a student may have in a large open area for exercise (e.g., gym or outside) and how that may impact the students' ability to respond to directives/instructions.
Extinction Withdrawal or removal of reinforcers in order to reduce the behavior.	0 group design studies and 11 single-case studies	No modifications recommended.
Functional Behavioral Assessment (FBA) FBA consists of describing the problem behavior, identifying antecedent or consequent events that control the behavior, developing a hypothesis of the function of the behavior, and/or testing the hypothesis.	0 group design studies and 10 single-case design studies.	No modifications recommended.

(Continued)

TABLE 3.1 (*Continued*)

Evidence-Based Intervention	Level of Evidence	Potential Modifications or Considerations for d/Dhh Students
Functional Communication Training (FCT) Replacement of problem behavior with more appropriate communication that accomplishes the same function (as determined by FBA).	0 group design studies and 12 single-case studies	Be sure to remember the focus is on clear communication through replacement of behavior, not on the form of communication (e.g., spoken or signed). For example, raising a hand to request a break in the classroom versus stating or signing "I need a break."
Modeling Demonstration of a desired target behavior that results in imitation of the behavior by the learner and that leads to the acquisition of the imitated behavior.	1 group design study and 4 single-case studies	No modification recommended.
Naturalistic Intervention Intervention strategies that occur within the typical setting/activities/routines in which the learner participates.	0 group design studies and 10 single-case studies	No modification recommended.

Evidence-Based Intervention	Level of Evidence	Potential Modifications or Considerations for d/Dhh Students
Parent-Implemented Intervention Parents learn to deliver interventions in their home and/or community through a structured parent training program.	8 group design studies and 12 single-case studies	No modification recommended.
Peer-Mediated Instruction Typically developing peers interact with and/or help children with ASD to acquire new behavior, communication, and social skills by increasing social and learning opportunities within natural environments. Teachers systematically teach peers strategies for engaging children with ASD in positive and extended social interactions in both teacher-directed and learner-initiated activities.	0 group design studies and 15 single-case studies	Be sure to ensure communication modality compatibility between the d/Dhh student and peers for this intervention.

(Continued)

TABLE 3.1 (*Continued*)

Evidence-Based Intervention	Level of Evidence	Potential Modifications or Considerations for d/Dhh Students
Picture Exchange Communication System (PECS) Learners are initially taught to give a picture of a desired item to a communicative partner in exchange for the desired item. PECS consists of six phases, which are: 1. "how" to communicate 2. distance and persistence 3. picture discrimination 4. sentence structure 5. responsive requesting 6. commenting	2 group design studies and 4 single-case studies	Consider the addition of a two dimensional image of the sign for use with d/Dhh students who are also learning signed communication.
Pivotal Response Training (PRT) Pivotal learning variables (i.e., motivation, responding to multiple cues, self-management, and self-initiations) guide intervention practices that are implemented in settings that build on learner interests and initiative.	1 group design study and 7 single-case studies.	No modification recommended.

Evidence-Based Intervention	Level of Evidence	Potential Modifications or Considerations for d/Dhh Students
Prompting Verbal, gestural, or physical assistance given to students to help them acquire or engage in a targeted behavior or skill. Prompts are generally given by an adult or peer before or as a learner attempts to use a skill.	1 group design study and 32 single-case studies	Consider "verbal" prompts as signed or spoken phrases for d/Dhh students dependent on their communication modality.
Reinforcement An event, activity, or other circumstance occurring after a desired behavior, which leads to the increased occurrence of the behavior in the future.	0 group design studies and 43 single-case studies	No modification recommended.
Response/Interruption Redirection Introduction of a prompt, comment, or other distracters when an interfering behavior is occurring, which is designed to divert attention away from the interfering behavior and results in its reduction.	0 group design studies and 10 single-case studies	No modification recommended.
Scripting A verbal and/or written description about a specific skill or situation that serves as a model for a student. Scripts are usually practiced repeatedly before the skill is used in the actual situation.	1 group design study and 8 single-case studies	Consider combining this practice with video modeling to ensure access for d/Dhh students who use a manual mode of communication.

(Continued)

TABLE 3.1 (*Continued*)

Evidence-Based Intervention	Level of Evidence	Potential Modifications or Considerations for d/Dhh Students
Self-Management Instruction focusing on learners learning the difference between appropriate and inappropriate behaviors, accurately monitoring and recording their own behaviors, and rewarding themselves for behaving appropriately.	0 group design studies and 10 single-case studies	No modification recommended.
Social Narratives Narratives that describe social situations in some detail by highlighting relevant cues and offering examples of appropriate responding. Social narratives are individualized according to student needs and typically are quite short, perhaps including pictures or other visual aids.	0 group design studies and 17 single-case studies	Consider combining this practice with video modeling to ensure access ford/Dhh students who use a manual mode of communication.

Evidence-Based Intervention	Level of Evidence	Potential Modifications or Considerations for d/Dhh Students
Social Skills Training Group or individual instruction designed to teach students with ASD how to appropriately interact with peers, adults, and other individuals. Most social skill meetings include instruction on basic concepts, role-playing or practice, and feedback to help students with ASD acquire and practice communication, play, or social skills to promote positive interactions with peers.	7 group design studies and 8 single-case studies	Be sure to ensure communication modality compatibility among the d/Dhh student, peers, and teachers for this intervention.
Structured Play Group Small group activities characterized by a clear theme, with adults leading, prompting, or scaffolding as needed to support students' performance.	2 group design studies and 2 single-case studies	Be sure to ensure communication modality compatibility between the d/Dhh student and peers.
Task Analysis A process in which an activity or behavior is divided into small, manageable steps in order to assess and teach the skill.	0 group design studies and 8 single-case studies	No modification recommended.

(Continued)

TABLE 3.1 (*Continued*)

Evidence-Based Intervention	Level of Evidence	Potential Modifications or Considerations for d/Dhh Students
Technology-Aided Instruction Instruction or interventions in which technology is the central feature supporting the acquisition of a goal for the learner.	9 group design studies and 11 single-case studies	Ensure compatibility between technology used and assistive listening devices.
Time Delay In a setting or activity in which a student should engage in a behavior or skill, a brief delay is added between the opportunity to use the skill and any additional instructions or prompts. The purpose of the time delay is to allow the student to respond without having to receive a prompt and thus focuses on fading the use of prompts during instructional activities.	0 group design studies and 12 single-case studies	No modification recommended.

Evidence-Based Intervention	Level of Evidence	Potential Modifications or Considerations for d/Dhh Students
Video Modeling A visual model of the targeted behavior or skill (typically in the behavior, communication, play, or social domains), provided via video recording and display equipment to assist learning in or engaging in a desired behavior or skill.	1 group design study and 31 single-case studies	Ensure compatibility between technology used and assistive listening devices.
Visual Supports Any visual display that helps a student perform a desired behavior or skill independent of prompts.	0 group design studies and 18 single-case studies	Consider the addition of a two dimensional image of the sign for use with d/Dhh students who are also learning signed communication.

Note. Definitions modified from Wong et al. (2015). ASD = autism spectrum disorder; d/Dhh = d/Deaf or hard of hearing; DRA = differential reinforcement of alternative behavior; DRO = differential reinforcement of other behavior; DRI = differential reinforcement of incompatible behavior.

over time. While there may be growth, it is slow rather than following a continual positive trajectory. Each placement acts as an individual, isolated environment where students may learn small amounts in each setting, but this learning is unlikely to be maintained and may regress. Additionally, professionals who work with children with either ASD or sensory challenges are often inadequately prepared to provide services to those who have a dual-sensory diagnosis due to these children's very unique needs (Borders et al., 2014).

Borders et al. (2017) proposed an educational decision-making framework to use when working with students who are DWD. This framework includes EBPs utilizing a life-span perspective and person-centered planning (PCP). A life-span perspective takes into consideration teaching methodologies and how those impact the student's future (Borders et al., 2017). The PCP transition process begins around the age of 14 years. Teams use PCP to help an individual with disabilities solve problems and create a plan that helps the individual achieve their vision of their future. The PCP is a long-term plan that focuses on the individual's interests, strengths, and needs. As an integral part of the transition process, the PCP also incorporates community support systems that will be necessary when the student transitions to adulthood (Borders et al., 2017).

Transition Phases

In the United States, most professionals view transition plans for individuals with disabilities through the lens of IDEA (2004), where they are mandated by age 16 for any individual with an individualized education plan (IEP). Completing formal transition planning at that age ensures that an individual has the skills required to transition from high school to postsecondary education or employment. Transition planning is also required for children aged 2.5 years when exiting Part C services for Part B services (see Chapter 2 for details on these sections of IDEA). This type of transition plan includes the types of services that the child will receive, where the child will receive the services, and who will provide the services. The goal of Part C transition planning is to build a bridge for the child and family from early intervention services to early childhood services.

In one's lifetime, there are major transitions or developmental stages (e.g., graduation from high school) and countless smaller transitions (e.g., art class to the cafeteria; second grade to third grade; school week to the weekend). Transitions throughout the school day and from year to year can be a source of anxiety for individuals with ASD. Even though transition plans are not mandated during every transition in a child's life, planning is required for all transitions, regardless of the magnitude. Using the PCP framework and transition tools in all phases of educational programming ensures positive experiences and outcomes for the child.

The rigidity and inflexibility many individuals with ASD experience can increase the need to plan for transitions. Well-organized transition planning can also assist educational teams in ensuring that appropriate supports are put in place for the student and family (Hatfield et al., 2016; Koch & Rumrill, 2017). There are tools and practices (e.g., video modeling, schedules, visual supports) available to assist families and educational teams in supporting transitions.

Families and professionals should consider beginning the transition planning process as early as possible. One tool that can be helpful is Charting the LifeCourse™ (2017). This framework was developed to assist individuals with disabilities and their families in creating a vision for their lives. This tool further articulates what knowledge and skills should be developed, identifies necessary supports, and determines the steps needed to achieve their goals. The LifeCourse™ framework encourages individuals and families to "focus on a specific life stage, with an awareness of how prior, current, and future life stages and experiences impact and influence life trajectory" (University of Missouri-Kansas City Institute for Human Development, 2017, p. 2). This tool can be used throughout the individual's life and can be beneficial during the transition planning process.

Two additional tools that are recommended for transition planning are Making Action Plans (MAPS; Forest & Pearpoint, 1992; Vandercook et al., 1989) and Planning Alternative Tomorrows with Hope (PATH; Borders et al., 2017; Forest & O'Brien, 1993). Both these systems provide a structured means to plan for the future through the identification of strengths, needs, and goal setting and can be used as part of the IEP meeting or a PCP meeting.

CONCLUSION

As the prevalence of ASD has increased among the general public, educational teams have indicated a similar rise in the population of students who are d/Dhh. Accurately identifying ASD in students who are d/Dhh is difficult due to overlapping characteristics; however, whether or not a diagnosis of ASD is obtained, a child displaying ASD-type characteristics may benefit from a variety of instructional approaches. Professionals providing services to this population of learners are urged to look to adjacent fields when determining effective practices, specifically those from the field of ASD and severe and multiple disabilities, which have been developed to address communication, socialization, and behavioral needs. Families and professionals working with individuals who are d/Dhh-ASD, often need multiple means of support (e.g., parent groups, inter/transdisciplinary teams). The amount of available information is on the rise, but more is needed (see Resource section, Guardino, 2008; Guardino & Cannon, 2015) to better address the existing challenges with identification, assessment, and compilation of strategies specific to learners who are d/Dhh-ASD.

DISCUSSION QUESTIONS

1. Describe two to three challenges in identifying students who are d/Dhh and have ASD.
2. Explain the importance of diagnosing a child correctly the first time. What difficulties may arise if the diagnosis is not accurate?
3. Individuals with ASD often experience challenges communicating and socializing with others. How could these challenges be further exacerbated if the individual is also d/Dhh? What steps should be taken to help mitigate these challenges?
4. Identify the factors that must be considered when developing communication training methods for people who are d/Dhh with ASD. Provide an example of each training method. If needed, refer to the original sources cited within the chapter.
5. Describe the benefits of using antecedent interventions with students who are d/Dhh with ASD.

6. What are some steps that can be taken to support individuals who are d/Dhh and have ASD with the various transitions that occur throughout the school and/or workday?

Resources

Organizations

- **Clerc Center, Gallaudet University**
  - https://clerccenter.gallaudet.edu/national-resources/info/info-to-go/deaf-students-with-disabilities.html
- **Illinois Service Resource Center, Northbrook, IL**
  - http://www.isrc.us/deaf-plus
- **Organization of Autism Research**
  - https://researchautism.org/education/teachers-corner/
  - OAR's Teacher's Corner holds informational guides that teach educators how to support their autistic students and how to teach their classmates about autism.

Professional Development

- **The IRIS Center**
  - https://iris.peabody.vanderbilt.edu/
- **National Autism Resources**
  - https://www.nationalautismresources.com/classroom-materials-teaching-supplies/
  - A teacher hub for classroom supplies made specifically for students on the autism spectrum, ranging from fidget toys to sensory soothing tools.
- **National Professional Development Center on Autism Spectrum Disorders**
  - http://autismpdc.fpg.unc.edu/
- **Ohio Center for Autism and Low Incidence**
  - http://www.ocali.org/
- **TEACCH Autism Program**
  - https://teacch.com/resources/

- ○ TEACCH is operated by the University of North Carolina at Chapel Hill School of Medicine and provides teaching materials and assessment tools to educators with students on the autism spectrum.
- **Understanding DAD** (i.e., deafness and diversity)
  - ○ http://understandingdad.net/

Free Webinars

- **Assessment of Autism Spectrum Disorder With Children Who Are Deaf/Hard of Hearing–Part 1**
  - ○ https://www.youtube.com/watch?v=hs2GdnI6G8U
- **Autism and Deaf and Hard of Hearing Students**
  - ○ https://www.youtube.com/watch?v=zTJDPB_EMhk
- **Deafness With Autism for General Education Teachers**
  - ○ https://www.youtube.com/watch?v=sX9JcfaL5CQ
- **Supporting Students With a Dual Diagnosis of Deafness and Autism Spectrum Disorder–Part 1**
  - ○ https://www.youtube.com/watch?v=NHQ6lXCqKjY
- **Supporting Students With a Dual Diagnosis of Deafness and Autism Spectrum Disorder–Part 2**
  - ○ https://www.youtube.com/watch?v=h-p6ovA5Cp0&index=3& list=PL27q7YAI6RuuAa-yttgw6zJoKCsEMujT9&t=0s
- **Supporting Students With a Dual Diagnosis of Deafness and Autism Spectrum Disorder–Part 3**
  - ○ https://www.youtube.com/watch?v=IPODrzOeYmU&index= 4&list=PL27q7YAI6RuuAa-yttgw6zJoKCsEMujT9&t=0s
- **Supporting Students With a Dual Diagnosis of Deafness and Autism Spectrum Disorder–Part 4**
  - ○ https://www.youtube.com/watch?v=mRCFTxMFtTo&index =5&list=PL27q7YAI6RuuAa-yttgw6zJoKCsEMujT9&t=0s
- **Supporting Students With a Dual Diagnosis of Deafness and Autism Spectrum Disorder–Part 5**
  - ○ https://www.youtube.com/watch?v=1QiXF5UNTmU&index =6&list=PL27q7YAI6RuuAa-yttgw6zJoKCsEMujT9&t=0s

Articles/Newsletters

- **"Red Flags for Disabilities in Children Who Are Deaf/ Hard of Hearing," by Moeller and Wiley**
  - https://leader.pubs.asha.org/article.aspx?articleid=2289769
- **"A Summary of Current Understanding Regarding Children With Autism Spectrum Disorder Who Are Deaf or Hard of Hearing," by Swarkowski, Mood, Shield, Wiley, and Yoshinaga-Itano**
  - https://pdfs.semanticscholar.org/43ee/dee5ab-f4855af459a7f6c717cc0cad043032.pdf
- *Loud & Clear,* **Issue 2—Sensory Needs**
  - https://advancedbionics.com/content/dam/advancedbion-ics/Documents/Regional/US/libraries/Loud-and-Clear/Loud-&-Clear!-Newsletter/Loud-and-Clear!-Newsletter-Issue-2-Perspectives-on-Deafness-with-Autism.pdf
- *Loud & Clear,* **Issue 5—Communication Assessment and Intervention for the School Age Child**
  - https://advancedbionics.com/content/dam/advancedbionics/Documents/Regional/US/libraries/Loud-and-Clear/Loud-&-Clear!-Newsletter/Loud-and-Clear!-Newsletter-Issue-5.pdf
- *Loud & Clear,* **Issue 6—Addressing Behavioral Needs in Students Who Are Deaf or Hard of Hearing With Autism Spectrum Disorder**
  - https://advancedbionics.com/content/dam/advancedbionics/Documents/Regional/US/libraries/Loud-and-Clear/Loud-&-Clear!-Newsletter/Loud-and-Clear!-Newsletter-Issue-6.pdf

Parent Guides

- **Autism and Beyond**
  - https://autismandbeyond.researchkit.duke.edu/resources
  - A product of Duke University, Autism and Beyond is a site that holds the answers to many of the questions a parent of an autistic child may have. Some of the topics include how to get help for your child and for yourself as the parent.
- **Autism Now**
  - https://autismnow.org/

- ○ The Autism NOW Center, sponsored by The Arc; the website can keep the community up to date on the latest news and research regarding autism.
- **Autism Speaks**
  - ○ https://www.autismspeaks.org/tool-kit/parents-guide-autism
  - ○ A Parent's Guide to Autism is a downloadable family support tool kit that addresses frequently asked questions, diagnosis information, and child support advice.
- **Open Source Parenting-Special Needs: Deaf With Autism**
  - ○ https://osparenting.wordpress.com/ resources-deaf-autism- deafautism-resources/
  - ○ This resource allows parents to share information on children who are deaf with autism.

References

American Psychiatric Association. (2013). *Diagnostic and statistical manual of mental disorders* (5th ed.; DSM-5). https://doi.org/10.1176/appi.books.9780890425596

Autism Speaks Organization. (2020, March). Table: Severity levels of autism spectrum disorder. https://www.autismspeaks.org/autism-diagnosis-criteria-dsm-5

Baron-Cohen, S., Wheelwright, S., & Jolliffe, T. (1997). Is there a "language of the eyes"? Evidence from normal adults and adults with autism or Asperger syndrome. *Visual Cognition, 4*(3), 311–331.

Berard, G. (1993). *Hearing equals behavior.* Keats.

Birath, A. L., Le Beau, V. V., & McConkey Robbins, A. (Eds.). (2014). *Loud & Clear!* https://advancedbionics.com/content/dam/advancedbionics/Documents/Regional/US/libraries/Loud-and-Clear/Loud-&-Clear!-Newsletter/Loud-and-Clear!-Newsletter-Issue-2-Perspectives-on-Deafness-with-Autism.pdf

Borders, C. M., Bock, S. J., & Probst, K. M. (2016). A review of educational practices for deaf/hard of hearing students with comorbid autism. *Deafness & Education International, 18*(4), 189–205. https://doi.org/10.1080/14643154.2016.1255416

Borders, C. M., Bock, S. J., Probst, K., & Kroesch, A. (2017). Deaf/hard of hearing students with disabilities. In S. Lenihan (Ed.), *Preparing to teach, committing to learn: An introduction to educating children who are deaf/hard of hearing.* National Center for Hearing Assessment and Management, Utah State University. http://www.infanthearing.org/

Borders, C., Bock, S. J., & Szymanski, C. (2014). Teacher ratings of evidence-based practices from the field of autism. *Journal of Deaf Studies and Deaf Education, 20*(1), 91–100. https://doi.org/10.1093/deafed/enu033

Borders, C. M., Meinzen-Derr, J., Bauer, A., Embury, D. C., & Wiley, S. (2015). Students who are deaf with additional disabilities: Does educational label impact language services? *Deafness Education International, 17*(4), 204–218. https://doi.org/10.1179/1557069X 15Y.0000000006

Bradley, L. A., Krakowski, B., & Thiessen, A. (2008). With little research out there it's a matter of learning what works in teaching students with deafness and autism. *Odyssey: New Directions in Deaf Education, 9*(1), 26–18. https://files.eric.ed.gov/fulltext/EJ903164.pdf

Bruce, S. M., & Borders, C. (2015). Communication and language in learners who are deaf with additional disabilities: Theories, research, and practice. *American Annals of the Deaf, 160*(4), 368–384. https://doi.org/10.1353/aad.2015.0035

Carr, J., Xu, D., & Yoshinaga-Itano, C. (2014). Language Environmental Analysis Language and Autism Screen and the Child Development Inventory Social Subscale as a possible autism screen for children who are deaf or hard of hearing. *Seminars in Speech and Language, 35*, 266–275. https://doi.org/10.1055/s-0034-1389099

Cejas, I., Hoffman, M. F., & Quittner, A. L. (2015). Outcomes and benefits of pediatric cochlear implantations in children with additional disabilities: A review and report of family influences on outcomes. *Pediatric Health, Medicine, and Therapeutics, 6*, 45–63. https://doi.org/10.2147/PHMT.S65797

Celani, G., Battacchi, M. W., & Arcidiacono, L. (1999). The understanding of the emotional meaning of facial expressions in people with autism. *Journal of Autism and Developmental Disorders, 29*(1), 57–66.

Centers for Disease Control. (2018). *Autism spectrum disorder (ASD): Data & statistics.* https://www.cdc.gov/ncbddd/autism/data.html

Davis, T. N., Barnard-Brak, L., Dacus, S., & Pond, A. (2010). Aided AAC systems among individuals with hearing loss and disabilities. *Journal of Developmental and Physical Disabilities, 22*, 241–256. https://doi.org/10.1007/s10882-009-9180-6

Dawson, G., Meltzoff, A. N., Osterling, J., Rinaldi, J., & Brown, E. (1998). Children with autism fail to orient to naturally occurring social stimuli. *Journal of Autism and Developmental Disorders, 28*(6), 479–485.

Denmark, T., Swettenham, J., Atkinson, J., & Campbell, R. (2009). *What's in the face? The comprehension and production of facial expressions in sign language by deaf children with autism* [Paper presentation]. International Meeting for Autism Research (IMFAR), Chicago, IL.

Easterbrooks, S. R., & Handley, C. M. (2005). Behavior change in a student with a dual diagnosis of deafness and pervasive development disorder: A case study. *American Annals of the Deaf, 150*(5), 401–407. https://doi.org/10.1353/aad.2006.0001

Ferrell, K. A., Bruce, S., & Luckner, J. L. (2014). *Evidence-based practices for students with sensory impairments* (Document No. IC-4). University of Florida. https://ceedar.education.ufl.edu/innovation-configurations/

Fitzpatrick, E. M., Lambert, L., Whittingham, J., & Leblanc, E. (2014). Examination of characteristics and management of children with hearing loss and autism spectrum disorders. *International Journal of Audiology, 53*(9), 577–586. https://doi.org/10.3109/14992027.2014.903338

Forest, M., & O'Brien, J. (1993). *PATH: A workbook for planning positive possible futures: Planning alternative tomorrows with hope for schools, organizations, businesses, families.* Inclusion Press.

Forest, M., & Pearpoint, J. C. (1992). Putting all kids on the MAP. *Educational Leadership, 50*(2), 26–31.

Gallaudet Research Institute (GRI). (2013). *Regional and national summary report of data from the 2011–2012 Annual Survey of Deaf and Hard of Hearing Children and Youth.* http://research.gallaudet.edu/Demographics/2012_National_Summary.pdf

Gordon, A. (1991). Co-occurrence of deafness and infantile autism. *American Journal of Psychiatry, 148*(11), 1615b–1615. https://doi.org/10.1176/ajp.148.11.1615b

Guardino, C. A. (2008). Identification and placement for deaf students with multiple disabilities: Choosing the path less followed. *American Annals of the Deaf, 153*(1), 55–64. https://doi.org/10.1353/aad.0.0004

Guardino, C., & Cannon, J. E. (2015). Theory, research, and practice for students who are deaf and hard of hearing with disabilities: Addressing the challenges from birth to postsecondary education. *American Annals of the Deaf, 160*(4), 347–355. https://doi.org/10.1353/aad.2015.0033

Hatfield, M., Falkmer, M., Falkmer, T., & Ciccarelli, M. (2016). Evaluation of the effectiveness of an online transition planning program for adolescents on the autism spectrum: Trial protocol. *Child & Adolescent Psychiatry & Mental Health, 10,* 1–11. https://doi.org/10.1186/s13034-016-0137-0

Hobson, R. P. (1986). The autistic child's appraisal of expressions of emotion. *Journal of Child Psychology and Psychiatry, 27*(3), 321–342.

Hoevenaars-van den Boom, M. A. A., Antonissen, A. C. F. M., Knoors, H., & Vervloed, M. P. J. (2009). Differentiating characteristics of deafblindness and autism in people with congenital deafblindness and profound intellectual disability. *Journal of Intellectual Disability Research, 53*(6), 548–558. https://doi.org/10.1111/j.1365-2788.2009.01175.x

Individuals With Disabilities Education Act, 20 U.S.C. § 1400 (2004).

Jacobs, S., Roush, J., Munoz, K., & White, K. (2010, February). *Hearing screening in the neonatal intensive care unit: Current status and future needs* [Paper presentation]. National EHDI Conference, Chicago, IL.

Johansson, M., Gillberg, C., & Råstam, M. (2010). Autism spectrum conditions in individuals with Möbius sequence, CHARGE syndrome, and oculo-auriculo-vertebral spectrum: Diagnostic aspects. *Research in Developmental Disabilities, 31,* 9–24. https://doi.org/10.1016/j.ridd.2009.07.011

Jure, R., Rapin, I., & Tuchman, R. (1991). Hearing impaired autistic children. *Developmental Medicine and Child Neurology, 33*(12), 1062–1072.

Kellogg, E. C., Thrasher, A., & Yoshinaga-Itano, C. (2014). Early predictors of autism in young children who are deaf or hard of hearing: Three longitudinal case studies. *Seminars in Speech and Language, 35,* 276–287. https://doi.org/10.1055/s-0034-1389100

Koch, L. C., & Rumrill, P. D. (2017). Providing supportive transition services to individuals with autism spectrum disorder: Considerations for vocational rehabilitation professionals. *Journal of Vocational Rehabilitation, 47*(2), 207–222. https://doi.org/10.3233/JVR-170896

Krug, D. A., Arik, J. R., & Almond, P. J. (2008). *Autism screening instrument for educational planning* (3rd ed.; ASIEP-3) [Assessment instrument]. PRO-ED.

Leekam, S. R., Lopez, B., & Moore, C. (2000). Attention and joint attention in preschool children with autism. *Developmental Psychology, 36*(2), 261–273.

Leekam, S. R., & Ramsden, C. A. H. (2006). Dyadic orienting and joint attention in preschool children with autism. *Journal of Autism and Developmental Disorders, 36*(2), 185–197.

Loveland, K. A., Steinberg, J. L., Pearson, D. A., Mansour, R., & Reddoch, S. (2008). Judgments of auditory-visual affect congruence in adolescents with and without autism: A pilot study of a new task using fMRI. *Perceptual and Motor Skills, 107*(2), 557–575. https://doi.org/10.2466/pms.107.2.557-575

Lyons, J., Cappadocia, M. C., & Weiss, J. A. (2011). Social characteristics of students with autism spectrum disorders across classroom settings. *Journal of Developmental Disabilities, 17*(1), 77–82.

Mace, F. C., Pratt, J. L., Prager, K. L., & Pritchard, D. (2011). An evaluation of three methods of saying "no" to avoid an escalating response class hierarchy. *Journal of Applied Behavior Analysis, 44*(1), 83–94. https://doi.org/10.1901/jaba.2011.44-83

Malandraki, G. A., & Okalidou, A. (2007). The application of PECS in a deaf child with autism. *Focus on Autism and Other Developmental Disabilities, 22*(1), 23–32. https://doi.org/10.1177/10883576070220010301

Meinzen-Derr, J., Wiley, S., Bishop, S., Manning-Courtney, P., Choo, D., & Murray, D. (2014). Autism spectrum disorder in 24 children who are deaf or hard of hearing. *International Journal of Pediatric Otorhinolaryngology, 78*(1), 112–118. https://doi.org/10.1016/j.ijporl.2013.10.065

Mood, D., & Shield, A. (2014). Clinical use of the Autism Diagnostic Observation Schedule-Second Edition with children who are deaf. *Seminars in Speech and Language, 35*(4), 288–300. https://doi.org/10.1055/s-003401389101

Myck-Wayne, J., Robinson, S., & Henson, E. (2011). Serving and supporting young children with a dual diagnosis of hearing loss and autism: The story of four families. *American Annals of the Deaf, 156*(4), 379–390.

Ozonoff, S., Pennington, B. F., & Rogers, S. J. (1991). Executive function deficits in high-functioning autistic individuals: Relationship to theory of mind. *Journal of Child Psychology and Psychiatry, and Allied Disciplines, 32*(7), 1081.

Probst, K., & Borders, C. (2017). Comorbid deafblindness and autism spectrum disorder: Characteristics, differential diagnosis, and possible interventions. *Review Journal of Autism and Developmental Disorders.* https://doi.org/10.1007/s40489-016-0100-2

Rimland, B., & Edelson, S. M. (1994). The effects of auditory integration training on autism. *American Journal of Speech-Language Pathology, 3*(2), 16–24.

Ring, H. A., Baron-Cohen, S., Wheelwright, S., Williams, S. C. R., Brammer, M., Andrew, C., & Bullmore, E. T. (1999). Cerebral correlates of preserved cognitive skills in autism: A functional MRI study of embedded figures task performance. *Brain, 122*(7), 1305–1315. https://doi.org/10.1093/brain/122.7.1305

Roper, L., Arnold, P., & Monteiro, B. (2003). Co-occurrence of autism: Diagnostic considerations. *International Journal of Research and Practice [Autism], 7*(3), 245–253.

Rosenhall, U., Nordin, V., Sandström, M., Ahlsén, G., & Gillberg, C. (1999). Autism and hearing loss. *Journal of Autism and Developmental Disorders, 29*(5), 349–356.

Schopler, E. & Van Bourgondien, M. E. (2010). *Childhood Autism Rating Scale* (2nd ed.; CARS-2) [Assessment instrument]. Western Psychological Services.

Shield, A. (2010). *The signing of deaf children with autism: Lexical phonology and perspective taking in the visual-spatial modality* [Unpublished doctoral dissertation]. University of Texas, Austin.

Shield, A. (2014). Preliminary findings of similarities and differences in the signed and spoken language of children with autism. *Seminars in Speech and Language, 35*, 309–320.

Shield, A., & Meier, R. P. (2012). Palm reversal errors in native-signing children with autism. *Journal of Communication Disorders, 45*, 439–454. https://doi.org/10.1016/j.jcomdis.2012.08.004

Spezio, M. L., Adolphs, R., Hurley, R. S. E., & Piven, J. (2007). Abnormal use of facial information in high-functioning autism. *Journal of Autism and Developmental Disorders, 37*(5), 929–939.

Stiegler, L. N., & Davis, R. (2010). Understanding sound sensitivity in individuals with autism spectrum disorders. *Focus on Autism and Other Developmental Disabilities, 25*, 67–75.

Szarkowski, A., Flynn, S., & Clark, T. (2014). Dually diagnosed: A retrospective study of the process of diagnosing autism spectrum disorders in children who are deaf and hard of hearing. *Seminars in Speech and Language, 35*, 301–308. https://doi.org/10.1055/s-0034-1389102

Szarkowski, A., Mood, D., Shield, A., Wiley, S., & Yoshinaga-Itano, C. (2014). A summary of current understanding regarding children with autism spectrum disorder who are deaf or hard of hearing. *Seminars in Speech and Language, 35*(4), 241–259.

Szymanski, C. A., Brice, P. J., Lam, K. H., & Hotto, S. A. (2012). Deaf children with autism spectrum disorders. *Journal of Autism and Developmental Disorders, 42*(10), 2027–2037. https://doi.org/10.1007/s10803-012-1452-9

Tharpe, A. M., Bess, F. H., Sladen, D. P., Schissel, H., Couch, S., & Schery, T. (2006). Auditory characteristics of children with autism. *Ear and Hearing, 27*(4), 430–441. https://doi.org/10.1097/01.aud.0000224981.60575.d8

Trussell, J. W., & Easterbrooks, S. R. (2016). Morphological knowledge and students who are deaf or hard-of-hearing: A review of the literature. *Communication Disorders Quarterly, 38*(2), 67–77. https://doi.org/1525740116644889.

University of Missouri-Kansas City Institute for Human Development. (2017, February). *What is the Charting the Life Course?* http://www.lifecoursetools.com/

Vandercook, T., York, J., & Forest, M. (1989). The McGill Action Planning System (MAPS): A strategy for building the vision. *Research and Practice for Persons With Severe Disabilities, 14*(3), 205–215. https://doi.org/10.1177/154079698901400306

Vernon, M., & Rhodes, A. (2009). Deafness and autistic spectrum disorders. *American Annals of the Deaf, 154*(1), 5–14. https://doi.org/10.1353/aad.0.0072

Wong, C., Odom, S. L., Hume, K. A., Cox, C. W., Fettig, A., Kurcharczyk, S., Brock, M. E., Plavnick, J. B., Fleury, V. P., & Schultz, T. R. (2015). Evidence-based practices for children, youth, and young adults with autism spectrum disorder: A comprehensive review. *Journal of Autism and Developmental Disorders.* https://doi.org/10.1007/s10803-014-2351-z

Worley, J. A., Matson, J. L., & Kozlowski, A. M. (2001). The effects of hearing impairment on symptoms of autism in toddlers. *Developmental Neurorehabilitation, 14*(3), 171–176. https://doi.org/10.3109/17518423.2011.564600

Zane, T., Carlson, M., Estep, D., & Quinn, M. (2014). Using functional assessment to treat behavior problems of deaf and hard of hearing children diagnosed with autism spectrum disorder. *American Annals of the Deaf, 158*(5), 555–566. https://doi.org/10.1353/aad.2014.0008

4

Understanding the Needs of Children Who Are d/Deaf or Hard of Hearing With Disabilities Due to Genetic Causes

Susan M. Bruce, Catherine Nelson,
and Brent Stutzman

LEARNING OUTCOMES

Readers will:

- Define and state the difference between "prevalence" and "incidence."
- Name and describe the three primary inheritance patterns.
- Discuss the potential sensory, medical, and motor implications for children with Down syndrome, CHARGE syndrome, and Usher syndrome.
- Determine the educational implications for children with Down syndrome, CHARGE syndrome, and Usher syndrome.
- Recognize several resources to support children who are d/Deaf or hard of hearing with disabilities due to genetic causes.

Approximately 40%–50% of the population of children who are d/Deaf or hard of hearing (d/Dhh) have a disability (Gallaudet Research Institute, 2013; Guardino & Cannon, 2015). Thus, whenever a hearing loss is diagnosed, it is essential to conduct thorough health, genetic, and educational assessments to rule out the possibility of additional challenges (Schein & Miller, 2008) that may lead to the identification of a disability.

DOI: 10.4324/9781003252054-4

Sometimes, these challenges are additional outcomes associated with the syndromes that cause varying hearing levels. There are >400 genetic syndromic causes of deafness (Lomas et al., 2017), with some resulting in a disability. While detailed information about genetic syndromes can be useful to practitioners and parents, it is critical to remember that this information does not define or predict an individual's potential.

The authors present common inheritance patterns, followed by a discussion of three of the most common genetic syndromes that are associated with being d/Dhh with a disability (DWD). A brief introduction to each syndrome is followed by its prevalence and/or incidence. While these terms are sometimes used interchangeably in the professional literature, "prevalence" is the proportion of the population having a specific characteristic in a specified period of time, whereas "incidence" is the number of new cases in a specified time period (Ward, 2013). Prevalence is often expressed as a rate (such as 1 in 10,000) or as a percentage of the population who manifest a particular characteristic. Thus, in this article, the term "prevalence" is used when discussing how frequently a syndrome occurs in the general population or in the population of individuals who are d/Dhh. When that information is not available, the "incidence" will be presented. In addition to prevalence and incidence statistics, inheritance pattern(s) of each syndrome, sensory implications (eyes/visual impairment, ears/hearing loss), physical and medical implications, and educational implications will be presented. Resources are provided to further assist parents and professionals who work with children who are d/Dhh with syndromes.

GENETIC INHERITANCE PATTERNS

There are three primary genetic inheritance patterns: autosomal dominant, autosomal recessive, and X-linked. Autosomal dominant and autosomal recessive disorders involve genes located in the 22 nonsex-linked chromosome pairs, while X-linked disorders involve genes on the 23rd chromosome pair, also known as the X chromosome (Batshaw et al., 2013). When considering the relationship of inheritance patterns to syndromes, it is important to understand the statistical odds of having a child: (a) who manifests (has) the syndrome, (b) who is a carrier, or (c) is unaffected (neither manifests nor carries the syndrome). Syndromes may be caused by other inheritance patterns such as gene mutations and partial or whole chromosomal gains and deletions. When a single gene is involved, it is known as a monogenetic disorder. Some disorders are multifactorial, meaning that a variation in both a gene and ≥1 environmental factors resulted in the manifestation of the disorder.

GENETIC SYNDROMES AS CAUSES OF HEARING LOSS AND DISABILITIES

Down syndrome, CHARGE syndrome, and Usher syndrome are three genetic syndromes with a relatively high prevalence in the general population or d/Dhh population. The sensory, motor, health, and educational implications of each of these three syndromes are discussed in this section, along with six additional syndromes detailed in Table 4.1. It is important to recognize that characteristics associated with each syndrome will be expressed differently across individuals.

Down Syndrome

Down syndrome is an etiology of intellectual disability (ID), which may also cause hearing loss and visual impairments, along with other physical issues. Down syndrome was named after Dr. John Langdon Down, who—in 1866—wrote the first paper that articulated the distinct facial and other physical characteristics of individuals with this syndrome. The genetic basis of Down syndrome was identified in 1959 (Roizen, 2012). The prevalence of Down syndrome has been estimated as 1 in every 691 births (Tedeschi et al., 2015). Down syndrome is the third leading cause of deafblindness after CHARGE and Usher syndromes (National Center on Deaf-Blindness, 2020)

There are three types of Down syndrome: trisomy 21, translocation, and mosaicism. Each syndrome presents with a distinct inheritance pattern. About 95% of individuals with Down syndrome have trisomy 21, which is caused by the uneven division of chromosomes, resulting in three copies of chromosome 21 instead of two. The risk of having a child with trisomy 21 increases with maternal age. Translocation type involves "attachment of the long arm of an extra chromosome 21 to chromosomes

TABLE 4.1 Additional Syndromes Resulting in DWD

Syndrome	Incidence	Inheritance Pattern	Major Characteristics	Educational Implications
1p36 deletion syndrome (Heilstedt et al., 2003; Shapira et al., 1997)	>1 in 10,000†	Missing piece of chromosome 22 in each cell	• Sensorineural hearing loss • Visual impairment • Developmental delays (including motor) and intellectual disability • Seizures • Microcephaly • Flat area on back of skull • Feeding difficulties • Low muscle tone • Short fifth finger • Wide variation in other lower-frequency physical characteristics	Due to wide variability in clinical characteristics, one must consider the possibility of dual-sensory loss. A teacher of students with visual impairments (TVI) can support by conducting functional vision assessment (FVA) and learning media assessment (LMA) to get a better understanding of how to support learning (Bruce et al., 2015). An interprofessional collaborative team may be needed to help support language/speech and motor development as well as to advise on appropriate communication systems.

(Continued)

TABLE 4.1 (*Continued*)

Syndrome	Incidence	Inheritance Pattern	Major Characteristics	Educational Implications
Cornelia de Lange syndrome (CLS; Krantz et al., 2004; Sarimski, 1997, 2002)	1 in 10,000–50,000†	Autosomal dominant (complex inheritance with multiple chromosomes and mutations involved)	• Hearing loss • Visual impairment • Moderate-to-severe intellectual disability • Microcephaly • Feeding difficulties • Motor and language delays • Delays in growth • Distinctive face • Excess hair	Many children with CLS have limited use of speech and low rates of intentional communication, and they may rely on gestures and other nonverbal means of communication. CLS is also associated with self-injurious/aggressive behaviors, mimicry, and high energy/overactivity. There is a need for behavior support plans that help to build functional communication.
Treacher Collins syndrome (TCS; Åsten et al., 2014; Cobb et al., 2014; Dauwerse et al., 2011)	1 in 50,000†	Autosomal dominant	• Bilateral conductive hearing loss • Downward slanting eyes • Hypoplasia of facial bones (underdeveloped) • Cleft palate • Abnormalities in external ear shape	Children with TCS may have speech and language delays that are associated with hearing loss and oral abnormalities that impair speech production. Early exposure to sign language is key to providing early communication. Children with TCS are often bullied because of their appearance, increasing the need for psychological/socioemotional supports.

Syndrome	Incidence	Inheritance Pattern	Major Characteristics	Educational Implications
Trisomy 13 syndrome (Braddock et al., 2012; Bruce et al., 2015; Janvier & Watkins, 2013; Parker et al., 2003)	1 in 6,000†	• Nondisjunction (error in cell division)	• Mixed or conductive hearing loss • Ophthalmological issues • Severe intellectual disability • Polydactyly (extra fingers or toes) • Low muscle tone • Low birth weight • Low-set ears • Ongoing medical complications	Children with trisomy 13 and trisomy 18 will struggle with speech and may need alternative modes of communication. They may be prelinguistic expressively while having a small receptive vocabulary in sign language or speech. Children with trisomy 13 will develop gross and fine motor skills, and through imitation, this may help provide an avenue for learning manual communication modes as well as for participation in self-care in the home.

(Continued)

TABLE 4.1 (*Continued*)

Syndrome	Incidence	Inheritance Pattern	Major Characteristics	Educational Implications
Trisomy 18 syndrome (Braddock et al., 2012; Cereda & Carey, 2012; Parker et al., 2003)	1 in 3,000†	Nondisjunction	• Moderate-to-severe sensorineural hearing loss • Many associated ophthalmological issues (coloboma, microphthalmia, etc.) • Severe intellectual disability • High infant mortality (5–10% survive past first year) • Low birth weight • Heart anomalies • Ongoing medical complications	*Note:* Due to the high mortality rates and ongoing medical complications, there is an ongoing debate about the appropriateness of providing life-saving interventions for children with trisomy 13 and trisomy 18 (see Janvier & Watkins, 2013). Most children with trisomy 18 are nonambulatory, but they can still be expected to participate in routines at home and school.

Syndrome	Incidence	Inheritance Pattern	Major Characteristics	Educational Implications
Waardenburg syndrome (WS; Read & Newton, 1997; Waardenburg, 1951)	1 in 42,000†; deafness in ~20% of cases	Autosomal dominant (Types I–III), autosomal recessive (Type IV)	• Congenital sensorineural hearing loss • Distinctive iris pigmentation (full or partial heterochromia, or bright blue eyes) • White forelock of hair • Dystopia canthorum (wide nasal bridge)	The characteristics of WS, excluding hearing loss, are mostly related to appearance, and thus do not pose specific learning challenges. Type III WS sometimes presents with muscle and joint rigidity in hands/arms, which may require both medical intervention and communication adaptations if manual modes of communication prove challenging.

Note. †Estimates of incidence in live births.

14, 21, or 22" (Roizen, 2012, p. 308). Individuals with mosaicism have only some cells with the anomaly. Intellectual capacity is similar among individuals who have trisomy 21 and translocation, but it is higher in individuals with mosaicism, presumably due to some cells being typical (Roizen, 2012). A variety of prenatal tests identify Down syndrome, allowing parents an opportunity to prepare for an infant with special medical needs.

Sensory Implications

Estimates of the prevalence of children with Down syndrome who are d/Dhh have ranged from 15% in newborns (Tedeschi et al., 2015) to 60%–75% for children and adults (Roizen, 2012). Tedeschi et al. (2015) recommend continued monitoring of hearing (even when the previous testing was normal) due to findings of "fluctuating and progressive hearing loss in 45–90% of children and adolescents with Down syndrome" (p. 170). The hearing level may be sensorineural or conductive, including a progressive sensorineural hearing loss. Sensorineural (inner ear) anomalies include hypoplasia (underdeveloped) or dysplasia (differently developed) of the cochlea (the snail-shell-shaped bone of the inner ear) or cochlear nerve (Tedeschi et al., 2015). Conductive (middle and outer ear) anomalies include remnant tissue in the middle ear cavity, differences in the formation of the ossicles (the three bones in the middle ear that transmit sounds), dysfunction of the Eustachian tube (that connects the throat and the middle ear), and frequent otitis media (ear infections; Tedeschi et al., 2015). Mixed hearing levels, i.e., a combination of sensorineural and conductive losses, are also common in individuals with Down syndrome and have implications for individualized hearing technology needs.

Visual impairments occur in 30%–62% of children with Down syndrome (Centers for Disease Control and Prevention, 2020; Roizen, 2012). Visual anomalies include significant refractive errors, strabismus (crossed eyes), nystagmus (vertical or horizontal rapid movements of eyes), blepharitis (eyelid inflammation), ptosis (drooping eyelids), cataracts (clouding of a lens), esotropia (eye moves inward toward the nose), keratoconus (cornea thins and then bulges into a cone shape), and tear duct obstructions (Roizen, 2012; Sacks, 2016). Researchers have found that adults with similar levels of intellectual functioning, compared with adults with Down syndrome, struggled with neural processing in the area of visual flow (similar to those with Alzheimer's disease), which could result in difficulty identifying moving objects and ambulating around obstacles (Del Viva et al., 2015). Like hearing, vision must be monitored closely across the life span because acquired visual issues may arise.

Physical and Medical Implications

In addition to these sensory challenges, a variety of physical and medical conditions occur in children with Down syndrome. Congenital heart anomalies—most often, septal defects (holes) of the atrium or ventricles, endocardial cushion defect (involving the heart walls and chambers), and pulmonary vascular obstruction—occur in 44% of children with Down syndrome (Roizen, 2012; Sacks, 2016). Approximately 1%–2% of children with Down syndrome have congenital hypothyroidism, but more require thyroid hormone replacement in their childhood years (Roizen, 2012). Individuals with Down syndrome are commonly short in stature, with adult men being about 5' tall and women being about 4'5" tall (Bruce et al., 2015). Most children with Down syndrome have hypotonia (low muscle tone) and they may have orthopedic issues (Bruce et al., 2015) or hypothyroidism, putting them at risk to develop obesity. Children with Down syndrome are at a much higher risk for Type 1 diabetes. Epilepsy occurs in about 6% of children with Down syndrome (Roizen, 2012). Gastrointestinal issues occur in 6.7% of children with Down syndrome, sometimes due to a narrowing or blockage of the duodenum (a section of the small intestine). "Gastroesophageal reflux disease (GERD) is known to be common among children with Down syndrome" (Roizen, 2012, p. 311). More than half of children with Down syndrome will experience skin disorders, such as dermatitis, inflammation of the lips, dandruff, or dryness of the eyes (Roizen, 2012). Due to the risk of sleep apnea, a sleep study is recommended for all children with Down syndrome (Roizen, 2012). Adults with Down syndrome are predisposed to early onset Alzheimer's disease and dementia (Del Viva et al., 2015). Life expectancy is about 55 years for individuals with mild-to-moderate ID and 43 years for those with severe ID (Uppal et al., 2015). Children with Down syndrome have a complex set of health risks that require collaborative medical and educational teams.

Social-Emotional Implications

Children and adults with Down syndrome have relatively strong social skills and are often highly empathetic (Wren, 2014). They are at higher risk (than the general population) to develop behavioral, psychiatric, and social problems, yet, rarely exhibit highly aggressive behaviors (Roizen, 2012). Glenn et al. (2015) found that repetitive and routinized behaviors were higher in individuals with Down syndrome due to fears rather than being associated with mental health problems. Glenn et al. (2015) suggest that the desire for sameness may be a positive adaptive behavior that reduces cognitive load (the amount of information in working memory). About 10% of children with Down syndrome have autism (Dykens, 2007).

Educational Implications

In most cases, children with Down syndrome have a moderate ID. Gross motor development follows the same pattern as children without disabilities, albeit at a slower rate. When matched by mental age, auditory and visual types of attention appear to be similar to those in children without disabilities (Faught et al., 2016). Joint attention, which appears to be related to vocabulary acquisition, may be enhanced by reducing adult directedness and instead following the child's attentional lead (Zampini et al., 2015).

Receptive language is often more advanced than expressive language in children with Down syndrome, with about 10% of the language delay attributed to a lack of language exposure (Roizen, 2012). Spoken language is delayed, and in some instances, unfamiliar adults will have difficulty understanding the speech of individuals with Down syndrome, calling on the need for augmentative and alternative communication (e.g., sign language and speech-generating devices) developed by an interpersonal collaborative team that will consider the strengths and needs of each individual (Wilkinson & Na, 2015).

Children with Down syndrome have relative strengths in social skills, daily living skills, reading, and short-term visual memory (Wren, 2014). They generally exhibit strong visual motor skills and weak verbal short-term memory skills. Visual supports, such as picture cues and graphic organizers, allow learners with Down syndrome to build on their strengths. These learners may have more difficulty than age-matched peers without disabilities in completing mathematical tasks, with research seeking to clarify the causes of these difficulties (Abreu-Mendoza & Arias-Trejo, 2015).

While all children with disabilities are expected to master learning standards in the general curriculum, there are some specialized curricular materials developed for children with Down syndrome. The Down Syndrome Foundation of Orange County, California, developed a program with curricular materials known as The Learning Program (Down Syndrome Foundation of Orange County, 2004–2019), which offers materials on calendar, counting, literacy, and math (including money and number lines). Their website also includes a list of recommended applications ("apps") for mobile and tablet devices. Horstmeier (2004) developed a book on teaching math skills to children and adults with Down syndrome and others who benefit from a hands-on approach to learning. This text provides objectives, instructional procedures (including suggestions for generalization) to teach math skills such as number sense, counting, place value, addition, subtraction, multiplication, division, and calculator use.

The educational program should consider the relative strengths and needs of each child and may include instructional approaches and strategies that have been effective with children with ID, and in some cases, with children who are d/Dhh, visually impaired, or deafblind. The prognosis for positive life outcomes has greatly improved for children with Down syndrome due to (a) early identification, (b) improved medical care, (c) more inclusive schools and community placements, and (d) supported employment (Roizen, 2012). Appropriate management of health and sensory issues is critical to positive outcomes, requiring a collaborative team approach. Interprofessional collaborative practice calls on medical and school professionals to clarify roles, share expertise, and coordinate services to address the complex needs of their patients and students (Golum & Schreck, 2018; Ogletree, 2017).

CHARGE Syndrome

The term *CHARGE* was selected in 1981 to describe a cluster of physical anomalies that was originally known as an association and later identified as a syndrome when the genetic marker was identified (Hartshorne et al., 2011). Each letter in the acronym CHARGE stands for an associated anomaly: (C) ocular colobomas (missing tissue), (H) heart anomalies (of almost every type), (A) atresia of the choanae (blocked back of nasal passage) (RG) retardation of growth or development, and (E) ear anomalies with or without associated hearing loss (Busa et al., 2016). While these originally identified anomalies are still relevant, it was later understood that cranial nerve dysfunction (which may cause facial palsy and challenges with swallowing and aspiration) was also a major characteristic, creating a greater understanding of the impact on vision, hearing, and behavior. The following minor characteristics, appearing in ≥50% of the children, were also recognized as being important for diagnosis: (a) genital hypoplasia, (b) cardiovascular malformations, (c) growth deficiency, (d) distinctive facial features, (e) unique palmar crease, and (f) CHARGE behavioral profile. Other minor characteristics that appear in 15%–40% of the children include the following: (a) orofacial cleft (an opening in the oral structure); (b) tracheoesophageal fistula (an atypical physical connection between the esophagus and the trachea); and (c) renal (kidney) anomalies (Davenport & Hefner, 2011: Kohlhase, 2011). A diagnosis of CHARGE syndrome occurs when either four of the major characteristics occur without minor characteristics or when three major characteristics coexist with at least three minor characteristics (Kohlhase, 2011). Thus, individuals with CHARGE syndrome have a highly variable set of congenital anomalies with varying levels of severity and usually require extensive medical interventions (Busa et al., 2016). Vesseur et al. (2016) reported developmental delays in just over half of the children in their sample. Due to medical complications and the complexity of needs in these children, caution is warranted when identifying an ID.

The incidence of CHARGE syndrome is 1 in 10,000–15,000 live births (Bashinski, 2015). More than 90% of children with CHARGE syndrome experience both vision and hearing losses, known as deafblindness (Hartshorne et al., 2011). CHARGE syndrome is the most common hereditary cause of deafblindness, accounting for 924 of 2,401 children and youth having hereditary causes of deafblindness, among the total 9,635 children identified as deafblind in the national child count in the United States (National Center on Deaf-Blindness, 2017).

CHARGE syndrome is usually caused by an autosomal dominant inheritance pattern involving mutations in the *CHD7* gene (Pisaneschi et al., 2015). The diagnosis of CHARGE syndrome almost always occurs after the child is born (Busa et al., 2016); thus, there is little opportunity for advanced preparation on the part of the parents.

Sensory Implications

CHARGE syndrome is associated with every type of ear and hearing issue and a wide range of hearing abilities. The vast majority of children with CHARGE syndrome experience mixed hearing losses. The common anomalies within the inner ear that cause sensorineural hearing loss include malformed cochlea, malformed or missing semicircular canals, and reduced hair cell structures (Thelin, 2011). Missing semicircular canals and abnormalities of the auditory nerve result in severe balance problems, almost universally experienced by children with CHARGE syndrome (Brown, 2011). Ossicular abnormalities, Eustachian tube dysfunction, and middle ear infections are common causes of conductive hearing loss in individuals with CHARGE syndrome (Thelin, 2011). The pinna and ear canal of the external ear are often affected, making the fitting and wearing of hearing aids more difficult, although the unique shape of the external ear is often helpful in identification. Thelin (2011) reported the following hearing levels among this group: "15% typical hearing, 38% mild-moderately severe, and 47% severe-profound" (p. 29). Approximately 40% of individuals with CHARGE syndrome use listening and spoken language (Bashinski, 2015). To augment speech intelligibility, which may be affected due to physical characteristics that cause articulation issues (e.g., cleft, respiratory problems), communication devices, or sign language to increase communication may be used (Bashinski, 2015). Cochlear implants may be recommended, with the likely outcomes of improved awareness of sound and greater engagement with the environment, rather than improved spoken language (Bashinski, 2015).

As mentioned earlier, colobomas (a hole in the structure of the eye) are a major characteristic of CHARGE syndrome. Colobomas may occur in the iris, choroid, or retina. Microphthalmia (small and often malformed eye/s) is also common (Bruce et al., 2015). Anderzén-Carlsson (2015) reports the prevalence of colobomas and microphthalmia in individuals with CHARGE syndrome as being 73%–91%. It is critical to understand the impact of the coloboma on each child's visual field so that sign language, communicative displays, and other educational materials are visually accessible.

Brown (2011) describes individuals with CHARGE syndrome as being "truly multisensory impaired" (p. 169) because they experience reduced functioning in the vestibular system, proprioception system, and tactile sense in addition to being deafblind. It is critical to appreciate that these systems interact with one another and that the impact of these senses cannot be understood by adding the effects of one system to the effects of another. The interactive effects of vision and hearing may cause the functional use of either sense to be different from what one might anticipate given medical reports. Thus, functional assessment of vision and hearing are critical to understanding the accommodations required by each individual with CHARGE syndrome. This should include a learning media assessment, which will support the educational team to identify preferred learning channels, literacy modes, and accommodations. Through careful observation, the interprofessional collaborative team will identify the sensory strengths and needs of each individual in order to create meaningful activities and predictable environments that support individuals with CHARGE syndrome.

Physical and Medical Implications

CHARGE syndrome involves a complex set of physical characteristics that usually result in very high medical needs and multiple surgeries in early life. Tracheostomies, renal issues, genitourinary issues, growth deficiency, genital hypoplasia, bone issues, sleep apnea, and delayed puberty are among the health challenges experienced by these children (Bruce et al., 2015; Hartshorne et al., 2016). Feeding challenges are common due to cleft palate, choanal atresia, and other anatomical issues that may result in reflux or vomiting (Anderzén-Carlsson, 2015). These extensive health issues and associated hospitalizations result in fewer opportunities for typical early childhood experiences, undoubtedly taking a toll on development (Bashinski, 2015). Although most children with CHARGE syndrome learn to walk, low muscle tone and weak postural security (related to balance issues) can result in slow movement and exhaustion (Brown, 2011).

Social-Emotional Implications

Behavioral challenges in individuals with CHARGE syndrome are common and include anxiety, sensitivity to a variety of sensory inputs (visual, auditory, and tactile), and perseverative behavior (Bruce et al., 2015). Obsessive-compulsive disorder, autism spectrum disorder, attentional issues, tics, Tourettes, and executive dysfunction are common across individuals with CHARGE (Hartshorne et al., 2011).

Hartshorne (2011) described the CHARGE behavioral phenotype, explaining that these seven behavioral characteristics are associated with the syndrome rather than being learned:

> (1) low normal cognitive functioning, (2) very goal directed and persistent with a sense of humor, (3) socially interested but immature, (4) repetitive behaviors that increase under stress, (5) high levels of sensation seeking, (6) under conditions of stress and sensory overload, find it difficult to self-regulate and easily lose behavioral control, and (7) difficulty with shifting attention and transitioning to new activities; easily lost in own thoughts. (p. 319)

This behavioral phenotype is now accepted as one of the minor characteristics used when identifying CHARGE syndrome. Hartshorne et al. (2016) found that "aggression, tactile defensiveness, obsessive compulsive-like behaviors, and anxiety were the most common mental health challenges" (p. 2019) experienced by adolescents and adults with CHARGE syndrome, with some of these behaviors resulting in ongoing sleep difficulties.

When considering behavioral interventions, it is important to consider the cause of behavior (including health and environmental factors), ways to reduce stress and anxiety, and the role of sensory issues, including frustrations with balance (Nannemann et al., 2017). Positive behavior support plans will need to consider the influence of sensory-motor needs and include a component on teaching students when to select strategies that support them to feel calm and secure in specific environments. Bruce et al. (2018) identify eight strategies that were paired with elements of cognitive behavior therapy to support young adult students with CHARGE syndrome: (1) provide structure, (2) offer a positive classroom climate, (3) address sensory needs and sensory sensitivities, (4) reward on-task behavior, (5) plan transitions between activities and environments and prepare the student for these transitions, (6) teach what mature behavior looks like, (7) teach strategies to cope with feelings of anxiety, and (8) be thoughtful about the words (and intonation) and signs (including modulation of signs) expressed by adults.

Educational Implications

Deuce (2017) identified the unique strengths and needs of children with CHARGE syndrome. Strengths include the ability to learn concrete concepts based on lived experiences and problem-solving. Deuce (2017) reports that about half of the children use different modes for expressive and receptive communication and that they tend to relate better to adults than to peers (perhaps due to the greater predictability of adults). They struggle to express emotion and face issues with organization and poor memory (Deuce, 2017).

Children with CHARGE syndrome who are presymbolic (i.e., do not use symbols to communicate) may benefit from the van Dijk approach to assessment and instruction, a child-guided, developmental approach that is highly responsive to the child's emotional states and interests and that supports the development of more complex communication (Nelson & Bruce, 2019). Early literacy activities may be personalized (about the child's lived experiences), including experience books that are cocreated with the child and then repeatedly shared with the child (Bruce et al., 2016).

Instructional strategies include environmental arrangement and management that is considerate of the individual's sensory needs (including well-defined physical spaces for schoolwork and breaks), positive behavioral supports (such as offering the desired level of stimulation), creating predictable transitions and other routines (and teaching these through individualized daily schedules that may initially include object representations and/or pictures), providing sufficient time for processing information, supporting the learner to be organized within and across tasks, and alternating preferred and nonpreferred tasks (Deuce, 2017; Majors, 2011; Smith et al., 2010). The individual selection of assistive technologies is necessary due to the diverse needs and talents of the population.

Most children with CHARGE syndrome experience significant challenges with body awareness and with maintaining some body positions (due to balance issues), which are areas of development supported by physical therapists. To support participation in physical education, fitness, and sports, Lieberman (2011) suggests modifications of (a) the environment (e.g., lighting); (b) equipment (e.g., beepers to provide additional auditory information); (c) rules (e.g., the pace of the game); and (d) instruction (e.g., pairing verbal directions with demonstration).

Ferrell et al. (2014) articulated the state of evidence-based practices in deafness, blindness and visual impairment, and deafblindness across 12 areas of instruction. These practices were grounded in both the child-guided approach and the systematic instructional approach (based on principles from behavioral theory). Some of these practices apply to children with CHARGE syndrome. Nelson et al. (2022; see Chapter 6) provide additional information on approaches and strategies that are effective when teaching children who are deafblind. Each state or region has a deafblind project that may offer training and technical support to the educational team and family.

In looking at adolescent and adult outcomes, Hartshorne et al. (2016) found that individuals with CHARGE syndrome performed best on personal care tasks, yet most required support with everyday activities. About 25% in their sample lived independently, although some of these individuals required supports. Across the life span, individuals with CHARGE syndrome require an interprofessional collaborative approach.

Usher Syndrome

Usher syndrome is associated with congenital or progressive sensorineural hearing loss and progressive vision loss due to retinitis pigmentosa (RP), which involves a reduction of retinal cells, resulting in difficulty seeing at night or in dim light and diminished peripheral vision. Simpson (2013) describes three types of Usher syndrome, with the vast majority of individuals having the first or second type. Usher syndrome Type 1 (USH1) is associated with profound congenital hearing levels, lack of vestibular function (resulting in severe balance issues), and the onset of RP in childhood. Usher syndrome Type 2 (USH2) involves sloping moderate-to-severe hearing levels at birth, typical balance (no vestibular dysfunction), with the onset of RP between 10 and 20 years of age. Usher syndrome Type 3 (USH3) is distinguished because both the hearing and vision losses are progressive. Babies with USH3 are born with typical hearing and vision, with hearing loss being obvious by the teen years and the onset of vision loss being more variable (Keates, 2002). Individuals with USH1 may have gait issues resulting from vestibular dysfunction, whereas individuals with USH2 may have gait issues due to structural issues in the cerebellum (Domanico et al., 2015). Due to the profound hearing levels, children with USH1 may benefit from a cochlear implant, while individuals with USH2 generally benefit from hearing aids (Simpson, 2013).

Estimates of the prevalence of Usher syndrome in the U.S. population are in the range of 4–17 in 100,000 (National Institute on Deafness and Other Communication Disorders, 2017). It is estimated that 3%–6% of children with congenital deafness have Usher syndrome and that 70% of all individuals with Usher syndrome have USH2 (Keates, 2002). The Deaf-Blind National Child Count of 2018 identified 345 children with Usher syndrome, across all three types (National Center on Deaf-Blindness, 2020), accounting for approximately 12% of the hereditary causes of child-hood deafblindness in the United States. Furthermore, ≥50% of adults who are deafblind have Usher syndrome (Fakin et al., 2012). Usher syndrome has an autosomal recessive inheritance pattern, with men and women equally likely to be affected (Lenarduzzi et al., 2015). Thirteen genes have been linked to the three types of Usher syndrome (Mathur & Yang, 2015).

Sensory Implications

Individuals with Usher syndrome, regardless of type, experience visual impairments due to RP. In RP, the proteins that support retinal health are either greatly reduced or absent, which results in retinal deterioration

(Wallber, 2009). Retinal photoreceptor cells take in light and convert it to electrical signals that travel to other cells in the retina, then to the optic nerve, and then on to the brain, where the signals are converted to images. Both the rod cells and cone cells of the retina are photoreceptors and are impacted by RP. An electroretinogram (ERG) measures responses from the rod and cone cells and will detect RP. Rod cell degeneration results in difficulties with night vision, including the use of vision in dimly lit areas or in areas where lighting changes. The rod cell loss also impacts peripheral vision, resulting in what is commonly referred to as tunnel vision. Humans typically have a visual field of about 160° horizontally and 135° vertically (Ang, 2014). In the United States, legal blindness is denoted by a visual acuity of 20/200 or less (in which case, the denominator is larger) or by 20° or less of the remaining visual field. "Most individuals with Usher syndrome have remaining central vision of 5–10° in late adulthood" (Henricson et al., 2012, p. 1449). Wallber (2009) reports that about half of the individuals with USH1 and almost three-quarters of those with USH2 maintain 20/40 vision in a very small visual field in one or both eyes.

As vision deteriorates, walking and other forms of mobility, communication, reading mode, and general independence are impacted. It may be necessary to reconsider vocational choices or to provide modifications or accommodations to support one's vocation. Sometimes, individuals with RP avoid sports activities or choose to stay inside when light is dim outside. It is important to remember that peripheral vision involves vision not only from the sides of the body (which may result in the person being startled when others approach or bumping into door frames or other obstacles that appear to the side) but also above the head (as in tree limbs that may be hanging low) or below (resulting in safety issues with stairs, stages, and other platforms). As peripheral vision deteriorates, individuals who rely on visual receptive sign language may be observed stepping back farther to see their partner's signs. They may increase their head movements to visually capture more of the environment. It may be helpful if those in conversation with said individuals use a more restricted sign space. Some individuals with Usher syndrome will change their expressive forms of communication over time. Sauerburger (1993) aptly described the unique challenges of communicating through sign language as vision becomes more limited due to RP, from the early need for increased lighting

to visual tracking aided by holding the wrist of the communication partner as they sign, and the potential need for tactile sign language. The loss
of cone cells, which occurs later than the loss of rod cells, results in difficulties with acuity, color perception, and central vision. Cataracts (clouding of the lens) and macular cysts may compromise the remaining central
vision. The diagnosis of Usher syndrome tends to occur about 5–10 years
after a child has been identified as d/Dhh, pointing to the importance of
screening this population for Usher syndrome so that the vision loss can be
anticipated (Wallber, 2009).

Physical and Medical Implications

Other physical and medical characteristics associated with Usher syndrome
include central nervous system effects, loss of sense of smell, epilepsy, and—
in some cases—delayed development (Buethe et al., 2013; Simpson,
2013). Dammeyer (2012b) has found that sleep problems are common,
but that individuals with Usher syndrome are quite healthy with very few
hospitalizations.

Social-Emotional Implications

Individuals with USH1 may strongly identify with Deaf culture due to
being profoundly deaf at birth and communicating in a visually based
sign language (Wallber, 2009). Those with USH2 may initially identify
as being hard of hearing and may use spoken language as their primary
form of communication. Those with USH3 may initially view themselves
as hearing and sighted and will be reliant on spoken language and print.
Thus, dramatic self-identity transitions may be made, across the types, from
viewing oneself as d/Deaf to being a deafblind person, from identifying
as a hard of hearing person to a deafblind person, or a hearing/sighted
person to a deafblind person. As their vision loss progresses, children with
Usher syndrome need their parents and professionals to explain what is
happening in age-appropriate ways (Wallber, 2009).

In a review of studies conducted on the prevalence and nature of psychiatric disorders in individuals with Usher syndrome, Domanico et al.
(2015) reported highly variable findings. The research and clinical reports

they reviewed identified individual cases of anxiety, anger, isolation, distress, panic attacks, attention deficit hyperactivity disorder (ADHD), schizophrenia, aggression, or psychosis. Wahlqvist et al. (2013) studied a Swedish population of individuals with USH2. Their participants reported more physical and psychological health issues than the general population, including issues with headaches, anxiety, fatigue, and depression. Dammeyer (2012a) asserts the importance of addressing the hearing and vision levels as well as providing communication development supports as part of the intervention for intellectual and behavioral challenges. Wahlqvist et al. (2013) point out that the increase in vulnerability that can arise from accessing less information from the environment and from being more reliant on others are contributing factors to some of the psychological challenges reported. Caution is warranted when comparing health and psychological findings of hearing and sighted individuals with the results from individuals who are DWD or deafblind. Many of the reported findings may be unsurprising given the ongoing and progressive losses, isolation, and reshaping of identities experienced by individuals with Usher syndrome.

Educational Implications

Estimates of intellectual or other learning disabilities in individuals with Usher syndrome vary (Dammeyer, 2012b). Great caution should be exercised when diagnosing ID in individuals with Usher syndrome. Children with Usher syndrome may have some relative strengths when compared to children with other etiologies of d/Dhh or DWD. For example, Henricson et al. (2012) have found that children with USH1 developed better phonological working memory and phonological skills than other deaf children in their study (both groups had cochlear implants).

Communication (including literacy) and orientation and mobility (O&M) are two areas requiring the attention of educational teams serving children with Usher syndrome. Walber (2009) presents a helpful list of suggestions in the categories of communication, projected materials, computer and print accessibility, and general recommendations. She suggests that parents ensure appropriate home lighting, introduce O&M skills early (including the use of public transportation), and support their children in establishing relationships with adult role models who have Usher syndrome. Additional educational suggestions include reducing teacher movement (minimize visual demands), keep bright lights behind the student (including windows), maintain a physically organized classroom, avoid wearing patterns (reducing visual fatigue or dizziness), and appropriate use of interpreters (Washington Sensory Disabilities Services, 2010). In the school setting, O&M can be supported by providing appropriate orientation to the classrooms and other school environments, providing sighted guide support when needed, and offering early dismissal for transitions to the next classroom (Washington Sensory Disabilities Services, 2010). Individuals with Usher syndrome can remain independent travelers but will require specialized O&M instruction about how to interact with the public. For example, they may use a carefully sequenced set of print cards to interact with members of the public about making purchases, crossing streets, and other needs (Bourquin & Sauerburger, 2005). As their vision loss progresses, individuals with Usher syndrome will need instruction about new strategies and accommodations to accomplish daily activities and support for relationships (Luft, 2015), including communication strategies.

Some individuals with Usher syndrome will transition from being print readers to braille readers. Some adults may choose to use braille in limited ways, such as for labeling items that cannot otherwise be tactually distinguished. Braille may be accessed in hard copy or through electronic formats, such as refreshable braille displays. Assistive technologies provide options for the production of braille as well. Braille reading will require the individual to learn new tactile skills, the braille code, and the mechanics of braille reading, such as tracking braille across the page and reading braille with two hands (to maximize reading speed). The braille code includes 189 contractions, and there are rules about the use of these contractions when writing in braille (Emerson et al., 2009). The teacher of students with visual impairments (TVI) will teach braille to school-age children. Adults may seek support for braille reading through the Commission for the Blind in their state.

In 2017, the National Center on Deaf-Blindness (2020) in collaboration with the National Family Association for Deaf-Blind and the Usher Syndrome Coalition, sponsored two webinars on Usher syndrome (see

Resources). These webinars are free and will be helpful in identifying additional educational suggestions. Ferrell et al. (2014) articulated the state of evidence-based practices in deafness, blindness and visual impairment, and deafblindness. Some of these practices will be applicable to individuals with Usher syndrome. The reader is also referred to Nelson et al. (2022, see Chapter 6). Each state or region has a deafblind project that may offer training and technical support to the educational team and family. Children with Usher syndrome will benefit from an interprofessional collaborative team that responds to their changing needs.

Other Genetic Syndromes

Table 1 presents information on the following six additional syndromes that are etiologies of DWD: (1) Waardenburg syndrome, (2) Treacher Collins syndrome, (3) 1p36 deletion syndrome, (4) Cornelia de Lange syndrome, (5) trisomy 13 syndrome, and (6) trisomy 18 syndrome. Additional genetic syndromes that may cause DWD (that are not addressed in the narrative or the table) include the following: (a) Alport syndrome, (b) Alström syndrome, (c) Flynn-Aird syndrome, (d) Goldenhar syndrome, (e) Mohr-Tranegjaerg syndrome, (f) San Filliopo syndrome, and (g) Wolfram syndrome.

CONCLUSION

Understanding the strengths and needs of individuals who are DWD requires a deep appreciation of their disability and nondisability characteristics. The impact of DWD cannot be understood by simply adding up the effects of an individual's hearing level and their disability(ies). This is because our senses interact, reinforce each other, and impact all areas of development. Characteristics, such as resilience, coupled with appropriate educational experiences and other life experiences will greatly influence the potential for happiness and other positive life outcomes. Due to the prevalence of disabilities in the d/Dhh population, preservice preparation programs for teachers should include content on additional and multiple disabilities (Schein & Miller, 2008). In addition, school districts should provide professional development and parental supports for children who are DWD. Such efforts will support the development and implementation of programming that will support positive outcomes for all students.

DISCUSSION QUESTIONS

1. What is the difference between prevalence and incidence?
2. Name the three primary inheritance patterns. Which chromosome pairs are associated with each inheritance pattern?
3. Children with Down syndrome typically exhibit strong visual skills but weak short-term memory. What are some steps that could be taken to help them better learn daily routines and functional living skills?
4. Children with CHARGE syndrome experience reduced functioning in vision, hearing, proprioception, tactile abilities, and balance. As a professional, how can you encourage and support a child's ability to explore his or her world freely?
5. Using the seven behavioral characteristics of a person with CHARGE syndrome, what strategies might professionals use to assist during the transition from school to employment or postsecondary education?
6. Usher syndrome causes vision to deteriorate, which impacts mobility, communication, and general independence. What accommodations or modifications might a person need at home, school, and work to function independently throughout their lifetime?

RESOURCES

- **The Centre for Genetics Education**
  - ○ https://www.genetics.edu.au
  - ○ The Centre provides fact sheets that include figures and clear descriptions about the three primary inheritance patterns.

Down Syndrome

- **Down Syndrome Education International (DSE)**
  - ○ https://www.down-syndrome.org/en-us/
- **Down Syndrome International (DSi)**
  - ○ https://ds-int.org

- DSi is a charitable organization that seeks to improve the quality of life experienced by individuals with Down syndrome. The organization's goals include raising awareness about Down syndrome, providing resources to individuals, and representing individuals with this syndrome.
- **Global Down Syndrome Foundation**
  - https://www.globaldownsyndrome.org/our-story/
  - The foundation is dedicated to improving the lives of individuals through research, medical care, education, and advocacy. It supports the Linda Crnic Institute for Down Syndrome. The website contains information on Down syndrome, research, grants and grant opportunities, and conferences.
- **National Down Syndrome Affiliates in Action (DSAIA)**
  - https://www.dsaia.org/
  - DSAIA is a trade association with members from >80 organizations. Central to their mission is providing resources to support individuals with Down syndrome to meet their potential. Their website includes a resource library.
- **National Down Syndrome Society (NDSS)**
  - https://www.ndss.org/
  - NDSS is a human rights organization for individuals with Down syndrome and is involved with national advocacy and public policy. Its website provides information on Down syndrome through the life span and information on their legislative agenda.
- **National Association for Down Syndrome (NADS)**
  - http://www.nads.org/
  - NADS provides parent support, resource referral, public awareness, self-advocacy, and conferences and seminars. The website contains information on Down syndrome in the prenatal period, infants and toddlers aged 0–3 years, children aged 4–12 years, and teens and adults aged ≥13.
- **Down Syndrome Foundation of Orange County**
  - https://www.dsfoc.org/
  - This organization created The Learning Program (https://www.dsfoc.org/store/), which offers materials on calendars, counting, literacy, and math (including money and number lines). Their website also includes a list of recommended applications ("apps") for mobile and tablet devices.

Trisomy 13 and 18 Syndromes

- **International Trisomy Alliance**
  - https://www.internationaltrisomyalliance.com/
- **Support Organization for Trisomy 18, 13, and Related Disorders (SOFT)**
  - http://trisomy.org/
  - SOFT is an international organization with branches in several countries across the globe. It is a volunteer organization incorporated in 1980. The website contains information about trisomy, resources, information for professionals, publications, and upcoming events.
- **Trisomy 18 Foundation**
  - https://www.trisomy18.org/
  - The mission of the Trisomy 18 Foundation is to advance research and empower families. Its website contains information on the syndrome, upcoming events, and how families can connect with each other. Furthermore, individual families are highlighted.

1p36 Deletion Syndrome

- **1p36 Deletion Support & Awareness**
  - http://www.1p36dsa.org/
  - This support and awareness group was founded in 2009 by parents of children with 1p36 deletion. The website contains information on the syndrome, including how it is diagnosed, information on an annual national conference on the syndrome, web resources, and journal references.
- **National Institutes of Health Genetics Home Reference: 1p36 Deletion**
  - https://ghr.nlm.nih.gov/condition/1p36-deletion-syndrome
  - The website provides an overview of the syndrome including frequency, inheritance pattern, and diagnosis and management resources.

CHARGE Syndrome

- **National Center on Deaf-Blindness (NCDB)**
  - https://nationaldb.org/

○ https://www.chargesyndrome.org/wp-content/uploads/2020/12/Hey-I-reached-adulthood-now-what.pdf

○ NCDB provides technical assistance to state and multistate projects serving children and youth who are deafblind. It has national initiatives in early identification, family engagement, interveners and qualified personnel, literacy, and transition. It also conducts the National Deaf-Blind Child Count. The website below contains a list of resources specific to CHARGE syndrome.

- **Perkins eLearning**
  ○ https://www.perkinselearning.org/videos/webcast/charge-syndrome-overview
  ○ This resource from the Perkins School for the Blind contains a webcast by Pamela Ryan on CHARGE syndrome with full transcript.

- **The CHARGE Syndrome Foundation**
  ○ https://www.chargesyndrome.org/
  ○ The mission of the CHARGE Syndrome Foundation is to promote awareness, provide support programs to parents, build networks and partnerships, and invest in research. The website contains information for families, professionals, and researchers, including information on foundation-supported research, available grants, and upcoming events including the national CHARGE syndrome conference.

Usher Syndrome

- **American Speech-Language-Hearing Association (ASHA)**
  ○ https://www.asha.org/Articles/Understanding-Usher-Syndrome/
  ○ The ASHA website on Usher syndrome provides an overview of the clinical and genetic features of Usher syndromes and their various types. It also gives information on diagnosis and treatment, including specific educational strategies

- **Hearing Health Foundation**
  ○ https://hearinghealthfoundation.org/what-is-usher-syndrome

- **National Center on Deaf-Blindness 2017 Webinars on Usher Syndrome**
  ○ https://www.nationaldb.org/updates/2017-national-webinar-starting-a-national-dialogue-on-finding-children-with-usher-syndrome/

- ○ These webinars are free and will be helpful for identifying additional educational suggestions.
- **National Institute on Deafness and Other Communication Disorders**
  - ○ https://www.nidcd.nih.gov/health/usher-syndrome
- **National Eye Institute (National Institutes of Health)**
  - ○ https://nei.nih.gov/health/pigmentosa/pigmentosa_facts
  - ○ National Institutes of Health provides an overview of the essential facts of RP, including a definition, its effects on vision, inheritance patterns, prevalence rates, diagnosis, and treatment.
- **Usher Syndrome Coalition**
  - ○ https://www.usher-syndrome.org/about-the-coalition/
  - ○ The mission of the coalition is to raise awareness and accelerate research on Usher syndrome. It also provides support to individuals with Usher syndrome and their families, including how to make connections via conferences and social media.
- **Usher Syndrome Network, Deafblind International**
  - ○ http://usher.deafblindinternational.org/current-research/
  - ○ The Usher Syndrome Network is a network established under the umbrella of Deafblind International, an association of professionals who work with individuals who are deafblind, and their family members. The website provides information on the syndrome, links to medical and psychosocial publications, and information on international conferences.
- **Usher Syndrome Society**
  - ○ http://www.ushersyndromesociety.org/

Other Resources on Syndromes

- **National Institutes of Health: Genetic and Rare Diseases Information Center (GARD)**
  - ○ https://rarediseases.info.nih.gov/diseases
  - ○ GARD maintains a list of rare diseases, with information on each in both written and auditory form. In addition to information on diagnosis and treatment, a resource list is provided.
- **National Organization for Rare Disorders (NORD)**
  - ○ https://rarediseases.org/

o NORD is involved in providing information for patients and families, patient organizations, and clinicians and researchers. It is also involved nationally in policy and advocacy on behalf of rare syndromes. This website provides a comprehensive overview of various syndromes.

REFERENCES

Abreu-Mendoza, R. A., & Arias-Trejo, N. (2015). Numerical and area comparison abilities in Down syndrome. *Research in Developmental Disabilities, 41–42,* 58–65.

Anderzén-Carlsson, A. (2015). CHARGE syndrome—A five case study of the syndrome characteristics and health care consumption during the first year of life. *Journal of Pediatric Nursing, 30,* 6–16.

Ang, B. (2014). Visual field. *Vision and Eye Health.* http://www.vision-and-eye-health.com/visual-field.html

Åsten, P., Akre, H., & Persson, C. (2014). Associations between speech features and phenotypic severity in Treacher Collins syndrome. *BMC Medical Genetics, 15*(47), 47.

Bashinski, S. (2015). Communication programming for learners with CHARGE syndrome: Augmenting comprehension and expression. *Perspectives on Augmentative and Alternative Communication, 24,* 86–93.

Batshaw, M. L., Gropman, A., & Lanpher, B. (2013). Genetics and developmental disabilities. In M. L. Batshaw, N. J. Roizen, & G. R. Lotrecchiano (Eds.), *Children with disabilities* (7th ed., pp. 3–24). Brookes.

Bourquin, E., & Sauerburger, D. (2005). Teaching deaf-blind people to communicate and interact with the public: Critical issues for travelers who are deaf-blind. *RE:view, 137,* 109–116.

Braddock, B., McDaniel, J., Spragge, S., Loncke, F., Braddock, S. R., & Carey, J. C. (2012). Communication ability in persons with trisomy 18 and trisomy 13. *Augmentative and Alternative Communication, 28*(4), 266–277.

Brown, D. (2011). CHARGE syndrome—True multi-sensory impairment. In U. Horsch & A. Scheele (Eds.), *Compendium on CHARGE syndrome: Multidisciplinary and international perspectives* (pp. 169–188). Median-Verlag von Killisch-Horn GmbH.

Bruce, S. M., Bashinski, S. M., Covelli, A. J., Bernstein, V., Zatta, M. C., & Briggs, S. (2018). Positive behavior supports for individuals who are deafblind with CHARGE syndrome. *Journal of Visual Impairment & Blindness, 112,* 497–508.

Bruce, S., Brum, C., & Nannemann, A. (2015). Communication programming implications for individuals with genetic causes of severe disability and visual impairment. *Perspectives on Augmentative and Alternative Communication, 24,* 94–105.

Bruce, S. M., Janssen, M. J., & Bashinski, S. M. (2016). Individualizing and personalizing communication and literacy instruction for children who are deafblind. *Journal of Deafblind Studies on Communication, 2,* 73–87.

Buethe, P., Vohr, B. R., & Herer, G. R. (2013). Hearing and deafness. In M. L. Batshaw, N. J. Roizen, & G. R. Lotrecchiano (Eds.), *Children with disabilities* (7th ed., pp. 141–168). Brookes.

Busa, T., Legendre, M., Bauge, M., Quarello, E., Bretelle, F., Bilan, F., Sigaudy, S., Gilbert-Dussardier, B., & Philip, N. (2016). Prenatal findings in children with early postnatal diagnosis of CHARGE syndrome. *Prenatal Diagnosis, 36,* 561–567.

Centers for Disease Control and Prevention. (2020). *Data and statistics on Down syndrome.* https://www.cdc.gov/ncbddd/birthdefects/down-syndrome/data.html

Cereda, A., & Carey, J. C. (2012). The trisomy 18 syndrome. *Orphanet Journal of Rare Diseases, 7*(81), 1–14.

Cobb, A. R. M., Green, B., Gill, D., Ayliffe, P., Lloyd, T. W., Bulstrode, N., & Dunaway, D. J. (2014). The surgical management of Treacher Collins syndrome. *British Journal of Oral and Maxillofacial Surgery, 52,* 581–589.

Dammeyer, J. (2012a). Children with Usher syndrome: Mental and behavioral disorders. *Behavioral and Brain Functions, 8*(1), 1–5.

Dammeyer, J. (2012b). Development and characteristics of children with Usher syndrome and CHARGE syndrome. *International Journal of Pediatric Otorhinolaryngology, 76,* 1292–1296.

Dauwerse, J. G., Dixon, J., Seland, S., Ruivenkamp, C. A. L., van Haeringen, A., Hoefsloot, L. H., Peters, D. J. M., Clement-de Boers,

A., Daumer-Haas, C., Maiwald, R., Zweier, C., Kerr, B., Cobo, A. M., Toral, J. F., Jeannette, A., Hoogeboom, M., Lohmann, D. R., Hehr, U., Dixon, M. J., . . . Wieczorek, D. (2011). Mutations in genes encoding subunits of RNA polymerases I and III cause Treacher Collins syndrome. *Nature Genetics, 43*(1), 20–22.

Davenport, S. L. H., & Hefner, M. A. (2011). Overview and sensory issues. In T. S. Hartshorne, M. A. Hefner, S. L. H. Davenport, & J. W. Thelin (Eds.), *CHARGE syndrome* (pp. 3–12). Plural.

Del Viva, M. M., Tozzi, A., Bargagna, S., & Cioni, G. (2015). Motion perception deficit in Down syndrome. *Neuropsychologia, 75,* 214–220.

Deuce, G. (2017). The education of learners with CHARGE syndrome. *British Journal of Special Education, 44,* 376–393.

Domanico, D., Fragiotta, S., Cutini, A., Grenga, P. L., & Vingolo, E. M. (2015). Psychosis, mood, and behavioral disorders in Usher syndrome: Review of the literature. *Medical Hypothesis, Discovery and Innovation in Ophthalmology, 4,* 50–55.

Down Syndrome Foundation of Orange County. (2020, October 1). *The Learning Program.* https://www.dsfoc.org/online-courses/

Dykens, E. M. (2007). Psychiatric and behavioral disorders in persons with Down syndrome. *Mental Retardation and Developmental Disabilities Research Reviews, 13,* 272–278.

Emerson, R. W., Holbrook, M. C., & D'Andrea, F. M. (2009). Acquisition of literacy skills by young children who are blind: Results from the ABC braille study. *Journal of Visual Impairment & Blindness, 103,* 610–624.

Fakin, A., Zupan, A., Gavač, D., & Hawlina, M. (2012). Combination of retinitis pigmentosa and hearing loss caused by a novel mutation in PRPH2 and a known mutation in GJB2: Importance for differential diagnosis of Usher syndrome. *Vision Research, 75,* 71–76.

Faught, G. G., Conners, F. A., & Himmelberger, Z. M. (2016). Auditory and visual sustained attention in Down syndrome. *Research in Developmental Disabilities, 53–54,* 135–146.

Ferrell, K. A., Bruce, S., & Luckner, J. L. (2014). *Evidence-based practices for students with sensory impairments* (Document No. IC-4). http://ceedar.education.ufl.edu/tools/innovation-configurations/

Gallaudet Research Institute (GRI). (2013, August). *Regional and national summary report of data from the 2011–2012 Annual Survey of Deaf and Hard of Hearing Children and Youth.* https://research. gallaudet.edu/demographics/

Glenn, S., Cunningham, C., Nananidou, A., Prasher, V., & Glenholmes, P. (2015). Routinised and compulsive-like behaviours in individuals with Down syndrome. *Journal of Intellectual Disability Research, 59*(11), 1061–1070.

Golum, F. D., & Schreck, J. S. (2018). The journey to interprofessional collaborative practice: Are we there yet? *Pediatric Clinics of North America, 65,* 1–12.

Guardino, C., & Cannon, J. E. (2015). Theory, research, and practice for students who are Deaf and hard of hearing with disabilities: Addressing the challenges from birth to postsecondary education [Special issue]. *American Annals of the Deaf, 160*(4), 347–355.

Hartshorne, N., Hudson, A., MacCuspie, J., Kennert, B., Nacarato, T., Hartshorne, T., & Blake, K. (2016). Quality of life in adolescents and adults with CHARGE syndrome. *American Journal of Medical Genetics, 170*(8), 2012–2021.

Hartshorne, T. (2011). Behavioral phenotype. In T. S. Hartshorne, M. A. Hefner, S. L. H. Davenport, & J. W. Thelin (Eds.), *CHARGE syndrome* (pp. 317–326). Plural.

Hartshorne, T. S., Hefner, M. A., Davenport, S. L. H., & Thelin, J. W. (2011). Introduction. In T. S. Hartshorne, M. A. Hefner, S. L. H. Davenport, & J. W. Thelin (Eds.), *CHARGE syndrome* (pp. xi–xv). Plural.

Heilstedt, H. A., Ballif, B. C., Howard, L. A., Lewis, R. A., Stal, S., Kashork, C. D., Bacino, C. A., Shapira, S. K., & Shaffer, L. G. (2003). Physical map of 1p36, placement of breakpoints in monosomy 1p36, and clinical characterization of the syndrome. *American Journal of Human Genetics, 72,* 1200–1212.

Henricson, C., Wass, M., Lidestam, B., Möller, C., & Lyxell, B. (2012). Cognitive skills in children with Usher syndrome type 1 and cochlear implants. *International Journal of Pediatric Otorhinolaryngology, 76,* 1449–1457.

Horstmeier, D. (2004). *Teaching math to people with Down syndrome and other hands-on learners: Basic survival skills.* Woodbine House.

Janvier, A., & Watkins, A. (2013). Medical interventions for children with trisomy 13 and trisomy 18: What is the value of a short disabled life? *Acta Paediatrica, 102,* 1112–1117.

Keates, B. J. B. (2002). Genes and syndromic hearing loss. *Journal of Communication Disorders, 35,* 355–366.

Kohlhase, J. (2011). Genetics of CHARGE syndrome. In U. Horsch & A. Scheele (Eds.), *Compendium on CHARGE syndrome: Multidisciplinary and international perspectives* (pp. 11–18). Median-Verlag von Killisch-Horn GmbH.

Krantz, I. D., McCallum, J., Descipio, C., Kaur, M., Gillis, L. A., Yaeger, D., Jukofsky, L., Wasserman, N., Bottani, A., Morris, C. A., Nowaczyk, M. J. M., Toriello, H., Bamshad, M. J., Carey, J. C., Rappaport, E., Kawauchi, S., Lander, A. D., Calof, A. L., Li, H.-H., . . . Jackson, L. G. (2004). Cornelia de Lange syndrome is caused by mutations in NIPBL, the human homolog of Drosophila melanogajster Nipped-B. *Nature Genetics, 36*(6), 631–635.

Lenarduzzi, S., Vozzi, D., Morgan, A., Rubinato, E., D'Eustacchio, A., Osland, T. M., Rossi, C., Graziano, C., Castorina, P., Ambrosetti, U., Morgutti, M., & Girotto, G. (2015). Usher syndrome: An effective sequencing approach to establish a genetic and clinical diagnosis. *Hearing Research, 320,* 18–23.

Lieberman, L. (2011). Resources for physical education, sports, and fitness for children with CHARGE. In U. Horsch & A. Scheele (Eds.), *Compendium on CHARGE syndrome: Multidisciplinary and international perspectives* (pp. 251–261). Median-Verlag von Killisch-Horn GmbH.

Lomas, G. I., Andrews, J. F., & Shaw, P. C. (2017). Deaf and hard of hearing students. In J. M. Kauffman, D. P. Hallahan, & P. C. Cullen (Eds.), *Handbook of special education* (2nd ed., pp. 338–357). Routledge.

Luft, P. (2015). Transition services for DHH adolescents and young adults with disabilities: Challenges and theoretical frameworks. *American Annals of the Deaf, 160*(4), 395–414.

Majors, M. (2011). Educational considerations for students with CHARGE syndrome. In U. Horsch & A. Scheele (Eds.), *Compendium* on *CHARGE syndrome: Multidisciplinary and international perspectives* (pp. 201–212). Median-Verlag von Killisch-Horn GmbH.

Mathur, P., & Yang, J. (2015). Usher syndrome: Hearing loss, retinal degeneration and associated abnormalities. *Biochimica et Biophysica Acta, 1852,* 406–420.

Nannemann, A. C., Bruce, S. M., & Covelli, A. (2017). Positive behavior supports for a young adult with CHARGE syndrome. *Journal of Visual Impairment & Blindness, 111,* 175–179.

National Center on Deaf-Blindness. (2020, October 1). *The 2018 National Child Count of Children and Youth who are Deaf-Blind.* https://www.nationaldb.org/products/national-child-count/report-2018/

National Eye Institute. (2020, October 1). *Facts about retinitis pigmentosa.* https://www.nei.nih.gov/learn-about-eye-health/eye-conditions-and-diseases/retinitis-pigmentosa

National Institute on Deafness and Other Communication Disorders. (2017). *Usher syndrome.* National Institutes of Health. https://www.nidcd.nih.gov/health/usher-syndrome

Nelson, C., & Bruce, S. M. (2019). Children who are deaf/hard of hearing with disabilities: Paths to language and literacy. *Education Sciences, 9,* 134. https://doi.org/10.3390/educsci9020134

Nelson, C., Bruce, S., & Barnhill, B. A. (2022). Future directions in the field of Deafblindness. In C. Guardino, J. E. Cannon, & P. V. Paul (Eds.), *Deaf and hard of hearing learners with disabilities: Foundations, strategies, and resources* (pp. 162–192). Routledge.

Ogletree, B. T. (2017). Addressing the communication and other needs of persons with severe disabilities through engaged interprofessional teams: Introduction to a clinical forum. *American Journal of Speech-Language Pathology, 26,* 157–161.

Parker, M., Budd, J., Draper, E., & Young, I. (2003). Trisomy 13 and trisomy 18 in a defined population: Epidemiological, genetic and prenatal observations. *Prenatal Diagnosis, 23,* 856–860.

Pisaneschi, E., Sirleto, P., Lepri, F. R., Genovese, S., Dentici, M. L., Petrocchi, S., Angioni, A., Digilio, M. C., & Dallapiccola, B. (2015). CHARGE syndrome due to deletion of region upstream of *CHD7* gene START codon. *BMC Medical Genetics, 16,* 78–83.

Read, A. P., & Newton, V. E. (1997). Waardenburg syndrome. *Journal of Medical Genetics, 34*(8), 656–665.

Roizen, N. J. (2012). Down syndrome. In M. L. Batshaw, N. J. Roizen, & G. R. Lotrecchiano (Eds.), *Children with disabilities* (7th ed., pp. 307–318). Brookes.

Sacks, S. Z. (2016). Educating students with visual impairments who have multiple disabilities: An overview. In S. Z. Sacks & M. C. Zatta (Eds.), *Keys to educational success: Teaching students with visual impairments and multiple disabilities* (pp. 3–64). American Foundation for the Blind.

Sarimski, K. (1997). Communication, social-emotional development, and parenting stress in Cornelia-de-Lange syndrome. *Journal of Intellectual Disability Research, 41*(1), 70–75.

Sarimski, K. (2002). Analysis of intentional communication in severely handicapped children with Cornelia-de-Lange syndrome. *Journal of Communication Disorders, 35*(6), 483–500.

Sauerburger, D. (1993). *Independence without sight or sound: Suggestions for practitioners working with deaf-blind adults.* American Foundation for the Blind.

Schein, J. D., & Miller, M. H. (2008). Genetics and deafness: Implications for education and life care of deaf students. *American Annals of the Deaf, 153*(4), 408–410.

Shapira, S. K., McCaskill, C., Northrup, H., Spikes, A. S., Elder, F. F. B., Sutton, V. R., Korenberg, J. R., Greenberg, F., & Shaffer, L. G. (1997). Chromosome 1p36 deletions: The clinical phenotype and molecular characterization of a common newly delineated syndrome. *American Journal of Human Genetics, 61*(3), 642–650.

Simpson, K. L. (2013). Appendix B: Syndromes and inborn errors of metabolism. In M. L. Batshaw, N. J. Roizen, & G. R. Lotrecchiano (Eds.), *Children with disabilities* (7th ed., pp. 757–802). Brookes.

Smith, K. G., Smith, I. M., & Blake, K. (2010). CHARGE syndrome: An educator's primer. *Education and Treatment of Children, 33,* 289–314.

Tedeschi, A. S., Roizen, N. J., Taylor, H. G., Murray, G., Curtis, C. A., & Parikh, A. S. (2015). The prevalence of congenital hearing loss in neonates with Down syndrome. *Journal of Pediatrics, 166,* 168–171.

Thelin, J. W. (2011). Hearing. In T. S. Hartshorne, M. A. Hefner, S. L. H. Davenport, & J. W. Thelin (Eds.), *CHARGE syndrome* (pp. 25–42). Plural.

Uppal, H., Chandran, S., & Potluri, R. (2015). Risk factors for mortality in Down syndrome. *Journal of Intellectual Disability Research, 59*(9), 873–881.

Vesseur, A., Langereis, M., Free, R., Snik, A., van Ravenswaaij-Arts, C., & Mylanus, E. (2016). Influence of hearing loss and cognitive abilities on language development in CHARGE syndrome. *American Journal of Medical Genetics, 170*(8), 2022–2030.

Waardenburg, J. P. (1951). A new syndrome combining developmental anomalies of the eyelids, eyebrows and nose root with pigmentary defects of the iris and head hair and with congenital deafness. *American Journal of Human Genetics, 3*(3), 195–253.

Wahlqvist, M., Möller, C., Möller, K., & Danermark, B. (2013). Physical and psychological health in persons with deafblindness that is due to Usher syndrome type II. *Journal of Visual Impairment & Blindness, 107,* 207–220.

Wallber, J. (2009). Understanding Usher syndrome. *American Speech-Language-Hearing Association.* https://www.asha.org/Articles/ Understanding-Usher-Syndrome/

Ward, M. M. (2013). Estimating disease prevalence and incidence using administrative data: Some assembly required. *Journal of Rheumatology, 40,* 1241–1243.

Washington Sensory Disabilities Services (2010). *Educational accommodations to consider for children, teens, and college students with Usher syndrome.* https://www.wsdsonline.org/

Wilkinson, K., & Na, J. Y. (2015). Interprofessional practice in developing an AAC system for children with Down syndrome. *Perspectives on Augmentative and Alternative Communication, 24,* 114–122.

Wren, S. (2014). *Down syndrome specific curriculum supports: Capitalizing on learning strength.* Down Syndrome Guild of Greater Kansas City. https://www.kcdsg.org/

Zampini, L., Salvi, A., & D'Odorico, L. (2015). Joint attention behaviors and vocabulary development in children with Down syndrome. *Journal of Intellectual Disability Research, 59*(10), 891–901.

5

Deaf and Hard of Hearing Learners With Intellectual Disabilities: Current Understandings and Remaining Challenges

Pamela Luft

LEARNING OBJECTIVES

Readers will:

- Identify the major etiologies of deafness and intellectual disability (ID), the perception of students who are deaf or hard of hearing (d/Dhh) with an ID (d/Dhh-ID) over time, and the challenges when deafness and an ID co-occur.
- Identify the challenges of assessment and identification of effective strategies when working with students who are d/Dhh-ID.
- Identify the placement options and opportunities for students who are d/Dhh-ID.
- Describe the various professionals working with learners who are d/Dhh-ID and their families.
- Delineate the ways in which a communication plan and Individual Education Plan (IEP) can be used to create a strengths-based curriculum and optimal educational plans for students who are d/Dhh-ID.

DOI: 10.4324/9781003252054-5

- Demonstrate ways to modify curricula incorporating accommodations, adaptations, and augmentations for students who are d/Dhh-ID across a range of abilities.
- Identify several assistive technology hardware devices or software that can be used to increase the independence of students who are d/Dhh-ID.

This chapter describes the issues, challenges, and promising practices when working with students who are d/Deaf or hard of hearing (d/Dhh) with intellectual disabilities (d/Dhh-ID). These students comprise approximately 14.8% of the d/Dhh population (Gallaudet Research Institute [GRI], 2013). Within this group, 8.8% have mild-to-moderate intellectual challenges, and 6.0% have developmental disabilities and more extensive learning challenges. Students with mild-to-moderate intellectual challenges are likely to have typical or nearly typical language, communication, and social skills so they can integrate with their d/Dhh peers in many ways. Their difficulties will arise with academic learning, with somewhat lower achievement across all content areas, although supplementary strategies and practice should allow them to achieve near-typical levels. Students with moderate-to-severe intellectual disabilities (IDs) typically have learning challenges that affect communication and social skills, as well as their academic achievement. Successful instruction will require supplementary strategies and some modification of learning goals, depending on their unique learning profiles. These two categories of students suggest the range of intellectual abilities to be considered in their educational and instructional programming.

These students are equally culturally diverse as they are d/Dhh, which affects their preferred language and communication choices, in addition to having potential effects on their interaction and social skills. They may use communication accommodations that include cochlear implants (CI) or hearing aids to support spoken language or use American Sign Language (ASL). Students with more significant intellectual challenges may require more supportive communication options and devices to include greater use of visual language and/or modalities.

Several health challenges or conditions that affect the general d/Dhh population may also be present among individuals who are d/Dhh-ID. These encompass physical/orthopedic, vision, or other chronic illnesses that will influence their educational planning (GRI, 2013). More recent national data on special education students in K–12 environments do not include information on additional conditions. However, Karchmer and Allen (1999) identified a number of functional limitations that affected more than half of the d/Dhh population, including those with additional disabilities (see Table 5.1).

Accurate educational planning should begin with a comprehensive understanding of each student's strengths and needs. Therefore, it is important to identify whether students who are d/Dhh-ID have functional limitations in addition to their intellectual challenges (Karchmer & Allen, 1999). Teachers, parents, and service providers should be observant of these functional limitations to ensure that instructional content and methods are appropriately designed to maximize student learning. Table 5.1

TABLE 5.1 Functional Limitations Within the d/Dhh K–12 Population

Number of Functional Limitations	%
1	10.6
2	15.4
3	10.1
4–5	17.2
6–9	11.0
Categories of Functional Limitations	%
Social/behavioral	27.5
Thinking/reasoning	32.9
Maintain attention to classroom tasks	35.1
Expressive communication	45.6
Receptive communication	46.9
Physical (vision, balance, use of limbs, and overall health)	41.0

Note. Adapted from Karchmer and Allen (1999).

illustrates that nearly half of learners who are d/Dhh will have expressive and/or receptive communication limitations, with nearly one-third having thinking/reasoning limitations, and more than one-fourth having social/behavioral limitations. These limitations may be more prevalent in association with certain causes of students' deafness and ID, particularly among some of the syndromes identified in the next section.

Etiologies of Learners Who Are d/Dhh-ID

Several causes of hearing loss include conditions that may concurrently result in an ID. These involve genetic or inherited factors, maternal infections, infections to newborns, or a combination of genetic and nongenetic causes. Approximately 3 per 1,000 infants are born with moderate, profound, or severe hearing levels. An additional 1 in 500 infants are born with or develop some level of hearing loss during early childhood (Centers for Disease Control and Prevention [CDC], n.d.). For many infants, the cause is unknown, although hearing losses are more common in those admitted to intensive care units at birth (National Conference of State Legislatures, 2011).

Improvements in accurate medical diagnoses and treatments influence the prevalence of certain etiologies. Students with more severe conditions are increasingly likely to survive beyond childhood, placing new demands on educational services and on families. Several causes of hearing loss and ID include maternal rubella, Rh incompatibility, measles, and cytomegalovirus (CMV). New medical interventions have resulted in substantial changes in the rate of reported cases. From 1982 to 1992, maternal rubella was reduced by 88.98%, Rh incompatibility decreased by 77.4%, and measles declined by 68.5%. However, CMV, not even reported in 1982, increased during 1987–1992 by 189.32% (Holt et al., 1994). CMV remains one of the most common nongenetic causes of hearing loss in developed countries and results in possible complications to the liver, lung, and spleen, as well as seizures, small head size, and IDs (CDC, n.d.; Shearer et al., 1993–2018). Overall, heredity remains the largest cause of hearing loss among the d/Dhh population (25.4%). An additional 10.1% is due to postpartum disease or injury and 8.2% due to issues during pregnancy, with the cause of deafness unknown for 57.1% (GRI, 2013). No specific data are available for the d/Dhh-ID population, so we estimate that these numbers are similar.

Genetic etiologies that cause hearing loss and IDs can involve a number of syndromes (Bruce et al., 2022, see Chapter 4) or genetic mutation, although 70%–80% of the d/Dhh population is nonsyndromic with no other conditions (CDC, n.d.; Cryns & Van Camp, 2004). More than 400 syndromes cause varying levels of hearing loss, as do 1,227 conditions. Identification of genetic conditions and syndromes continues to expand through improved medical and genetic testing (U.S. National Library of Medicine, n.d.).

IDENTIFICATION AND ASSESSMENT

The passage of the Universal Newborn Hearing Screening legislation in all 50 U.S. states and many territories (Shulman et al., 2010) has markedly improved the early identification of infants who are d/Dhh. Parents of infants who are d/Dhh-ID may notice delays with typical developmental milestones. The identification of an infant's ID is based on the Individuals With Disabilities Education Act (IDEA) of the United States, which defines ID as follows:

> Intellectual disability means significantly subaverage general intellectual functioning, existing concurrently with deficits in adaptive behavior and manifested during the developmental period, that adversely affects a child's educational performance. The term "intellectual disability" was formerly termed "mental retardation." (IDEA, 2004, § 300.8 [c] [6])

Early intervention personnel are trained to track developmental milestones and should request additional state or local services, as needed. Many of the parent–infant programs make visits to the home and utilize this environment to teach family members strategies for supporting and enhancing language/communication and developmentally appropriate skills. Several websites with developmental milestones are listed in the resources section of this chapter.

Upon a child's third birthday, those who have been receiving infant-toddler services transition to school-based preschool programs. These programs are funded by the U.S. Department of Education to serve students with documented disabilities, primarily those with developmental disabilities (Jackson et al., 2022, see Chapter 2). Many of these children have significant physical, cognitive, communication, social-emotional, or adaptive development challenges (U.S. Department of Education, 2016, 2017a). Due to the small population size, students who are d/Dhh-ID have been placed in classrooms with children who have developmental disabilities (Hands & Voices, 2014). However, preschool services provided through centralized or consortium services across districts may result in a designated classroom with a trained teacher of d/Dhh (TDHH). A designated classroom allows for instruction by a TDHH who understands the unique language, communication, and preacademic learning needs of students who are d/Dhh-ID. In an inclusive preschool classroom, the TDHH may consult with general or special education teachers regarding specialized strategies to meet the unique needs of children who are d/Dhh-ID.

Regardless of the student's educational placement, children who are d/Dhh-ID require services that address their hearing levels as well as their ID. Typically, this is best met by a TDHH who has the specialized training to support both the development of language/communication skills and their intellectual needs. At a minimum, all preschool children who are d/Dhh, regardless of having an ID or not, should be on the caseload of a TDHH, who may travel between school districts to consult with and oversee the provision of appropriate educational services (Jackson et al., 2017).

Developmental Impacts

Being d/Dhh may affect a child's ability to acquire the language within his or her environment, as well as information about the world and how it operates (Luft, 2016). Acquiring a fluent language is essential to interpersonal communication in order for children to develop the cognitive schemata that become the basis of further intellectual development (Paul & Whitelaw, 2011; Zwiebel & Mertens, 1985). Children acquire critical linguistic content and the foundational constructs of all subsequent academic curricula and societal expectations during infancy. Conversations about the neighborhood, families, animals, seasons, and so on lead to the acquisition of early social studies, science, and math concepts, which d/Dhh children often miss or poorly understand, potentially compromising subsequent academic achievement (Luft, 2016).

Essential knowledge is transmitted through language, including psychosocial, behavioral, and sociocultural expectations, for successfully participating in the world (Luft, 2016). Language fluency is increasingly important for children's development across Jean Piaget's stages of cognitive development, including concepts of object permanence, abstract representations through words and images, understanding the perspectives of others, logical thinking, and engaging in hypothetical thinking and deductive reasoning (Beins, 2012; Crain, 2011). Erik Erikson's stages of psychosocial development also depend on language for developing concepts of trust, autonomy, confidence, and initiative in order to develop a strong identity and maintain relationships. Conversely, children unable to achieve these goals often mistrust, doubt, feel inferior, and experience role confusion and isolation (Crain, 2011; Stevens, 1983).

Assessment Challenges

The newborn hearing screening and follow-up programs have been successful in identifying the presence and extent of an infant's hearing loss (Holte et al., 2012). However, identifying and diagnosing the extent of ID can be much more challenging in that most assessments rely on communication. Differentiating between the impact of hearing loss on development and the effects of having an ID can be extremely challenging (Cawthon, 2015; Lewis, 2003; Miller et al., 2015). The effects of one often influence the other, with many assessment tasks utilizing interrelated cognitive and linguistic abilities. Some d/Dhh students' ID may not be accurately assessed until they attain foundational communication abilities. Some needs may not be recognized until learners struggle with typical academic or preacademic activities.

Few developmental assessments have been designed to address the unique language and communication issues of d/Dhh children (Case, 2008; Martin & Mounty, 2005; Miller et al., 2015). Although accommodations are permitted to make assessments accessible to d/Dhh learners, these accommodations do not compensate for linguistic or experiential gaps (Johnson & Mitchell, 2008; Loew et al., 2005; Thurlow et al., 2008).

Parents, teachers, and service providers should recognize that accurate assessment requires skilled diagnosticians or psychologists. These professionals should also have experience working with d/Dhh children across a range of ages, languages, and communication modalities, as well as varying levels of ID and related learning challenges (Miller et al., 2015). Finding professionals with multiple specializations can be difficult and often requires teachers and service professionals to contact regional or national resource centers or seek other means of multidisciplinary collaboration. Some of these centers are listed under the Resources section of this chapter.

Obtaining accurate and age-appropriate assessments at birth—and as the child matures—is critical to ensuring that infant–toddler, early childhood, and subsequent school-based programs are appropriately designed to meet individual learning challenges. This process should begin with audiological assessments that include pure-tone, discrimination, and functional listening evaluations of different environments (Johnson et al., 2013). A battery of assessments should also include observations and interviews of parents, teachers, and others who may have important insights regarding the child's learning abilities and response to instruction (Flexer et al., 2013). Given the distinctive learning and achievement profiles of children who are d/Dhh-ID, a comprehensive assessment report is warranted to ensure accurate outcomes and subsequent planning.

There is a lack of assessments specifically designed for d/Dhh children. However, if everyone with whom the child interacts is alert to distinct or potentially unrecognized strengths and needs, these should be shared with other members of the multidisciplinary team. Results then can be operationalized into functional and academic activities for home and school. Assessments such as the ARC's Self-Determination Scale, adolescent version (Wehmeyer & Kelchner, 1995), the American Institutes for Research (AIR) Self-Determination Scale, Student Form (AIR, n.d.), and the Transition Assessment and Goal Generator (TAGG; Martin et al., 2015) address pretransition, self-determination, and independence skills that are important to address throughout a child's educational program. The TAGG is an online assessment with an ASL version.

Instructional Strategies

Placement Considerations

As a result of the various syndromic, congenital, or postpartum causes of deafness, as well as the particular family and regional characteristics, each learner who is d/Dhh-ID brings unique strengths and challenges to the educational environment. The task for the IEP team is to identify and/or create high-quality, appropriate yet challenging education that supports and maximizes the child's strengths. However, many TDHHs do not feel prepared to work with d/Dhh students with disabilities (DWD; Guardino, 2015; Soukup & Feinstein, 2007). Particularly in local school districts, IEP teams may need to collaborate across districts to find the necessary dual or multiple disability expertise (Luft, 2015, 2016). This becomes particularly important for teams working with students with significant intellectual challenges and with additional functional, health, physical, or vision disabilities.

A communication plan is an important tool for addressing the individualized language and communication skills of learners who are d/Dhh-ID. Mandated in 16 states, communication plans can effectively and efficiently meet the IDEA (2004) requirements that each d/Dhh child's IEP addresses their unique language and communication needs (Luft & Amiruzzaman, 2018). These plans promote careful analysis of communication and accommodation preferences across environments, thereby individualizing their supports and services. Considering that >85% of K–12 d/Dhh students attend their local public-school program, communication plans are especially important to ensure that their communication needs are adequately met.

Parents and teachers must examine classroom placements across the full continuum of options in order to select the environment that provides appropriate, yet high, learning expectations. Planning should focus on the individual child's abilities and needs, rather than fitting the child into currently available programming (Johnson et al., 2013). Placements should provide ongoing access to peers with whom the student can communicate freely, an essential criterion for full integration into the school community and to prevent isolation (Alasim, 2018; Tsach & Most, 2016). Social integration skills and opportunities remain important to each student's

K–12 and post-high-school programming, regardless of additional learning challenges.

Each student's IEP should ensure that they receive sufficient educational services and supports in the classroom. Within local programs, the assigned TDHH may be an itinerant teacher serving students across schools and districts. The remaining educational services for students who are d/Dhh-ID may be provided in an inclusive setting with a general education teacher. Small group/self-contained or resource classrooms with a TDHH can provide more intensive, disability-specific services for students who are d/Dhh or d/Dhh-ID; but low population numbers often prevent the formation of such classes, except in consortium programs across districts.

Another placement option is a residential or separate school for d/Dhh students. Historically, these have been valued for providing specialized training and content to meet the unique communication and learning challenges of students who are d/Dhh and DWD (Bull & Bullis, 1991; Moores, 1978; Osgood, 2008). These schools often have sufficient student numbers to provide special classes with experienced teachers who may have the expertise to focus on the academic and instructional needs of learners who are d/Dhh-ID.

Optimizing Outcomes

Due to the nature of individualized learning profiles, the planning for students who are d/Dhh-ID should be child-centered and strengths-based, with a perspective that seeks to optimize their potential successes and adult outcomes. Historically, there has been a potential for professionals to underestimate students' abilities. This may still occur and lead to higher rates of placement into programs that do not align with students' potential (Wagner et al., 2006). These students have previously been steered into "custodial" environments, with little attention to their development and learning abilities (Ewing & Jones, 2003). Those students with very low academic achievement were, at times, mislabeled as educational "failures" (Harmon et al., 1998; Wheeler-Scruggs, 2003).

Low expectations that reduce access to quality instruction for students who are d/Dhh-ID, as well as their struggles to pass state graduation tests, may restrict future employment options and opportunities to attend postsecondary training. Students who are d/Dhh, whether with an ID or not, may be challenged by requirements that include a graduation test (Thurlow et al., 2010). More positively, 19 states have identified alternative requirements to the standard graduation tests (Thurlow et al., 2010) offering an achievable option to these students.

During the IEP process, a vocational rehabilitation counselor should be included at the mandated age for transition planning (16 years is the federally mandated age, while several states begin at 14; Workforce Innovation and Opportunity Act, 2014) or younger, depending upon expected outcomes. This is more than an option—it is strongly recommended and is the reason for the transition legislation—to establish adult service agency links through school-based IEP meetings. A rehabilitation counselor with a background in deafness (e.g., rehabilitation counselor for the deaf) is ideal to ensure that appropriate vocational rehabilitation services are provided. These services further support students' participation in their choice of postsecondary employment and community activities.

IEP Planning Supports

The IEP provides a range of further supports for students who are d/Dhh-ID through the category of Related Services: (a) speech-language pathology, (b) audiology, (c) interpreting, (d) psychological services, (e) physical and occupational therapy, (f) recreation and therapeutic recreation, (g) early identification and assessment, (h) counseling services and rehabilitation counseling, (i) orientation and mobility services, and (j) medical services for diagnosis or evaluation. Related services also include school health or nursing services, social work, and parent counseling and training (Ohio Department of Education, 2014).

All of these instructional and related services are central to ensuring that students who are d/Dhh-ID are provided with positively focused, optimally challenging, and appropriate curriculum and learning activities. The IEP's Related Services can be used to provide (a) training for parents or teachers, (b) communication access to extracurricular activities, and (c) opportunities to interact with peers and staff with whom the student can communicate directly. If communication remains a concern, implementing a communication plan is essential. All these steps help to ensure that the educational achievement of each student who is d/Dhh-ID leads to successful adulthood and to opportunities to participate in the school and broader community.

Communication Plans

Earlier, this chapter described the use of a communication plan to support the language and communication preferences of students who are d/Dhh-ID and to ensure access to teachers and peers with whom they can interact freely. Parents and teachers can request use of a communication plan (see Figure 1 for an example, pp. 146–147; Hands & Voices, 2018).

For states/districts that do not mandate the use of a communication plan, IEP team members are encouraged to include such a plan. The benefits of the plan include linking communication with the IEP to guarantee provision of needed services. Modifications or adaptations to instructional methods, materials, techniques, media, physical settings, or environments are included in the IEP to support the communication plan. These modifications may be necessary for students to be able to accomplish IEP goals and objectives (Dayton, KY, Schools, 2014; Indiana Department of Education, 2018). This communication plan should be integrated with the IEP's complete list of instructional supports and services needed by the students, based on a comprehensive evaluation of their abilities and needs.

Multilevel Model of Support

A guide for identifying and implementing supports and services can be found in Wehmeyer et al.'s (2002) multilevel model of least-to-most support needs. This multilevel process is used to ensure that curriculum-based instruction is appropriately modified, challenging, and supportive for students with ID. The steps to the model are described below.

Step 1

The model begins with an evaluation assessing whether the standard curriculum is appropriate without modifications. If modifications are needed, the first step calls for professionals to consider using assistive technology to ensure access. For students who are d/Dhh-ID, assistive technology could involve the use of hearing aids, CIs, assistive listening devices, the use of sign language interpreters, and/or real-time captioning (see the section on Assistive Technology and Accommodations).

Step 2

If the student continues to struggle with instructional tasks, the second step is to identify appropriate curricular accommodations. An "accommodation" allows a student to complete the same assignments or tests as other students but with flexible timing, formatting, setting, scheduling, response options, and/or presentation choices (PACER Center, 2015). Students who are d/Dhh-ID may benefit from accommodations, such as (a) chapter summaries, (b) peer readers, (c) text material that is rewritten for easier reading and to bridge conceptual levels, (d) use of shorter assignments, (e) repetition and highlighting of keywords, (f) visual aids and manipulatives, (g) additional time, or (h) alternatives for long writing assignments (e.g., models, posters, panoramas, collections, or signed/oral presentations).

Step 3

If further support is required, the third step is to augment the curriculum with additional resources and supplementary materials to provide additional practice and learning. One option is to use a functional curriculum that focuses on critical life skills for adulthood (Wehmeyer et al., 2002), in lieu of the standard curriculum. Alwell and Cobb (2009) found support for the use of functional curricula across disabilities, ages, and gender, as strategies to address students' needs not met by other modifications. Ayres et al. (2011) further emphasized that the question is not whether students with significant ID can learn particular curricular standards, but at what cost, when it eliminates the instruction needed to become independent and self-determined adults.

Strategies and Expectations for Academic Progress

Professionals should maintain high expectations and always strive to help learners reach their developmental potential across all domains (e.g., academic, cognitive, psychosocial, and behavioral), regardless of a

Legal Name of Student	State Student ID (SASID)	Date of Birth	Date

COMMUNICATION PLAN FOR STUDENT WHO IS DEAF/HARD OF HEARING OR DEAF-BLIND

The IEP team has considered each area listed below, and has not denied instructional opportunity based on the amount of the child's/student's residual hearing, the ability of the parent(s) to communicate, nor the child's/student's experience with other communication modes. To the extent appropriate, the input about this child's/student's communication and related needs as suggested from adults who are deaf/hard of hearing has been considered. 300.324(a)(2)(iv) 4.03(6)(A)

1. Language and Communication

1. a. The child's/student's **primary language** is one or more of the following.
Check all that apply.

Receptive   **Expressive**
☐ ☐ English
☐ ☐ Native language (ASL, Spanish etc), specify _____
☐ ☐ Combination of several languages
☐ ☐ Minimal language skills; no formal primary language

Describe:

Action Plan, if any:

1. b. The child's/student's **primary communication mode** is one or more of the following. Supports 300.116(e).
Check all that apply and if more than one applies, explain.

Receptive:
☐ Auditory
☐ Speechreading
☐ Fingerspelling
☐ Tactile/objects
☐ Home signs
☐ Other, please explain _____

☐ American Sign Language
☐ Cued Speech/Cued English
☐ Gestures
☐ Picture symbols/pictures/photographs

☐ Signing Exact English/Signed English
☐ Conceptual signs (Pidgin Signed English or Conceptually Accurate Signed English)

Expressive:
☐ Spoken language
☐ Conceptual signs (Pidgin Signed English or Conceptually Accurate Signed English)
☐ Tactile/objects
☐ Cued Speech/Cued English

☐ American Sign Language
☐ Fingerspelling
☐ Home signs
☐ Pictures symbols/pictures/photographs
☐ Other, please explain _____

☐ Signing Exact English/Signed English
☐ Gestures

Explanation for multiple modes of communication, if necessary:

Legal Name of Student	State Student ID (SASID)	Date of Birth	Date
1. **c.** What supports are needed to increase the proficiency of parents and family members in communicating with the child's/student? Parent Counseling Training 300.34(8)(i) and (iii) *Issues considered:* *Action Plan, if any:*			
2. Describe the child's/student's need for deaf/hard of hearing adult role models and peer groups in sufficient numbers of the child's/student's communication mode or language. Document who on the team will be responsible for arranging for adult role model connections and opportunities to interact with peers. (Section 3. 22-20-108 CRS II) 300.116 Placement Determination *Opportunities considered: ECEA proposed 4.03(6)(a)(iii)* *Action Plan, if any:*			
3. An explanation of all educational options provided by the administrative unit and available for thechild/student has been given. Placement determination 300.115 and 300.116 *Placements explained:* *Describe how the placement options impact the child's communication access and educational progress:*			
4. Teachers, interpreters, and other specialists delivering the communication plan to the child/student must have demonstrated proficiency in, and be able to accommodate for, the child's/student's primary communication mode or language. ECEA 3.04(1)(f) *Considerations:* *Action Plan, if any:*			
5. The communication-accessible academic instruction, school services, and extracurricular activities the child/student will receive have been identified. The team will consider the entire school day, daily transition times, and what the child/student needs for full communication access in all activities. *Considerations* 300.324(a)(2)(iv) Communication plan. 300.107 Non-academic settings. 300.101 FAPE: *Action Plan, if any:*			

FIGURE 5.1 Communication plan for students who are deaf/hard of hearing or deafblind (Hands & Voices, 2018)

learner's intellectual functioning level. Table 5.2 (pp. 149–151) outlines the instructional strategies and expectations for academic progression based upon students' needs: mild, moderate, and severe. The goal is to maximize the attainment of skills so that each student is able to meet age-appropriate societal expectations, participate in the community, and lead an independent adult life (Luft, 2015).

Assistive Technology and Accommodations

Assistive technology includes any piece of equipment, product, software, or system that is used to increase, maintain, or improve the functional capabilities of a child with a disability (IDEA, 2004). Assistive technology devices provide important supports to ensure appropriately challenging instructional services for students who are d/Dhh-ID. These devices or services are listed in the specially designed instruction portion of the IEP, but they do not include devices that require surgery, such as a CI (IDEA, 2004). The IEP can also list assistive technology services that include "any service that directly assists a child with a disability in the selection, acquisition, or use of an assistive technology device" (IDEA, 2004, § 1401 [2]). These services encompass evaluation, selection, purchase, fitting or adapting of a device to assist with child/adult use, and classroom support of technology (Ohio Department of Education, 2014).

Some examples of assistive technology for students who are d/Dhh-ID include modified cell phones (Jitterbug [simplified menu options] or Firefly [picture/image-based recognition for phone or email access]), although these phones must be appropriately programmed (Stock et al., 2011). Cell phones allow for ongoing contact with family members and service providers, which helps to increase independence. Computer-based video instruction may also be used to teach independent community access, such as the use of public transportation. Global positioning systems (i.e., GPS) can also be incorporated into phones to assist with navigation between locations. Public venues such as zoos and amusement parks, as well as restaurants, are increasingly using icon-based, touch-screen kiosks for information and maps, which can assist students with ID.

Assistive technologies can enhance many activities of (a) daily living, (b) environmental control, (c) recreation, (d) reading, (e) learning and

TABLE 5.2 Instructional Expectations and Strategies Relative to Students' Needs

Students' Needs	Instructional Expectations for Academic Progression	Select Strategies
Mild learning challenges	• Minimal modifications to the learning environment and curriculum • Learners should be expected to achieve the same foundational academic skills as their d/Dhh peers • Preschoolers should acquire the same preacademic, cognitive, psychosocial, and behavioral content • Academic modifications should support learning within the standard curriculum (Wehmeyer et al., 2002) • Secondary instruction should include transition planning that encourages postsecondary training, employment, and independent living outcomes at levels similar to those of d/Dhh peers • Postsecondary instruction should provide opportunities to attend a community college or vocational–technical program that provides job-ready skills, and the ability to live independently in the community	• Provide additional practice opportunities • Break tasks into smaller learning steps

(Continued)

TABLE 5.2 (*Continued*)

Students' Needs	Instructional Expectations for Academic Progression	Select Strategies
Moderate learning challenges	• Require more intensive supports and modifications to learning content (Wehmeyer et al., 2002) • Preschoolers should achieve most of the essential preacademic, cognitive, psychosocial, and behavioral content as do their d/Dhh peers with mild ID, but instruction in academic skills may require accommodation to ensure success (Wehmeyer et al., 2002) • Learners should be expected to acquire the essential academic skills that prepare them for employment, to live independently or with some supports, and engage in many of the typical adult activities within their communities • At the secondary level, their academic program should take a functional and community-based approach that integrates post-high-school plans for academic, employment, and independent living skills instruction that operationalizes their vision for a successful adulthood	• Use manipulatives to support instruction and/or the child's responses • Curricular accommodations may include the use of a graphic organizer that color codes a process, using a computer program, and/or adding color cues to highlight information • Adapt learning goals of a lesson to focus on functional skills (e.g., real-world manipulatives, role-play) • A vocational or rehabilitation counselor for the deaf (RCD) works with the learner to provide vocational training and independent community living (Moore, 2001, 2002; Test et al., 2009)

Students' Needs	Instructional Expectations for Academic Progression	Select Strategies
Significant learning challenges	• Require academic content to be modified at a more extensive level • Learners should be expected to achieve many of the foundational skills needed to be successful in work and living environments • In preschool, teaching appropriate socialization behaviors across various home and community environments is essential • Learners may be included in the standard curriculum with accommodations or modifications of activities • Elementary and secondary school programming should focus on foundational and functional academic skills with opportunities to apply learning in various environments (i.e., home, work, and community) • Adult goals may require periodic or ongoing supports from agency professionals, including long-term services from vocational rehabilitation • Provide learners the option to live in a group home with other d/Dhh individuals for socialization opportunities and ongoing support services • Learners should be expected to demonstrate progress in activities that prepare them for independent employment and living opportunities	• Allow more practice and time to learn skills • Teachers and parents can teach daily living skills, such as self-care and household care, beginning with classroom and home chores

studying, (f) composition of written material, (g) communication, and (h) computer access (Braddock et al., 2004). Personal support technologies (e.g., personal digital assistants, smartphones, and tablets) increase independence, productivity, and quality of life for those with ID across educational, vocational, or daily living tasks through scheduled prompts. Other possibilities include picture-based email programs and adapted internet browsers. In addition, the IEP team may want to include the services of a rehabilitation engineer or technologist to comprehensively assess the student's strengths and challenges to determine the assistive technology/ies that can remove or ameliorate barriers, to support increased independence and adult success (Luft, 2016; U.S. Department of Education, 2017b).

What Challenges Remain?

Although challenges remain, this chapter outlines the potential of students who are d/Dhh-ID. A majority of this population attending public school programs may have limited access to specialized professionals with expertise in both deafness and ID. Larger and consortium-based programs serving d/Dhh students across several districts may have greater capacity and access to such professionals. Yet, services often remain organized around either the general or an adapted curriculum, with few options in between (Luft, 2013, 2014). Parents, teachers, and other IEP team members may struggle to find appropriate communication and educational services and supports. In addition, many TDHHs lack training for working with students who are d/Dhh-ID and feel unprepared to meet their range of academic, social-emotional, and behavioral needs (Guardino, 2015; Soukup & Feinstein, 2007). Schools for the deaf tend to have greater expertise in disability-specific services and functional academic, employment, and daily living approaches, compared with services in the public school programs (Luft, 2013, 2014, 2016, 2017; Punch et al., 2006; Punch et al., 2004; Stinson & Kluwin, 2003). However, schools should have collaborative and/or consultation service models, making specialty expertise available to multidisciplinary IEP teams for educating learners who are d/Dhh and those with other disabilities, including ID.

A final challenge is for all team members to maintain high expectations regarding the abilities of d/Dhh-ID students. Teams may encounter low expectations and custodial programming due to historical patterns of underserving learners who are d/Dhh-ID (Bowe, 2003; Ewing & Jones, 2003). Yet, providing a range of services remains beneficial and cost-effective (Bowe, 2004) and aligns with the positive outcomes guaranteed by IDEA (2004). Skillful use of the IEP and communication plans ensure that learners who are d/Dhh-ID receive the supports and services that lead them toward a fulfilling adulthood that is appropriately tailored to enhance their abilities and meet their needs. Many learners are able to work and live independently in the community, and a range of agency services can provide intermittent or long-term supports as needed. Educational programming should maximize all students' academic and functional skills to allow participation in communities of their choice, to the extent that they desire.

DISCUSSION QUESTIONS

1. Explain the importance of having a comprehensive assessment of these students and how this affects instructional planning. Identify several of the difficulties in obtaining accurate and valid assessments, even when accommodations are provided.

2. Describe the importance of utilizing multiple perspectives of a child's abilities when creating their learning and achievement profile and while creating an optimal instructional plan. Compare and contrast the planning outcomes when using few versus multiple perspectives in making such plans.

3. Describe the purpose of a communication plan and how it is used to support the needs of students who are d/Dhh-ID. Identify how specific plan elements can be integrated into the IEP and identify the key IEP sections that support this. Provide at least one example of each.

4. Explain why it is important to plan with a child's strengths in mind rather than focusing on needs. Compare the planning outcomes of focusing on strengths versus needs.

5. Describe the curricular modification steps that Wehmeyer et al. (2002) prescribe for designing appropriately challenging and supportive instruction. Provide an example for each step.

RESOURCES

Organizations

- **American Association on Intellectual and Developmental Disabilities**
  - o http://aaidd.org/

Websites

- **Developmental Milestones: Centers for Disease Control and Prevention**
  - o https://www.cdc.gov/ncbddd/actearly/milestones/index.html
  - o https://www.cdc.gov/ncbddd/actearly/pdf/check-lists/Checklists-with-Tips_Reader_508.pdf
- **Language Milestones: American Speech-Language-Hearing Association**
  - o https://www.asha.org/public/speech/development/chart/

Regional or National Resource Centers

- **Ablelink Technologies**
  - o https://www.ablelinktech.com/index.php?id=8
- **Centers for Disease Control and Prevention**
  - o https://www.cdc.gov/ncbddd/hearingloss/free-materials/parentsguide508.pdf
  - o A parent's guide to genetics and hearing loss.
- **Gallaudet University**
  - o https://www.gallaudet.edu/
- **Hands & Voices.** *Communication plan.*
  - o http://www.cohandsandvoices.org/newsite/wp-content/uploads/2018/03/CO_R_Guide_3-12-2018.pdf
- **Laurent Clerc National Deaf Education Center, Gallaudet University**
  - o http://www3.gallaudet.edu/clerc-center.html
- **National Deaf Center on Postsecondary Outcomes**
  - o https://www.nationaldeafcenter.org/
- **National Technical Institute for the Deaf, Rochester Institute for Technology**
  - o http://www.ntid.rit.edu/
- **PACER Center**
  - o http://www.pacer.org

Readings

- *American Annals of the Deaf* (2015), *160*(4), 347–426. [Special issue on disability]. https://muse.jhu.edu/issue/32584
- ASHA–Intellectual Disabilities and Hearing Loss. https://www.asha.org/practice-portal/clinical-topics/intellectual-disability/
- *Odyessy* (2019). Deaf Students with Disabilities: A functional approach for parents and teachers, 76–80. https://clerccenter.gallaudet.edu/national-resources/documents/clerc/odyssey/2019_issue/ODYSSEY2019_SchleyTrussell.pdf

REFERENCES

Alasim, K. N. (2018). Participation and interaction of deaf and hard-of-hearing students in inclusion classroom. *International Journal of Special Education, 33,* 493–506.

Alwell, M., & Cobb, B. (2009). Functional life skills curricular interventions for youth with disabilities: A systematic review. *Career Development for Exceptional Individuals, 32*(2), 82–93.

American Institutes for Research. (n.d.). *AIR self-determination assessments.* http://www.ou.edu/education/centers-and-partnerships/zarrow/self-determination-assessment-tools/air-self-determination-assessment

Ayres, K. M., Lowrey, K. A., Douglas, K. H., & Sievers, C. (2011). I can identify Saturn but I can't brush my teeth: What happens when the curricular focus for students with severe disabilities shifts. *Education and Training in Autism and Developmental Disabilities, 45*(1), 11–21.

Beins, B. C. (2012). Jean Piaget: Theorist of the child's mind. In W. E. Pickren, D. A. Dewsbury, & M. Wertheimer (Eds.), *Portraits of pioneers in developmental psychology* (pp. 89–107). Psychology Press.

Bowe, F. G. (2003). Transition for deaf and hard-of-hearing students: A blueprint for change. *Journal of Deaf Studies and Deaf Education, 8,* 485–493.

Bowe, F. G. (2004). Economics and adults identified as low-functioning deaf. *Journal of Disability Policy Studies, 15*(1), 43–49.

Braddock, D., Rizzolo, M. C., Thompson, M., & Bell, R. (2004). Emerging technologies and cognitive disability. *Journal of Special Education Technology, 19*(4), 49–56.

Bruce, S. M., Nelson, C., & Stutzman, B. (2022). Understanding the needs of children who are d/Deaf or hard of hearing with disabilities due to genetic causes. In C. Guardino, J. E. Cannon, & P. V. Paul (Eds.), *Deaf and hard of hearing learners with disabilities: Foundations, strategies, and resources* (pp. 96–132). Routledge.

Bull, B., & Bullis, M. (1991). A national profile of school-based transition programs for deaf adolescents. *American Annals of the Deaf, 136,* 339–348.

Case, B. J. (2008). Accommodations to improve instruction and assessment of deaf students. In R. C. Johnson & R. E. Mitchell (Eds.), *Testing deaf students in an age of accountability* (pp. 51–62). Gallaudet University Press.

Cawthon, S. (2015). From the margins to the spotlight: Diverse deaf and hard of hearing student populations and standardized assessment accessibility. *American Annals of the Deaf, 160*(4), 385–394.

Centers for Disease Control and Prevention. (n.d.). A parent's guide to genetics and hearing loss. National Center on Birth Defects and Developmental Disabilities. https://www.cdc.gov/ncbddd/hearingloss/freematerials/parentsguide508.pdf

Crain, W. (2011). *Theories of development: Concepts and applications.* Prentice-Hall.

Cryns, K., & Van Camp, G. (2004). Deafness genes and their diagnostic applications. *Audiology and Neurotology, 9*(1), 2–22.

Dayton, KY, Schools. (2014). *IEP and lesson plan development handbook, section 1: Specially designed instruction/supplementary aids and Services.* https://www.dayton.k12.ky.us/userfiles/2/Documents/2015- 16/SpEd/IEP_Developments/iep%20and%20lesson%20plan%20development%20handbook2.pdf

Ewing, K. M., & Jones, T. W. (2003). An educational rationale for deaf students with multiple disabilities. *American Annals of the Deaf, 148*(3), 267–271. https://doi.org/10.1353/aad.2003.0019

Flexer, R. W., Luft, P., & Queen, R. M. (2013). Transition assessment. In R. W. Flexer, R. M. Baer, P. Luft, & T. J. Simmons (Eds.), *Transition planning for secondary students with disabilities* (4th ed., pp. 95–123). Pearson.

Gallaudet Research Institute. (2013). *Regional and national summary report of data from the 2011–12 Annual Survey of Deaf and Hard of Hearing Children and Youth.* https://www.gallaudet.edu/office-of-international-affairs/demographics.

Guardino, C. (2015). Preparing professionals to work with children who are D/deaf with disabilities [Special issue]. *American Annals of the Deaf, 160*(4), 415–426.

Hands & Voices. (2014). *Communication consideration A to Z: Preschool programs.* http://www.handsandvoices.org/comcon/articles/preschool.htm

Hands & Voices. (2018). Communication plan for students who are deaf or hard of hearing or deafblind. http://www.cohandsandvoices.org/newsite/wp-content/uploads/2018/03/CO_R_Guide_3-12-2018.pdf

Harmon, M., Carr, N., & Johnson, T. (1998). Services to low functioning deaf and hard of hearing persons. In *1998 PEPNet conference proceedings: Empowerment through partnerships* (pp. 290–300). University of Tennessee.

Holt, J., Hotto, S., & Cole, K. (1994). *Demographic aspects of hearing impairment: Questions and answers* (3rd ed.). Gallaudet University.

Holte, L., Walker, E., Oleson, J., Spratford, M., Moeller, M. P., Roush, P., Ou, H., & Tomblin, J. B. (2012). Factors influencing follow-up to newborn hearing screening for infants who are hard of hearing. *American Journal of Audiology, 21*(2), 163–174.

Indiana Department of Education (2018). *Specially designed instruction.* https://www.doe.in.gov/sites/default/files/specialed/specially-designed-instruction.pdf

Individuals With Disabilities Education Act 20 U.S.C. § 1400 *et seq.*

Jackson, B., Paulson, A., & Raschke, S. (2017). *Teachers of students who are deaf or hard of hearing: A critical resource needed for legal compliance.* Council for Exceptional Children, Division for Communication Disabilities and Deafness.

Jackson, R. L. W., Ammerman, S. B., & Trautwein, B. A. (2022). Infants and toddlers who are d/Deaf or hard of hearing with a developmental delay or are at risk for developmental delays. In C. Guardino, J. E. Cannon, & P. V. Paul (Eds.), *Deaf and hard of hearing learners with disabilities: Foundations, strategies, and resources* (pp. 25–62). Routledge.

Johnson, C. D., DesGeorges, J., & Seaver, L. (2013). *Educational advocacy for students who are deaf or hard of hearing.* Hands & Voices.

Johnson, R. C., & Mitchell, R. E. (2008). Introduction. In R. C. Johnson & R. E. Mitchell (Eds.), *Testing deaf students in an age of accountability* (pp. 1–15). Gallaudet University Press.

Karchmer, M. A., & Allen, T. E. (1999). The functional assessment of deaf and hard of hearing students. *American Annals of the Deaf, 144*(2), 68–77.

Lewis, V. (2003). *Development and disability* (2nd ed.). Blackwell.

Loew, R., Cahalan-Laitusis, C., Cook, L., & Harris, R. (2005). Access considerations and the provision of appropriate accommodations: A research perspective from a testing organization. In J. L. Mounty & D. S. Martin (Eds.), *Assessing deaf adults: Critical issues in testing and evaluation* (pp. 37–53). Gallaudet University Press.

Luft, P. (2013). Independent living services for deaf and hard of hearing students: Results of a nation-wide survey of school programs. *Journal of Applied Rehabilitation Counseling, 44,* 18–27.

Luft, P. (2014). A national survey of transition services for deaf and hard of hearing students. *Career Development and Transition for Exceptional Individuals, 37,* 177–192. https://doi.org/10.1177/2165143412469400

Luft, P. (2015). Transition services for DHH adolescents and young adults with disabilities: Challenges and theoretical frameworks. *American Annals of the Deaf, 160*(4), 395–414.

Luft, P. (2016). *Promoting positive transition outcomes: Effective planning for deaf and hard of hearing young adults.* Gallaudet University Press.

Luft, P. (2017). What is different about deaf education? Examining children and their contexts. *Journal of Special Education, 51,* 27–37. https://doi.org/10.1177/0022466916660546

Luft, P., & Amiruzzaman, S. (2018). Examining states' responses to the IDEA special factors requirements for DHH students. *Journal of Disability Policy Studies, 29*(1), 32–42.

Martin, D. S., & Mounty J. L. (2005). Overview of the challenge. In J. L. Mounty & D. S. Martin (Eds.), *Assessing deaf adults: Critical issues in testing and evaluation* (pp. 3–10). Gallaudet University Press.

Martin, J., Hennessey, M., McConnell, A., Terry, R., & Willis, D. (2015). *The Transition Assessment and Goal Generator (TAGG).* University of Oklahoma, Zarrow Center. https://tagg.ou.edu/tagg/

Miller, M. S., Thomas-Presswood, T. N., Metz, K., & Lukomski, J. (2015). *Psychological and psychoeducational assessment of deaf and hard of hearing children and adolescents.* Gallaudet University Press.

Moore, C. L. (2001). Disparities in job placement outcomes among deaf, late-deafened, and hard-of-hearing consumers. *Rehabilitation Counseling Bulletin, 44,* 144–150.

Moore, C. L. (2002). Relationship of consumer characteristics and service provision to income of successfully rehabilitated individuals who are deaf. *Rehabilitation Counseling Bulletin, 45,* 233–239.

Moores, D. F. (1978). *Educating the deaf: Psychology, principles, and practices.* Houghton Mifflin.

National Conference of State Legislatures. (2011). *Newborn hearing screening laws.* http://www.ncsl.org/research/health/newborn-hearing-screening-state-laws.aspx

Ohio Department of Education. (2014). *Ohio administrative code: Chapter 3301–51, education of students with special needs.* http://codes.ohio.gov/oac/3301-51.

Osgood, R. L. (2008). *The history of special education: A struggle for equality in American public schools.* Praeger.

PACER Center (2015). *ACTion sheet: PHP-c49a,* http://www.pacer.org/parent/php/PHP-c49a.pdf

Paul, P. V., & Whitelaw, G. (2011). *Hearing and deafness: An introduction for health and education professionals.* Jones & Bartlett.

Punch, R., Creed, P. A., & Hyde, M. (2006). Career barriers perceived by hard-of-hearing adolescents: Implications for practice from a mixed-methods study. *Journal of Deaf Studies and Deaf Education 11*(2), 224–237.

Punch, R., Hyde, M., & Creed, P. A. (2004). Issues in the school-to-work transition of hard of hearing adolescents. *American Annals of the Deaf, 149*(1), 28–38.

Shearer, A. E., Hildebrand, M. S., & Smith, R. J. H. (1993–2018). *Hereditary hearing loss and deafness overview.* University of Washington, GeneReviews. https://www.ncbi.nlm.nih.gov/books/NBK1434/

Shulman, S., Besculides, M., Saltzman, A., Ireys, H., White, K. R., & Forsman, I. (2010). Evaluation of the universal newborn hearing screening and intervention program. *Pediatrics, 126*(Supplement 1), S19–S27.

Soukup, M., & Feinstein, S. (2007). Identification, assessment, and intervention strategies for deaf and hard of hearing students with learning disabilities. *American Annals of the Deaf, 152*(1), 56–62. https://doi.org/10.1353/aad.2007.0014

Stevens, R. (1983). *Erik Erikson: An introduction.* St. Martin's Press.

Stinson, M. S., & Kluwin, T. N. (2003). Educational consequences of alternative school placements. In M. Marschark & P. E. Spencer (Eds.), *Oxford handbook of deaf studies, language, and education* (Vol. 1, pp. 52–64). Oxford University.

Stock, S. E., Davies, D. K., Wehmeyer, M. L., & Lachapelle, Y. (2011). Emerging new practices in technology to support independent community access for people with intellectual and cognitive disabilities. *NeuroRehabilitation, 28*(3), 261–269.

Test, D. W., Fowler, C. H., Richter, S. M., White, J., Mazzotti, V., Walker, A. R., Kohler, P., & Kortering, L. (2009). Evidence-based practices in secondary transition. *Career Development for Exceptional Individuals, 32*, 115–128. https://doi.org/10.1177/0885728809346960

Thurlow, M. L., Johnstone, C., Thompson, S. J., & Case, B. J. (2008). Using universal design research and perspectives to increase the validity of scores on large-scale assessments. In R. C. Johnson & R. E. Mitchell (Eds.), *Testing deaf students in an age of accountability* (pp. 63–75). Gallaudet University Press.

Thurlow, M. L., Vang, M., & Cormier, D. (2010). *Earning a high school diploma through alternative routes.* Synthesis Report 76. National Center on Educational Outcomes, University of Minnesota. University of Minnesota.

Tsach, N., & Most, T. (2016). The inclusion of deaf and hard-of-hearing students in mainstream classrooms. In M. Marschark, V. Lampropoulou, & E. K. Skordilis (Eds.), *Diversity in deaf education* (pp. 355–380). Oxford University Press.

U.S. Department of Education. (2016). *Programs: Preschool grants for children with disabilities.* https://www2.ed.gov/programs/oseppsg/index.html

U.S. Department of Education. (2017a). *39th Annual Report to Congress on the Implementation of the Individuals With Disabilities Education Act, 2017.* Office of Special Education and Rehabilitative Services.

U.S. Department of Education. (2017b). *Careers in rehabilitation: Rehabilitation engineering.* https://www2.ed.gov/students/college/aid/rehab/carengin.html

U.S. National Library of Medicine. (n.d.). *Genetics home reference: Your guide to understanding genetic conditions.* https://ghr.nlm.nih.gov/condition

Wagner, M., Newman, L., Cameto, R., & Levine, P. (2006). *The achievement and functional performance of youth with disabilities: A report from the National Longitudinal Transition Study-2 (NLTS2).* Institute of Educational Sciences, National Center for Special Education Research, U.S. Department of Education. http://www.nlts2.org/reports/2006_07/index.html

Wehmeyer, M. L., Lance, G. D., & Bashinski, S. (2002). Promoting access to the general curriculum for students with mental retardation: A multi-level model. *Education and Training in Mental Retardation and Developmental Disabilities, 37*(3), 223–234.

Wehmeyer, M., & Kelchner, K. (1995). *The Arc's Self-Determination Scale, Adolescent Version.* The Arc of the United States. http://www.thearc.org/document.doc?id=3670; http://www.ou.edu/education/centers-and-partnerships/zarrow/self-determination-assessment-tools/arc-self-determination-scale

Wheeler-Scruggs, K. (2003). Discerning characteristics and risk factors of people who are deaf and low functioning. *Journal of Rehabilitation, 69*(4), 39–46.

Workforce Innovation and Opportunity Act. P.L. 113-128 (2014).

Zwiebel, A., & Mertens, D. M. (1985). A comparison of intellectual structure in deaf and hearing children. *American Annals of the Deaf, 130*(1), 27–31.

6

Future Directions in the Field of Deafblindness

Catherine Nelson, Susan M. Bruce,
and Brooke A. Barnhill

LEARNING OBJECTIVES

Readers will:

- Understand the definition and demographics of the deafblind (DB) population of learners.
- Learn information from the existing body of literature of instructional strategies to use with students who are DB.
- Delineate important issues, such as early identification and intervention, assessment, placement, and transition to postsecondary life.
- Realize the need for personnel development, family support, and school and community inclusion.

The Individuals With Disabilities Education Improvement Act (IDEIA, 2004) defines deafblindness as "concomitant hearing and visual impairments, the combination of which causes such severe communication and other developmental and educational needs that they cannot be accommodated in special education programs solely for children with deafness or children with blindness" (2010, § 300.8 [c] [2]). A child who is deafblind (DB) typically has difficulty learning in an educational environment that emphasizes vision. Similarly, without

DOI: 10.4324/9781003252054-6

significant adaptations and supports, a child who is d/Dhh and has a visual impairment is unlikely to benefit from a program that stresses use of auditory information (van Dijk et al., 2010). Therefore, in 1990, the Conference of the International Association for the Education of Deafblind Persons (now Deafblind International) passed a resolution for the hyphenated word "deaf-blind" to become the singular word "deafblind." This resolution made clear that deafblindness is not deaf plus blind but, rather, constitutes a unique disability with individualized needs. However, programs funded under IDEIA utilize the hyphenated term "deaf-blind."

Population of Learners Who Are Deafblind

As reported by the National Deaf-Blind Child Count, 9,635 children and youth from birth to age 22 years were identified as deafblind in 2016 by state and multistate deafblind projects in the United States (Schalock, 2017). Although having one of the lowest incidences among the disability groups, deafblindness is also one of the most heterogeneous, with wide variations in the degree of vision and hearing levels. Approximately 99% of children identified as deafblind have some residual vision and hearing. The sensory losses are frequently accompanied by additional disabilities, including physical and/or cognitive disabilities, complex medical needs, and behavioral challenges. Such additional disabilities have been identified in about 90% of the deafblind child population, and almost 43% of this population has four or more additional disabilities (Schalock, 2017). Because the vision and hearing senses interact with each of the body's systems, the presence of additional disabilities multiplies the effects of deafblindness (van Dijk et al., 2010).

According to the 2016 National Deaf-Blind Child Count, complications from prematurity comprised the most common cause of deafblindness, at 10.7% of the population of learners ages 0–22 years. However, >75 etiologies were also identified in the count. Together, hereditary syndromes accounted for 44.4% of the identified etiologies. Three of the most prevalent syndromes, namely, Down, Usher (types 1, 2, and 3), and CHARGE (acronym for coloboma of the eye, heart defects, atresia of the choanae, retardation of growth and development, and ear abnormalities and deafness), are described in Chapter 4 (Bruce et al., 2022). Prenatal complications include cytomegalovirus (CMV) infection, hydrocephaly, and microcephaly. Postnatal causes include asphyxia, severe head injury, and meningitis (Schalock, 2017).

Deafblindness can be congenital (present from birth) or adventitious (acquired later in life). The distinction is important because individuals who later acquire deafblindness had vision and/or hearing previously to help them learn and master concepts and communication (Nelson & Bruce, 2016). However, individuals with progressive vision and/or hearing loss may struggle to learn new compensatory skills in communication and literacy (Bruce, 2005). Students who are deafblind communicate through many and varied modes. The various communication modalities include (a) American Sign Language (ASL), (b) tactile sign, (c) oral language, (d) augmentative and alternative communication, and (e) nonsymbolic communication through facial expressions and body movements. Regardless of the presence or absence of other disabilities, etiology, or communication mode, deafblindness may present specific challenges to development.

Impacts of Deafblindness

Vision and hearing, the two senses that allow individuals to gather information at a distance, interact inextricably in development (Bruce & Borders, 2015). Therefore, deafblindness impacts many developmental domains. In 2004, Silberman et al. detailed the following interrelated impacts on development and learning.

Attachment

The infant with congenital deafblindness may be unable to make eye contact with others or recognize caregivers' voices and facial expressions. This difficulty may, in turn, affect the development of trust, security, communication, and social skills (Miles & Riggio, 1999).

Social Connectedness and Experiences

Connections with people, actions, and the world beyond the personal body are enabled through vision and hearing. The individual who is deafblind may feel very isolated unless they are within physical reach of another person. Individuals who are d/Deaf or hard of hearing (d/Dhh) can see someone signing at a distance; the individual who is deafblind is unable to do so and may be unable to overhear conversations and observe others in a room. In addition, it may be difficult for individuals who are deafblind to know when new people have entered the room or a conversation, when different people have started talking, and when conversations have ended (Miles & Riggio, 1999).

Incidental Learning

Typically, incidental learning occurs through visual and auditory observation. When individuals with vision enter a room, they can see approximately how big the room is, the arrangement of things and people within the room, how many people are in it, and who is present. Individuals with hearing can detect voices that are familiar and use this information to find friends. They can overhear the types of things people are talking about and adjust their conversations accordingly. Such incidental learning allows for enhanced experiences and learning without direct intervention. Even with an interpreter, an individual who is deafblind may miss out on much of this environmental information unless there is someone available to also interpret the environment to the individual.

Concept Development

A child who is deafblind may have difficulty developing early concepts such as body image and concept of self. Learning that objects exist even when there is no direct contact with them (object permanence) is also difficult when the child does not see or hear objects as they come and go. Without the interplay of the distance senses, gaining complete and accurate information necessary for understanding object properties and how they fit into the larger world can be problematic. More abstract concepts may present particular challenges. For example, what are clouds or rainbows if you cannot see them and cannot explore them tactually? Moreover, it may be challenging to develop skills such as categorization in the absence of seeing similarities and differences.

Communication

Development of communication and language is significantly impacted by deafblindness. Individuals who are deafblind are often unable to see a communication partner's facial expressions and gestures or use environmental information to determine the topic of conversation. Delays in motor development, combined with the sensory losses discussed earlier, result in reduced opportunities to interact with objects and associate experiences with symbols, words, and concepts (Miles & Riggio, 1999). Further, children who are deafblind often have few communication partners and have reduced opportunities to learn communication through observation and imitation of others. Therefore, they may have insufficient opportunities to understand and practice interaction skills, which results in a need for direct instruction (Parker et al., 2008). Without such instruction, communicative acts by the child who is deafblind may be few in number, difficult for others to understand, and perceived as inappropriate by communication partners (Miles, 1999; Silberman et al., 2004).

Motor Skills

An infant's early exploration is motivated by information coming from vision and hearing. An infant sees something of interest and wants to physically reach it. The infant may hear an interesting sound and want to explore it further. Thus, the infant begins to crawl, pull to standing, and later, walk. Further, if the child has developed object permanence, they may be motivated to seek objects that are out of view and risk moving to a new space. In the absence of this motivation, motor skills of children who are deafblind are frequently delayed (Fraiberg, 1968; Wagner et al., 2013).

Access to Sensory Information

Researchers estimate that >80% of learning is achieved through vision (Rosenblum, 2010). Vision provides information about the environment, people, relationships, actions, and objects. That which cannot be immediately observed can be seen in pictures or videos. In a similar vein, with limited hearing, it is difficult to access communication and completely understand environmental information. Further, it is challenging to simultaneously listen to multiple auditory inputs, such as a person talking and traffic noises. The world of an individual who is deafblind is limited to what is in the range of touch, smell, or proprioception (information received from muscles, joints, and the balance organ of the inner ear, which allows for awareness of the relative position and movement of the body).

In the remainder of this chapter, we address the above challenges by introducing the extant literature base and identify strategies implemented with learners who are deafblind. Areas covered include early identification and intervention, assessment, educational placement and teams, instructional supports and strategies, and finally transition. The chapter concludes with a discussion of the need for family support, personnel development, and school and community inclusion.

Early Identification and Intervention

Early identification is crucial to meeting the needs of children who are deafblind and ameliorating the impacts of dual sensory impairments (Anthony, 2016; Parker et al., 2011; Purvis, et al., 2014). In early infancy, infants begin to move, interact with others, and learn about their world. Through early intervention, enhanced information can be provided to the child's brain during the most critical period for neurodevelopment. If sensory losses are detected early, medical interventions—including medications and surgery—can be implemented. Vision and hearing can be augmented through corrective lenses (including contact lenses and glasses), hearing aids, frequency-modulated (FM) systems, and cochlear implants (Anthony, 2016), although the effectiveness of these devices varies per child. The standard for early detection of hearing levels is screening by 1 month (universal newborn hearing screening), audiological evaluation by 3 months, and enrollment in early intervention programs by 6 months of age (Joint Committee on Infant Hearing, 2007). Currently, there is no system for universal newborn vision screening; however, the American Academy of Ophthalmology recommends that a physician examine a newborn's eyes for general health and conduct a red reflex test. The red reflex test involves shining light into the eyes and observing the subsequent reddish reflection of light from the back of the eye that appears in a healthy eye (Anthony, 2016).

If children who are d/Dhh, including children who are deafblind, do not receive appropriate early opportunities to learn language, they will likely experience delays in communication, cognition, reading, and social-emotional development (Joint Committee on Infant Hearing, 2007). Further, in the absence of early intervention, congenital deafblindness can have a negative impact on joint attention, reciprocity, and mutual enjoyment of social interactions (Chen, 2004). The infant–caregiver relationship is primary in early development and is the most important context for early learning. This relationship can be threatened, as infants who are deafblind are often less responsive than their peers without disabilities, and their frequently idiosyncratic or individual, nontypical communications may be difficult to read. Thus, mutually enjoyable interactions between infants and caregivers are reduced (Klein et al., 2000).

In addition to medical interventions such as surgery and low vision aids, effective early intervention involves teaching caregivers needed skills to support both social interactions and child development. Early intervention for children who are deafblind is typically provided in the home setting through Part C of IDEA (Schalock, 2017). Early intervention services should be provided by professionals who have specific expertise in combined vision and hearing loss as well as early intervention (Anthony, 2016). Other professionals who might be involved in the early intervention process include speech-language pathologists, audiologists, and orientation and mobility specialists.

Assessment

Central to effective educational practices for children and youth who are deafblind are comprehensive, accurate assessments (Rowland et al., 2010). Educational assessments for students with disabilities, including deafblindness, serve four major purposes: (a) determine eligibility; (b) inform the design of Individualized Education Programs (IEPs), including goal formulation; (c) guide instructional planning and implementation; and (d) evaluate the effectiveness of the educational program (Riggio & McLetchie, 2008; Rowland, 2009). However, because of the low incidence and the heterogeneous nature of the population, assessing children and youth who are deafblind is very challenging. Assessment challenges may be magnified by the presence of additional disabilities (Rowland et al., 2010; Silberman et al., 2004; van Dijk et al., 2010).

Standardized or norm-referenced tests that purport to measure intelligence quotient (IQ) or provide mental age equivalencies are particularly problematic, and there are currently no standardized assessments that measure intelligence that are specifically developed for, or standardized on, children who are deafblind (Holte et al., 2006; Mar, 1996; Riggio & McLetchie, 2008; van Dijk et al., 2010). Accommodations for vision and hearing levels are sometimes suggested in standardized assessments, but once implemented, they may alter standardized procedures. Therefore, the results of such assessments must be interpreted with caution. In addition, such accommodations do not account for the impact that deafblindness and concomitant disabilities can have on every area of development (Nelson et al., 2002; van Dijk et al., 2010). For example, children with limited vision may not understand how testing materials such as miniature objects relate to their larger referents. Children with limited receptive language may be unable to see or hear what is being asked of them. Unfamiliar settings and materials can create anxiety, and difficulty in establishing new relationships can lead to reduced test performance if the test administrator is unfamiliar (Nelson et al., 2002, 2009; van Dijk et al., 2010). Moreover, it is critical that comprehensive evaluations include a variety of assessment instruments that are administered by a team of professionals with expertise in sensory disabilities (Riggio & McLetchie, 2008; Rowland et al., 2010). Listed in the following sections are elements of quality assessments, components of comprehensive evaluations, and examples of assessment instruments that are appropriate for children who are deafblind.

Essential Elements of Quality Assessments of Children and Youth Who Are Deafblind

Quality assessment practices include several essential elements. They

- promote familiarity with the children and how they communicate (Nelson et al., 2002, 2009);

- utilize dynamic assessments to gain a full understanding of the child's abilities (Bruce et al., 2016; Nelson et al., 2010);
- are comprehensive, ongoing, and include authentic measures such as observation of children in their everyday environments and activities (Riggio & McLetchie, 2008; Rowland, 2009);
- occur across a variety of natural environments, including home, community, and school (Riggio & McLetchie, 2008; Rowland, 2009);
- consider a variety of communication forms, interpretations, and responses based upon the child's communications (Riggio & McLetchie, 2008);
- consider a child's preferences, strengths, and temperamental characteristics, including how they learn best (Nelson et al., 2002; Rowland, 2009);
- require an interdisciplinary team, including family members, teachers, therapists, and psychologists (Rowland, 2009);
- actively engage families in the assessment process by considering the cultures and values of all team members (Riggio & McLetchie, 2008);
- address the reason for referral and parental concerns when reporting results (Nelson et al., 2009; Rowland, 2009);
- drive ongoing planning and implementation of the student's IEP based on assessment data (Riggio & McLetchie, 2008); and
- base the accommodations on the unique needs and characteristics of each student rather than on their disability label (Horvath et al., 2005).

Components of Comprehensive Evaluations

A comprehensive evaluation of children and youth who are deafblind involves many components and varied assessments (Bruce et al., 2016). Some assessments, such as formal, standardized tests are administered directly to the child, while other types of assessment are accomplished through observation, interviews, and portfolios. Discussed in this chapter are developmental scales, ecological scales, communication assessments, and functional assessments of hearing, vision, and behavior.

Developmental scales provide information on how a child is progressing along a developmental continuum. A few developmental scales, appropriate for ages 0–8 years, have been developed specifically for children who are deafblind or children with visual impairments and multiple disabilities. Two commonly used developmental scales are the Callier Azusa G Scale (Stillman, 1978) and the INSITE Developmental Checklist (Morgan, 1989).

Ecological scales examine current child performance in an activity and environment, compared with the level of desired performance. The discrepancy between what is happening and what is desired is then analyzed in order to make the needed environmental modifications, implement adaptations, and/or provide additional instruction. Some dynamic assessments are child-guided in that the assessor follows the child's lead as playful interactions and routines are established to demonstrate underlying developmental abilities and/or learning processes (Nelson et al., 2002, 2009; van Dijk et al., 2010). An example of this type of assessment is the van Dijk Child-Guided Approach to Assessment (Nelson et al., 2002, 2009).

Communication is one of the more frequently researched areas of deafblind education (Bruce et al., 2016). As such, there are several evidence-based methods for assessing the communication of children and youth who are deafblind. The most widely researched and used is the Communication Matrix (Rowland, 2004), an observational communication assessment that is available as a free online resource (see the Resources section). The Matrix is useful for children and youth of any age who are at the earliest stages of communication, and it is designed to be used longitudinally to measure progress across time.

Functional assessments investigate how a child is performing in selected skill areas. Generally, such assessments include observations of students across environments and over an extended period of time. These assessments are important because they document how children who are deafblind use vision and hearing within routines and the possible reasons behind challenging behaviors. Functional vision assessments look at (a) visual acuity, (b) visual field, (c) color vision, (d) contrast sensitivity, (e) eye motility, (f) ocular motor behaviors, (g) visual-motor behaviors, (h) depth perception, and (i) visual perception (Bruce, Sacks, & Brum, 2016). Functional hearing assessments generally use observations of daily routines as well as interviews with caregivers and teachers to assess the child's responses to sounds. Naturally occurring sounds, including speech sounds, come from a variety of directions and from differing distances. Functional routines are advantageous because they are usually comfortable and provide a variety of sounds of varying intensity and frequency (Graves & Montgomery, 2016).

When children are exhibiting challenging behaviors that interfere with learning and social relationships, a functional behavior assessment (FBA) is often appropriate. There are many tools available, but most FBAs include observations and interviews to determine what comes before the occurrence of the challenging behavior (antecedent), what predicts it, the form of the behavior, and its consequences (Denno, 2016). In so doing, the FBA attempts to determine the function of the behavior and why the child is exhibiting such behavior (Cejas et al., 2022, see Chapter 8). A comprehensive assessment should inform the development of the IEP, including student educational placement and educational teams.

PLACEMENT AND EDUCATIONAL TEAMS

Educational Placements

Educational settings for students who are deafblind represent a continuum of placements. The IEP team must consider this continuum, based upon the learner's educational needs as indicated by assessment results, rather than disability. Learners who are deafblind might be educated all day or part of the day in the general education setting. Other educational settings include special classes located in general education settings, separate schools, or separate classrooms designed for children with severe disabilities, children who are d/Dhh, or children who are blind/visually impaired. Some learners who are deafblind receive their services in day schools, residential settings, or because of health concerns, in hospital or home settings. Regardless of placement, students can participate in the general curriculum and statewide assessments aligned with grade-level standards.

According to National Deaf-Blind Child Count data, in 2016, 30% of children who are deafblind between the ages of 3 and 5 years were served at least part of the day in general early childhood programs, almost double the percentage from the previous decade. Further, >61% of students older than 5 years of age identified as deafblind were served at least part of the school day in a general education classroom in their local school; this percentage has almost doubled in the past decade. Twenty-five percent of school-aged students in the Child Count participated in the general education curriculum and statewide assessments (Schalock, 2017).

Educational Teams

Regardless of the setting, students who are deafblind require specialized services for the dual sensory losses as well as possible other disabilities. Learners should have an IEP or Individualized Family Service Plan (IFSP; for ages 0–3 years) developed by a team that has at least one member with expertise in deafblindness (Parker et al., 2011). In a few states (Utah, Texas, and Illinois), the role of the teacher of the deafblind (TDB) is officially recognized as the expert. In other states, the expertise often comes from professionals serving on federal or state grant-funded deafblind projects. These projects provide technical assistance to schools and professionals serving children who are deafblind (Nelson & Sanders, 2014; Parker & Nelson, 2016). In addition, students who are deafblind may need very low staff-to-student ratios to ensure access to information and engagement (Parker et al., 2011). Some students will have a sign language interpreter, but others may require an intervener (Parker et al., 2011; Parker & Nelson, 2016).

An intervener is a paraprofessional who has specific knowledge and skills in deafblindness and provides one-on-one support to the individual who is deafblind. The intervener helps the student access communication and information in the environment, provides experiences to support concept development, and helps others interact with the student (Silberman et al., 2004). Because interveners are paraprofessionals with limited curricular expertise and responsibility, it is important that they receive ongoing support and supervision from professionals with expertise in deafblindness (Parker & Nelson, 2016). Other professionals who might be members of the IEP or IFSP team include a certified orientation and mobility specialist, teacher of students with visual impairments, teacher of the d/Dhh, audiologist, speech and language pathologist—and depending on disabilities—physical and occupational therapists.

Unfortunately, there is a shortage of personnel with the knowledge, skills, and expertise needed to teach learners with deafblindness and, thus, many students are served by personnel with little-to-no specialized training or experience (Grisham-Brown et al., 2018; Parker et al., 2011;

Parker & Nelson, 2016). In many areas, the federally funded state deaf-blind projects provide the only expertise in deafblindness through ongoing assistance, training, and support to IEP and IFSP teams throughout their respective states (Grisham-Brown et al., 2018; Parker et al., 2011). While there remains a need for certified TDBs, the role, as previously mentioned, is not widely recognized, and there are few universities that offer teacher training programs in deafblindness (Parker & Nelson, 2016). Therefore, in order to meet the current needs of students who are deafblind and ensure that the sparse qualified resources are maximized, interprofessional collaboration among team members (Ogletree, 2017) and consultative coaching are critical (Grisham-Brown et al., 2018).

Interprofessional collaboration promotes integrated, cohesive education to students through interaction and knowledge-sharing among professionals. Such collaborative practice requires a shift from discipline-specific roles. Professionals must be secure and competent in their knowledge base, have effective communication skills, have professional curiosity, and be able to collaboratively problem-solve to maximize student outcomes (Cloninger, 2017; Ogletree, 2017). Consultative coaching is a reciprocal process that includes reflection, discussion, and problem-solving among team members. Through both interprofessional collaboration and consultative coaching, the collective expertise of the teams can be greater than the sum of its parts.

EDUCATIONAL APPROACHES AND STRATEGIES

Because of the diverse population of students who are deafblind, educational strategies are multifaceted. However, ultimately, the student who is deafblind must be able to fully access information, communicate with teachers and peers, receive feedback, and engage as well as learn from the curriculum (Ferrell et al., 2014; Parker et al., 2011). Therefore, effective educational programs for children and youth who are deafblind involve specialized instructional strategies and environmental modifications and accommodations.

Instructional Approaches and Strategies

Two approaches that are widely used in the education of children and youth who are deafblind are child-guided approaches and systematic instructional approaches (Ferrell et al., 2014). Child-guided approaches follow the lead and interests of the child. As trust is built between the child and the communication partner, interactive dialogs are formed (Janssen et al., 2003; MacFarland, 1995). Systematic instructional approaches are behavioral and utilize direct, explicit instruction that is highly structured and sequenced (Brady & Bashinski, 2008; Collins, 2012).

Child-Guided Approach

The child-guided approach is often the foundation for strategies used in the field of deafblindness and is based on the work of Jan van Dijk and colleagues in the Netherlands (Silberman et al., 2004). The approach is conversational as the child and the communication partner (e.g., parent, teacher, intervener) follow each other's actions in a give-and-take conversational manner. Gradually, the resulting dialogs become more symbolic as the child's language evolves. The communication partner responds to the child's behaviors, no matter how small or atypical (MacFarland, 1995). Briefly, the approach, as outlined by MacFarland (1995) and van Dijk et al. (2010), includes: (a) following the child's lead and movements to build turn-taking interactions; (b) asking the child to follow the teacher's lead and movements as imitation and more complex movement and communication sequences are built; (c) utilizing concrete and tangible referents to characterize activities, people, and emotions; (d) using sequential memory strategies such as calendar systems and experience books to help the child understand the sequential nature of events and time; and (e) supporting the move from idiosyncratic, nonsymbolic communication to symbolic communication, achieved through the gradual introduction of symbolic language with concomitant fading of nonsymbolic communication within natural routines.

Systematic Instructional Approaches

Systematic approaches involve careful manipulation of teaching variables such as prompting, provision of opportunities, and consequences. These approaches have been successfully applied to teaching skills (particularly communication) and reduction of challenging behaviors that some students who are deafblind experience. Examples of successful systematic approaches include least-to-most prompting hierarchy, increased wait time, prelinguistic milieu teaching, and positive behavioral support strategies.

Least-to-most prompting hierarchies begin with the use of the least intrusive or controlling prompt necessary to prompt and promote the desired behavior. More intrusive prompts are gradually added only when the less-intrusive form is not sufficient to elicit the desired behavior (Nelson et al., 2013; Wolf Heller et al., 1996). For example, a prompting sequence might begin with a gesture, proceed to a verbal cue, be followed by a tangible or visual cue, then a full model, and finally, if needed, a partial or full physical prompt.

Related to prompting hierarchy is increasing the wait time between the prompt and the expected response. Students who are deafblind often need more time because they must piece together information from reduced input sources (vision and hearing). Therefore, it is important to allow the individual sufficient time to respond to the presented information and communications (Downing & Eichinger, 2011; Johnson & Parker, 2013). Johnson and Parker (2013) found that a wait time of at least 5 seconds between prompts increased appropriate responses by children with sensory impairments, including deafblindness.

Prelinguistic milieu teaching involves modeling, provision of opportunities for communication and skill development, and delayed prompting within highly motivating social and play routines (Brady & Bashinski, 2008). Adults reinforce the child's communicative behavior, such as gestures, by providing highly contingent responses. Systematic approaches, such as these, are also widely used to help students who exhibit challenging behaviors that interfere with learning and/or social interactions.

It is not uncommon for students who are deafblind to exhibit challenging behaviors, partly because the lack of vision and hearing makes the world an unpredictable place in which they feel that they have little control

(Nelson et al., 2013; Silberman et al., 2004). In addition, they may not have effective means to communicate with others to express choices or displeasure and may experience sensory overload (Hartshorne & Schmittel, 2016). Positive behavior support (PBS) is one systematic approach that has been shown to ameliorate challenging behaviors. PBS involves the following: (a) a clear description of the behavior; (b) an analysis (FBA) to determine the function of the behavior; (c) formulation of a hypothesis for why the individual is performing the behavior; (d) lifestyle enhancements; (e) environmental modifications to make the world more safe and predictable; (f) implementation of positive strategies, including contingent reinforcement of desired behaviors and teaching alternative and more appropriate skills and modes of communication; and (g) constant reevaluation of the effectiveness of the plan (Denno, 2016; Silberman et al., 2004). For further information about PBS and FBA, see Chapter 8 (Cejas et al., 2022). In addition to these outlined approaches, tactile instructional strategies and environmental modifications and accommodations can help the student who is deafblind receive information about the world and provide them with a means of communication (Downing & Chen, 2003; Miles, 2003).

Tactile Strategies

Children and youth who receive inadequate input from vision and hearing must rely on information from other senses. Therefore, tactile input can effectively augment vision and hearing to increase received information (Downing & Eichinger, 2011). Tactile strategies include the use of touch and object cues, hand-under-hand prompting, and tactile communication.

Touch and Object Cues. Touch and object cues are a tactile form of receptive communication as well as a viable means for understanding the world. Touch and object cues that occur naturally in the environment are more effective than artificial cues and are more readily learned. Hence, the use of real objects practiced within natural routines will provide students with a more salient way to understand their world (Downing & Eichinger, 2011). For example, assisting a child to touch their wheelchair before being placed in it provides information about what is to happen. Giving a child a cup to hold and manipulate can signal that it is snack time. Moreover, a communication partner might use a touch cue such as tapping a child under the arm to let them know that they are going to be lifted up.

Hand-Under-Hand Prompting. The hands of a person who is deafblind become critically important as they may effectively function as the person's eyes and ears. The hands allow for access to objects, people, and language, which are not accessible without vision and hearing (Miles, 2003). Persons interacting with individuals who are deafblind must be careful not to overly control or manipulate their hands. Often, prompting of children with disabilities has involved "hand-over-hand" manipulation. However, the exclusive use of such hand-over-hand touch can lead to passivity and avoidance of reaching out to explore the world to gain information. Miles (2003) suggests that the most skillful way of touching the child is the "hand-under-hand" touch, wherein the partner's hand is under the child's hand or alongside the hand. Thus, the touch is noncontrolling and does not interfere with the child's sensory experience as they touch an object.

Tactile Communication. Tactile forms of communication are many and varied. Tangible objects can be used by children who are at a nonsymbolic level of communication. Tangible symbol use is advantageous because they are permanent, they can be manipulated, and they link naturally to their referent (Rowland & Schweigert, 2000). The use of tangible symbols should require simple motor responses from the child, such as a touch or looking at the object, and the objects should be able to be reduced in size over time to increase portability.

Tactile ASL or tactile interpretation methods used by interpreters, interveners, and individuals who are deafblind vary. "Hands-on signing" involves the receiver's hand placed lightly on the back of the hands of the signer. In this way, signs are read through touch and movement. "Tracking" involves learners placing their hands on the wrist or forearms of signers as they track the signs visually. This method is generally used by learners with limited fields of vision.

Protactile ASL is a relatively new form of tactile communication used by individuals who are deafblind. Protactile ASL involves constant touch or connection, and social cues such as laughs, smiles, and yawns are provided through various touches. For example, a tap on the hand indicates that the communicator is nodding. Protactile communication is particularly useful when individuals who are deafblind are communicating with each other or are in groups of three or four.

Environmental Modifications and Accommodations

Environmental Modifications

Educational environments and activities should be predictable, meaningful, motivating, salient, and accessible for the learner who is deafblind (Nelson et al., 2013, 2016). However, if activities are dependent on both vision and hearing, they may not be very meaningful for a child who is deafblind. In the absence of the distance senses of vision and hearing, students who are deafblind may not be able to anticipate an activity, understand what it is about, or know when it is over. Therefore, instructional planning and delivery should include specific information to assist the students in understanding the sequence of the activity. In addition, modifications to instructional group size and enhanced visual and auditory stimuli are important for ensuring access and participation (Downing & Eichinger, 2011). Instructional groups need to be small enough that the student can access information and be fully engaged with instructional content. This engagement can be accomplished through one-on-one teaching, grouping 2–4 students, or having peers work together in cooperative learning groups (Downing & Eichinger, 2011).

Accommodations and Assistive Technology

Visual information can be enhanced through the use of preferential seating (e.g., sitting closer to instructional materials), attention to lighting (e.g., having light come over the shoulder rather than in front of the eyes), enlarged print, and increased contrast (e.g., print color is distinct from background color). The auditory environment can be enhanced by increasing the signal-to-noise ratio to ensure that the teacher's voice is louder than background noise, obtaining the student's attention prior to speaking, and changing the seating arrangement. For example, arranging seating in a "U" formation can allow students visual access to the teacher and others. In addition, if an interpreter is utilized, careful attention to physical placement is important to ensure that the student can access the interpreter or comfortably utilize tactual signing. Interpretation is often provided on a one-to-one basis.

Accommodations including various assistive technologies (ATs) for hearing, vision, and communication can assist in giving students who are deafblind an equitable educational experience. AT can be low tech (e.g., handheld braille labeler) or high tech, such as the Deafblind Communicator, an electronic device with a braille keyboard and a refreshable braille display. The braille can be read by the person who is deafblind as they write and can also be transmitted in text form to the smartphone of a sighted communication partner. Smartphones can also be paired with refreshable braille displays so that the individual who is deafblind can send and receive email and text messages.

ATs for access to auditory information include hearing aids, FM systems, cochlear implants, tactile alerting devices, and captioning. AT for access to visual information includes braille watches, braillewriters, refreshable braille display, braille printers and notetakers, braille translation software, and computer screen readers. Various technologies using tablet devices are being used in educational settings with students who are deafblind. Although technology has allowed information and communication access in ways that were unimaginable a few decades ago, it is important that the student who is deafblind be involved in the decision-making process surrounding technology use. Technology should not be based upon cognitive abilities but, rather, student needs. Teachers charged with technology implementation should receive training in how to most effectively implement and integrate the AT within the curriculum and instructional setting (Hartmann & Weismer, 2016; Parker et al., 2011).

In 2014, Ferrell et al. conducted a systematic analysis of research to identify the level of evidence for instructional practices used with children who are d/Dhh, visually impaired, and deafblind, for the Collaboration for Effective Educator, Development, Accountability, and Reform Center (CEEDAR). The review contains the current level of evidence for deafblind strategies across the curriculum and is available online (see Resources section).

POSTSECONDARY TRANSITION

Successful transitions from school to adult life are similar across youth, including those who are deafblind. While planning for transitions, educators must examine the quality of life rather than have a singular focus on employment outcomes. A person with a high quality of life will have meaningful choices, self-determination, effective communication skills, friendships and other relationships, as well as be able to participate within society and communities (McLetchie & Zatta, 2014). Research has consistently demonstrated the importance of youth and family involvement in the transition process (Cmar et al., 2017). Transition planning has gradually shifted from an approach that is system-driven to one that is person-centered. In a system-driven approach, available services are identified and fit with the individual. In a person-centered planning approach, teams include the individual, family, friends, and other persons involved in the individual's life. The team envisions what they would like to see happen in the domains discussed herein and identifies the needed supports to attain those goals. Transition planning should therefore be an ongoing, person-centered process with family involvement and should consider the individual's abilities, strengths, and preferences.

A key component of planning is self-determination or the ability to consider options and make appropriate decisions about one's own life. Moreover, students should be given opportunities to be active participants in IEP planning and have frequent opportunities to make personal choices throughout their education as well as within the transition planning process. Transition planning should involve the following domains: (a) vocational education and planning; (b) postsecondary planning; (c) independent or supported living; and (d) community participation (Zatta & McGinnity, 2016). Through collaborative, person-centered transition planning, the ultimate goal of a high quality of life may be achieved.

Finally, a successful transition to adulthood includes community identification and advocacy. The deafblind community is one that is rich and vibrant, comprising individuals who come from disparate and distinct cultures with different languages. Some individuals are from the Deaf culture who acquired blindness later; others are deaf with acquired blindness but from a hearing culture; some individuals are deafblind from birth or early childhood; and still others were blind but later acquired deafness. However, through common needs and interests, consumer advocacy communities that include all of the groups have emerged (Guilory Miller, 2015). Such consumer advocacy groups include the American Association of the Deaf-Blind, Deafblind International, and the Deaf-Blind Division of the National Federation of the Blind. The identified needs advocated by the deafblind advocacy groups include the following: (a) availability of, and access to, support services providers (individuals trained to act as links between individuals who are deafblind and their environment); (b) availability of trained interpreters in a variety of settings; (c) increased access to technology; (d) increased employment opportunities; (e) increased community services, including housing and transportation; and (f) increased access to health care and healthcare providers with specific knowledge of individuals who are deafblind (Lascek et al., n.d.)

FUTURE DIRECTIONS IN THE FIELD OF DEAFBLINDNESS

The population of children and youth who are deafblind is very heterogeneous but shares a common need for specialized services and supports to receive an appropriate education that is commensurate with students with vision and hearing. The majority of the students who are deafblind have multiple, often complex, disabilities and are educated in home communities and local schools (Nelson & Bruce, 2016; Schalock, 2017). Therefore, there is an increasing need in the field of deafblindness for family support, educational personnel with expertise in deafblindness, and high-quality inclusive practices in school and community.

The impact of having a child who is deafblind is unique for every family, and recent research has found that having a child with disabilities has many positive effects on families, including personal growth, positive impacts on siblings, awareness of disabilities, openness to diversity, and family unity (Hastings & Taunt, 2002). Research has also found that families of children with disabilities frequently experience toxic stress, which is both physically and emotionally damaging (Pottie & Ingram, 2008). Further, families of children with deafblindness and multiple disabilities face unique challenges (Correa-Torres & Bowen, 2016). Ensuring that effective supports and personnel are available to families is important in child adjustment and development. Further, support mechanisms should focus on families, including siblings and extended family members. Family supports may include help with stress management skills, parenting skills, communication strategies, and problem-solving skills. In addition, educators must be culturally responsive in their educational practices to ensure respect for the diverse cultures of children who are deafblind (Correa-Torres & Bowen, 2016).

As students are increasingly receiving their education in their home communities, the need for teachers and other service providers with specific expertise in deafblindness has accelerated. Although the need for such expertise has been recognized over several decades, the formalization of the roles of the TDB and the intervener has remained elusive. However, national competencies for both roles were developed and recognized by the Division on Visual Impairments and Blindness of the Council of Exceptional Children in 2009 (Parker & Nelson, 2016). As the field advances, Parker and Nelson (2016) propose that states develop Comprehensive Systems of Personnel Development for Children and Youth Who Are Deafblind. The proposed systems would involve state-level planning, coordination, and evaluation of standards of practice, preservice and in-service training, leadership development, and expanded research efforts. Further, recruitment efforts need to be undertaken to ensure that the diversity of teachers and related service providers serving students who are deafblind reflects the diverse ethnicity of the student population (Correa-Torres & Bowen, 2016; Parker & Nelson, 2016).

Because the majority of children on the Deaf-Blind Child Count are served at least part of the day in general education classrooms (Schalock, 2017), there is a need for increased knowledge to maximize student learning in inclusive classrooms. Unique supports include an adaptation of sensory information, provision of experiential learning, sensory development activities, assistive technology, and orientation and mobility training. Creative, evidence-based methods must ensure that children are meaningfully involved in the curriculum and have opportunities to have social interactions and form social relationships (Goetz, 1995). Moreover, high-quality inclusive environments should be thoughtfully designed using the principles of Universal Design for Learning principles (Guardino & Cannon, 2022, see Chapter 1) that consider technology and learning goals (Hartmann & Weismer, 2016). Finally, inclusion must be thought of beyond the classroom. Children and youth who are deafblind need opportunities to fully participate in a variety of community environments and activities to ensure a lifelong quality of life.

DISCUSSION QUESTIONS

1. What forms of communication are used by individuals who are deafblind? What are some factors that may influence their communication mode?
2. Deafblindness impacts development in many areas. What are three domains of development and learning that are impacted by deafblindness?
3. Why is it important for families to be involved in the assessment process?
4. What are some challenges that children who are deafblind might face in a general education setting?
5. Describe two to three environmental modifications and/or accommodations that are important for deafblind students?

RESOURCES

- **Active Learning Space**
  - http://activelearningspace.org/
  - An organization that provides instruction on how to create environments that support children with sensory impairments and other disabilities to be active participants in learning.
- **American Printing House for the Blind (APH)**
  - http://www.aph.org/
  - APH provides resources, services, and products to families, professionals, and individuals with vision impairments, including deafblindness. Students who are deafblind may also be eligible to access materials from APH through the Federal Quota Program.
- **CEEDAR Center Innovation Configuration: Evidence-Based Practices for Students With Sensory Impairments**
  - http://ceedar.education.ufl.edu/wp-content/uploads/2014/09/IC-4_FINAL_03-30-15.pdf
  - The Collaboration for Effective Educator, Development, Accountability, and Reform Center (CEEDAR) Center National Resource and Technical Assistance Center supports knowledge and use of evidence-based practices in special education. This report specifically focuses on the evidence base behind strategies for students with sensory impairments, including those with deafblindness.

- **Communication Matrix: Assessment and Community**
  - https://communicationmatrix.org/
  - A free, online assessment tool that measures the expressive communication skills of individuals with severe and multiple disabilities, including deafblindness. The assessment measures progress, offers suggestions for instruction, and is available in practitioner and parent versions.
- **Helen Keller National Center for Deaf-Blind Youths & Adults**
  - https://www.helenkeller.org/hknc
  - A national resource center that provides training and resources to individuals who are aged ≥16 years and are deafblind, as well as those who serve them.
- **The National Center on Deaf-Blindness**
  - https://nationaldb.org/
  - A national resource center for families and professionals that provides information and technical assistance to support children and youth who are deafblind. It contains an in-depth online library, state deafblind project contact information, and a list of ongoing and archived webinars.
- **The National Family Association for Deaf-Blind**
  - http://nfadb.org/
  - A national nonprofit family organization that seeks to connect, educate, and empower families of individuals who are deafblind.
- **Open Hands, Open Access: Deaf-Blind Intervener Modules**
  - https://moodle.nationaldb.org/
  - This resource contains 28 modules that illustrate and teach content related to working with individuals who are deafblind. The modules are free, present online, and, after registration, are available to anyone who is interested in learning more about working with individuals who are deafblind.
- **Perkins School for the Blind**
  - http://www.perkinselearning.org/
  - Contained in this website are online resources for professional development activities, as well as information and teaching strategies to support individuals who are deafblind.
- **Texas School for the Blind and Visually Impaired (TSBVI)**
  - http://www.tsbvi.edu/online-learning

○ TSBVI provides online resources, videos, webinars, courses, and forms to support families and practitioners who serve individuals who are deafblind.

REFERENCES

Anthony, T. L. (2016). Early identification of infants and toddlers with deafblindness. *American Annals of the Deaf, 161*(4), 412–423.

Brady, N. C., & Bashinski, S. M. (2008). Increasing communication in children with concurrent vision and hearing loss. *Research & Practice for Persons With Severe Disabilities, 33*(1–2), 59–70.

Bruce, S. M. (2005). The impact of congenital deafblindness on the struggle to symbolism. *International Journal of Disability, Development and Education, 52*(3), 233–251.

Bruce, S. M., & Borders, C. (2015). Communication and language in learners who are deaf with disabilities: Theories, research, and practice. *American Annals of the Deaf, 160*(4), 368–384.

Bruce, S. M., Nelson, C., Perez, A., Stutzman, B., & Barnhill, B. A. (2016). The state of research on communication and literacy in deafblindness. *American Annals of the Deaf, 161*(4), 424–443.

Bruce, S. M., Nelson, C., & Stutzman, B. (2022). Understanding the needs of children who are d/Deaf or hard of hearing with disabilities due to genetic causes. In C. Guardino, J. E. Cannon, & P. V. Paul (Eds.), *Deaf and hard of hearing learners with disabilities: Foundations, strategies, and resources* (pp. 96–132). Routledge.

Bruce, S., Sacks, S. Z., & Brum, C. (2016). Assessment of students who have visual impairments and multiple disabilities. In S. Z. Sacks & M. C. Zatta (Eds.), *Keys to educational success* (pp. 101–147). AFB Press.

Cejas, I., Sarangoulis, C. M., Mestres, A., Nelson, J. A., & Quittner, A. L. (2022). Assessment and intervention with learners who are d/Deaf or hard of hearing with emotional and behavioral challenges. In C. Guardino, J. E. Cannon, & P. V. Paul (Eds.), *Deaf and hard of hearing learners with disabilities: Foundations, strategies, and resources* (pp. 230–261). Routledge.

Chen, D. (2004). Young children who are deaf-blind: Implications for professionals in deaf and hard of hearing services. *Volta Review, 104*(4), 273–284.

Cloninger, C. J. (2017). Designing collaborative educational services. In F. P. Orelove, D. Sobsey, & D. Gilles (Eds.), *Educating students with severe and multiple disabilities: A collaborative approach* (pp. 1–25). Brookes.

Cmar, J. L., McDonnall, M. C., & Markoski, K. M. (2017). *In-school predictors of post-school employment for youth who are deaf-blind.* The National Research and Training Center on Blindness and Low Vision, Mississippi State University.

Collins, B. C. (2012). *Systematic instruction for students with moderate and severe disabilities.* Brookes.

Correa-Torres, S. M., & Bowen, S. K. (2016). Recognizing the needs of families of children and youth who are deafblind. *American Annals of the Deaf, 161*(4), 454–461.

Definition of a Child With a Disability: Deafblindness. 34 C.F.R. § 300.8. (2011). https://www.govinfo.gov/content/pkg/CFR-2011-title34-vol2/pdf/CFR-2011-title34-vol2-sec300-8.pdf

Denno, L. (2016). Positive strategies for behavioral intervention. In S. Z. Sacks & M. C. Zatta (Eds.), *Keys to educational success* (pp. 451–484). AFB Press.

Downing, J. E., & Chen, D. (2003). Using tactile strategies with students who are blind and have severe disabilities. *Teaching Exceptional Children, 36,* 56–60.

Downing, J., & Eichinger, J. (2011). Instructional strategies for learners with dual sensory impairments in integrated settings. *Research & Practice for Persons With Severe Disabilities, 36*(3–4), 150–157.

Ferrell, K. A., Bruce, S., & Luckner, J. L. (2014). *Evidence-based practices for students with sensory impairments* (Document No. IC-4). http://ceedar.education.ufl.edu/tools/innovation-configurations/

Fraiberg, S. (1968). Parallel and divergent patterns in blind and sighted infants. *Psychoanalytic Study of the Child, 23,* 264–300.

Goetz, L. (1995). Inclusion of students who are deaf-blind: What does the future hold? In N. G. Haring & L. T. Romer (Eds.), *Welcoming students who are deaf-blind into typical classrooms* (pp. 3–17). Brookes.

Graves, A., & Montgomery, C. (2016). *Informal functional hearing evaluation (IFHE).* Texas Schools for the Blind and Visually Impaired Outreach Programs. http://www.tsbvi.edu/images/outreach/Documents/IFHEDocument-NCDB.pdf

Grisham-Brown, J., Degirmenci, H. D., Snyder, D., & Luiselli, T. E. (2018). Improving practices for learners with deaf-blindness: A consultation and coaching model. *Teaching Exceptional Children, 50*(5), 263–271.

Guardino, C., & Cannon, J. E. (2022). Approaches and frameworks that support students who are d/Deaf or hard of hearing with a disabilities. In C. Guardino, J. E. Cannon, & P. V. Paul (Eds.), *Deaf and hard of hearing learners with disabilities: Foundations, strategies, and resources* (pp. 1–24). Routledge.

Guilory Miller, C. (2015, April). The deaf-blind dilemma. *Braille Monitor.* https://nfb.org/images/nfb/publications/bm/bm15/bm1504/bm150402.htm

Hartmann, E., & Weismer, P. (2016). Technology implementation and curriculum engagement for children and youth who are deafblind. *American Annals of the Deaf, 161*(4), 462–473.

Hartshorne, T. S., & Schmittel, M. C. (2016). Social-emotional development in children and youth who are deafblind. *American Annals of the Deaf, 161*(4), 444–453.

Hastings, R. P., & Taunt, H. M. (2002). Positive perceptions in families of children with developmental disabilities. *American Journal on Mental Retardation, 107*, 116–127.

Holte, L., Glidden Prickett, J., Van Dyke, D. C., Olson, R. J., Lubrica, P., Knutson, C. L., Knutson, J. F., & Brennan, S. (2006). Issues in the evaluation of infants and young children who are suspected of or who are deaf-blind. *Infants & Young Children, 19*(3), 213–227.

Horvath, L. S., Kampfer-Bohach, S., & Farmer Kearns, J. (2005). The use of accommodations among students with deafblindness in large-scale assessment systems. *Journal of Disability Policy Studies, 16*(3), 177–187.

Individuals With Disabilities Improvement Education Act Amendments of 2004. P.L. 108–446, 20 U.S.C. § 1400 *et seq.* (2006 & Supp. V. 2011).

Janssen, M. J., Riksen-Walraven, J. M., & van Dijk, J. P. M. (2003). Contact: Effects of an intervention program to foster harmonious interactions between deaf-blind children and their educators. *Journal of Visual Impairment & Blindness, 97*, 215–229.

Johnson, N., & Parker, A. T. (2013). Effects of wait time when communicating with children who have sensory and additional disabilities. *Journal of Visual Impairment and Blindness, 107*, 363–374.

Joint Committee on Infant Hearing. (2007). Year 2007 position statement: Principles and guidelines for early hearing detection and intervention programs. *Pediatrics, 120*(4), 898–921. https://doi.org/10.1542/peds.2007-2333

Klein, M. D., Chen, D., & Haney, M. (2000). *Promoting learning through active interaction: A guide to early communication with young children who have multiple disabilities.* Brookes.

Lascek, S., Pope, J., & Ruzenski, S. (n.d.). *Trends and unresolved issues impacting individuals who are deaf-blind.* American Association of the Deaf-Blind and the Helen Keller National Center. http://aadb.org/information/ncd/ncd_introduction.html

MacFarland, S. Z. (1995). Teaching strategies of the van Dijk curricular approach. *Journal of Visual Impairment and Blindness, 89*, 222–228.

McLetchie, B., & Zatta, M. (2014). *To live, to love, to work, to play: Blending quality of life into the curriculum.* https://www.perkinselearning.org/videos/webcast/live-love-work-play-blending-quality-life-curriculum

Mar, H. (1996). *Psychological evaluation of children who are deaf-blind: An overview with recommendations for practice.* DB-Link: The National Information Clearinghouse on Children Who Are Deaf-Blind. https://nationaldb.org/library/page/26

Miles, B. (2003). *Talking the language of the hands to the hands.* DB-Link; The National Information Clearinghouse on Children who are Deaf-Blind. http://documents.nationaldb.org/products/hands.pdf

Miles, B. (1999). What is communication? In B. Miles & M. Riggio (Eds.), *Remarkable conversations* (pp. 8–19). Perkins School for the Blind.

Miles, B., & Riggio, M. (1999). Understanding deafblindness. In B. Miles & M. Riggio (Eds.), *Remarkable conversations* (pp. 22–37). Perkins School for the Blind.

Morgan, E. (1989). *The INSITE developmental checklist: A comprehensive developmental checklist for multihandicapped sensory impaired infants and young children age 0–6.* SKI*HI Institute.

Nelson, C., & Bruce, S. M. (2016). Critical issues in the lives of children and youth who are deafblind. *American Annals of the Deaf, 161*(4), 406–411.

Nelson, C., Greenfield, R., Hyte, H., & Shaffer, J. (2013) Stress, behavior, and children and youth who are deafblind. *Research and Practice for Persons With Severe Disabilities, 38*(3), 139–156.

Nelson, C., Hyte, H. A., & Greenfield, R. (2016). Increasing self-regulation and classroom participation of a child who is deafblind. *American Annals of the Deaf, 160*(5), 496–509.

Nelson, C., Janssen, M., Oster, T., & Jayaraman, G. (2010). Reliability of the van Dijk assessment for children with deaf-blindness. *AER Journal, 3*(3) 71–80.

Nelson, C., & Sanders, D. (2014). Collaboration to ensure effective education of students who are deafblind. *Visual Impairment and Deafblind Education Quarterly, 59*(5), 26–35.

Nelson, C., van Dijk, J., McDonnell, A., & Thompson, K. (2002). A framework for understanding young children with severe multiple disabilities: The van Dijk approach to assessment. *Research and Practice for Persons With Severe Disabilities, 27*(2), 97–111.

Nelson, C., van Dijk, J., Oster, T., & McDonnell, A. P. (2009). *Child-guided strategies: The van Dijk approach to assessment for understanding children and youth with sensory impairments and multiple disabilities.* American Printing House for the Blind.

Ogletree, B. T. (2017). Addressing the communication and other needs of persons with severe disabilities through engaged interprofessional teams: Introduction to a clinical forum. *American Journal of Speech-Language Pathology, 26,* 157–161.

Parker, A. T., Grimmett, E. S., & Summers, S. (2008). Evidence-based communication practices for children with visual impairments and additional disabilities: An examination of single-subject design studies. *Journal of Visual Impairment and Blindness, 102,* 540–532.

Parker, A. T., McGinnity, B. L., & Bruce, S. M. (2011). *Educational programming for students who are deaf-blind.* Division on Visual Impairments, Council for Exceptional Children. https://higherlogicdownload.s3.amazonaws.com/SPED/d2199768-679e-41f6-aa2a-e9d3b5b748c8/UploadedImages/Position%20Papers/DVI%20Deafblindness%20Position%20Paper.pdf

Parker, A. T., & Nelson, C. (2016). Toward a comprehensive system of personnel development in deafblind education. *American Annals of the Deaf, 161*(4), 486–501.

Pottie, G., & Ingram, K. M. (2008). Daily stress, coping, and well-being in parents of children with autism: A multilevel modeling approach. *Journal of Family Psychology, 22*, 855–864.

Purvis, B., Malloy, P., Schalock, M., McNulty, K., Davies, S., Stremel Thomas, K., & Udell, T. (2014). *Early identification and referral of infants who are deaf-blind.* National Center on Deaf-Blindness. https://files.eric.ed.gov/fulltext/ED548232.pdf

Riggio, M., & McLetchie, B. (2008). Assessment. In M. Riggio & B. McLetchie (Eds.), *Deafblindness: Educational service guidelines* (pp. 35–45). Perkins School for the Blind.

Rosenblum, L. D. (2010). *The extraordinary powers of our five senses: See what I am saying.* Norton.

Rowland, C. (2004). *Communication matrix.* https://communicationmatrix.org/

Rowland, C. (2009). *Assessing communication and learning in young children who are deafblind or have multiple disabilities.* http://www.designtolearn.com/uploaded/pdf/DeafBlindAssessmentGuide.pdf

Rowland, C., & Schweigert, P. (2000). Tangible symbols, tangible outcomes. *Augmentative and Alternative Communication, 16*, 61–78.

Rowland, C., Stillman, R., & Mar, H. (2010). Current assessment practices for young children who are deaf-blind. *AER Journal Research and Practice in Visual Impairment and Blindness, 3*(3), 63–71.

Schalock, M. (2017). *The 2016 national child count of children and youth who are deaf-blind.* National Center on Deaf-Blindness. http://cb4cb5aa6990be188aff-8017fda59b77ece717432423a4f3bbdf.r43.cf1.rackcdn.com/2016-National-Deaf-Blind-Child-Count-Report-PDF-FINAL.pdf

Silberman, R., Bruce, S., & Nelson, C. (2004). Children with sensory impairments. In F. P. Orelove, D. Sobsey, & R. Silberman (Eds.), *Educating children with multiple disabilities* (4th ed., pp. 193–247). Brookes.

Stillman, R. D. (1978). *The Callier Azusa G Scale.* Callier Center for Communication Disorders.

van Dijk, R., Nelson, C., Postma, A., & van Dijk, J. (2010). Deaf children with severe multiple disabilities: Etiologies, intervention, and assessment. In M. Marschark & P. E. Spencer (Eds.), *Oxford handbook of deaf studies, language, and education* (Vol. 2, pp. 171–192). Oxford University Press.

Wagner, M. O., Haibach, P. S., & Lieberman, L. J. (2013). Gross motor skill performance in children with and without visual impairments. *Research in Developmental Disabilities, 34*(10), 3246–3252.

Wolf Heller, K., Allgood, M. H., Ware, S., & Castelle, M. D. (1996). Use of dual communication boards at vocational sites by students who are deaf-blind. *RE:view, 27,* 180–190.

Zatta, M., & McGinnity, B. (2016). An overview of transition planning for students who are deafblind. *American Annals of the Deaf, 161*(4), 474–485.

7

Learners Who Are d/Deaf and Hard of Hearing With a Learning Disability

Joanna E. Cannon, Caroline Guardino, Amanda Clements, and Stephanie W. Cawthon

LEARNING OBJECTIVES

Readers will:

- Recognize that a learning disability (LD) is the disability with the highest incidence rate among d/Deaf or hard of hearing (d/Dhh) learners.
- Understand the various terminologies and conflicting definitions associated with LDs.
- Describe the assessment process of identifying an LD with learners who are d/Dhh.
- Understand assessment considerations necessary to identify an LD with a student who is d/Dhh.
- Discuss the trends in research across the decades on learners who are d/Dhh with an LD.
- Review strategies, practices, and accommodations to utilize with learners who are d/Dhh-LD, given the level and complexity of their individualized needs.
- Acquire resources to use when working and collaborating with learners who are d/Dhh-LD, their families, and other professionals.

DOI: 10.4324/9781003252054-7

Children who are deaf or hard of hearing (d/Dhh) are a diverse and heterogeneous group. They differ in many ways, including the age at onset and identification of their hearing levels, communication modality, auditory technology usage, language development, school placement, and cultural identity. Approximately 40%–50% of the d/Dhh population have a disability(ies), further diversifying their individualized needs (Gallaudet Research Institute [GRI], 2013; for an in-depth discussion regarding the challenges of determining demographics across a low-incidence field, see Guardino & Cannon, 2015). This chapter discusses the terminology surrounding LD and is a synthesis of the existing research and literature regarding students who are d/Dhh with an LD (d/Dhh-LD). The authors address the ongoing challenges of identification as well as recommend strategies and resources beneficial to caregivers and educators.

Learners Who Are d/Dhh With an LD

The abbreviation "LD" is used throughout this chapter to refer to the general class of learning disabilities that arise across all cognitive domains and all subsets of learning disabilities (i.e., dyslexia, auditory processing disorder, dyscalculia; see Table 7.1). The abbreviation "SLD," which stands for specific LD, will be used to refer to the subset of LDs that primarily involves disorders of reading, math, and language.

LD is the most prevalent disability category for children who are d/Dhh, at a rate of approximately 7.2% of the U.S. d/Dhh population (GRI, 2013; Guardino & Cannon, 2015; Mitchell & Karchmer, 2010). This aligns with the prevalence rates of students with LDs in the general education population, ranging from 3% to 10% (National Joint Committee on Learning Disabilities [NJCLD], 2016). However, researchers have noted that LD prevalence may be higher in the d/Dhh population than in the hearing population (Edward & Crocker, 2008; McCracken et al., 2008; Soukup & Feinstein, 2007) for at least three reasons. First, many of the causes of varying hearing levels may also cause neurological disorders (e.g., meningitis, rubella, cytomegalovirus, prematurity; Calderon, 1998; Edwards, 2010; Mauk & Mauk, 1992; Morgan & Vernon, 1994) and may affect the educational, social, and language skills, as well as self-esteem, of learners who are d/Dhh-LD. Second, in the last 2 decades, many d/

Dhh students who were not making adequate academic progress were not assessed to determine whether they had an LD given the exclusionary factors in the Individuals With Disabilities Education Act (IDEA, 2004; Caemmerer et al., 2016; Edwards, 2007, 2010). Third, students who may have benefitted from a psychoeducational evaluation were not eligible because of the misinterpretation of the law (Roth, 1991) and the fear of mislabeling. To determine accurate prevalence rates, professionals must first be able to define the characteristics of LDs in learners who are d/Dhh.

Defining LDs

There is a wide variety of terminology used to define LDs in the field of special education. Table 7.1 provides definitions of various terms used to describe LDs at both the macro- and microlevels. Defining an LD is complex because the disability is multifaceted, and competing definitions have conflated the debate over the specific criteria of an SLD.

In the United States, the federal definition of an SLD is:

> a disorder in one or more of the basic psychological processes involved in understanding or in using language, spoken or written, that may manifest itself in the imperfect ability to listen, think, speak, read, write, spell, or to do mathematical calculations, including conditions such as perceptual disabilities, brain injury, minimal brain dysfunction, dyslexia, and developmental aphasia. (IDEA, 2004, § 300.8 [c] [10])

The definition becomes further complicated for students who are d/Dhh-LD, with the stipulation that "specific learning disabilities do not include learning problems that are primarily the result of visual, hearing, or motor disabilities, of intellectual disability, of emotional disturbance, or of environmental, cultural, or economic disadvantage" (IDEA, 2004, § 300.8 [c] [10]). In comparison, the NJCLD (2016) definition of LDs helps to clarify the sensory challenges included in the U.S. IDEA definition.

> Learning disabilities is a general term that refers to a heterogeneous group of disorders manifested by significant difficulties in the

TABLE 7.1 Terminology Associated With Learning Disabilities

Terminology	Definition
Learning disability	Neurodevelopmental learning issues in reading, writing, math, organization, focus, listening comprehension, social skills, motor skills, or a combination of these. These issues are not the result of low intelligence, low vision or hearing levels, or lack of access to quality instruction.
Specific learning disability	Neurodevelopmental disorder in which a person has difficulty learning or using academic skills (e.g., reading, writing, math). The learning difficulties cannot be attributed to other aspects of development, cognitive functioning, emotional behavior disorders, or cultural, economic, or environmental disadvantage.
Auditory processing disorder (APD)	Sensory disorder that makes it difficult to understand language, although vision and hearing levels are in the typical range.
Dyslexia	A specific learning disability in reading in which a person has difficulty decoding single words, leading to issues with reading, writing, and spelling.
Dyspraxia	A developmental coordination disorder in which a person has difficulty in planning and performing fine motor skill tasks (e.g., writing, tying shoelaces, buttoning a coat).
Dyscalculia	A specific learning disability in math in which a person has a difficulty in grasping number-related concepts (e.g., using symbols and functions to solve problems).

Terminology	Definition
Dysgraphia	A specific learning disability in written expression in which a person has difficulty forming letters or writing within a defined space (e.g., writing legibly, at age-appropriate speed, synthesizing thoughts).
Nonverbal learning disabilities	Neurological disorder that originates in the right hemisphere of the brain, in which a person has difficulty with visual-spatial, intuitive, organizational, evaluative, and holistic processing functions (i.e., recognizing and responding to nonliteral or unspoken language, such as sarcasm or body language) as well as issues with abstract reasoning and gross motor coordination.
Executive functioning disorders	Neurological disorder in which a person has difficulty with mental skills or cognitive processes to accomplish tasks (e.g., planning ahead, prioritizing, self-monitoring behavior, beginning and transitioning between activities).

Note. Adapted from http://www.ldonline.org/; https://www.ncld.org/executive-summary.

acquisition and use of listening, speaking, reading, writing, reasoning, or mathematical abilities. These disorders are intrinsic to the individual, presumed to be due to central nervous system dysfunction, and may occur across the lifespan. Problems in self-regulatory behaviors, social perception, and social interaction may exist with learning disabilities but do not by themselves constitute a learning disability. Although learning disabilities may occur concomitantly with other disabilities (for example, sensory impairment, intellectual disabilities, emotional disturbance), or with extrinsic influences (such as cultural or linguistic differences, insufficient or inappropriate instruction), they are not the result of those conditions or influences. (NJCLD, 2016)

This definition recognizes that some students who are d/Dhh, despite having language delays, can also have an LD that is caused by neurological dysfunction. Given the conflicting definitions of LD, it is not surprising that professionals are challenged with identifying LD in children who are d/Dhh. Unfortunately, this has been an ongoing challenge for decades.

Challenges in Identifying LDs

When evaluating d/Dhh students, professionals often debate the characteristics of an LD that are relevant and applicable, primarily because of conflicting definitions. Laughton (1989) offered a definition with characteristics explicit to learners who are d/Dhh-LD.

[Learners who are d/Dhh-LD] have significant difficulty with acquisition, integration, and use of language and/or non-linguistic abilities. Disorders are presumed to be caused by coexisting conditions of central nervous system dysfunction and peripheral sensorineural hearing loss and not by either condition exclusively. Can vary in its manifestations and degree of severity and can affect education, communication, self-esteem, socialization, and/or daily living skills throughout life. (p. 5)

In many educational settings, having dual eligibility for special education services is not standard practice, and a primary disability is often limited to one. The restriction of one primary disability may lead to the underidentification of a secondary disability if needs are not differentiated between deafness and the LD. Consequently, when an LD is not identified, learners may not receive the supports they need to be academically or socially successful. This may be especially true for those d/Dhh learners with emotional behavior disorders (EBD) because of the frequency with which they experience LD (Cejas et al., 2022, see Chapter 8 for further information regarding d/Dhh learners with EBD). Further investigation is needed in order to provide appropriate strategies and supports to learners who are d/Dhh-LD and their families (Morgan & Vernon, 1994).

Early detection of any language-related challenges is critical since the gaps between the academic successes of students who are d/Dhh and peers with typical hearing appear to widen as children grow (Nelson & Crumpton, 2015; Sligar et al., 2013). Early signs of learning difficulties may appear in the preschool years (e.g., difficulty learning names of letters or counting objects; Mauk & Mauk, 1992), but they can only be reliably identified after starting elementary school. An LD is understood to be a cross-cultural and chronic condition that typically persists into adulthood, albeit with cultural differences and developmental maturation. Possible indicators of an LD with students who are d/Dhh include challenges with: (a) auditory perception and receptive language skills, (b) sequential organization ability, (c) lower overall grades and tests scores, (d) math calculation skills, and (e) attention and memory (Berent et al., 2000; Caemmerer et al., 2016; Isaacson, 1996).

Conducting educational evaluations of d/Dhh children requires specialized training and experience. Teasing apart the impact of the hearing levels and the learning patterns regarding the achievement of a d/Dhh child can be very challenging (Wiley, 2014). Yet professionals must persevere in the process, knowing that appropriate identification can help practitioners select appropriate curriculum materials and instructional strategies (Soukup & Feinstein, 2007).

ASSESSMENT CONSIDERATIONS

A transdisciplinary, asset-based approach provides a holistic evaluation of learners, particularly those with complex learning needs (Jackson et al., 2015). Collaboration across speech-language pathologists, audiologists, teachers for all academic subjects, school psychologists, and other professionals working with the student (Edwards, 2010; McCracken et al., 2008) is necessary to provide a detailed and comprehensive examination of students' strengths, needs, and supports (see Cawthon, 2015, for further information regarding assessment reliability, examiner qualifications, and language). The results of the examination should be considered across linguistic, cultural, and cognitive domains so that the construct of an LD within the societal and cultural norms is acknowledged and approached with caution (Mauk & Mauk, 1998; see Table 7.2).

Teachers of d/Dhh learners often report that they can identify a student who is not making progress at the same rate as their peers, despite suspected average intelligence and receiving the same instructional practices (Roth, 1991). Teachers report issues across memory, visual perception, and attention (Laughton, 1989), as well as stagnated progress in at least one subject area. Under a multitiered system of support model (MTSS; Hoover et al.,

TABLE 7.2 Assessment Considerations Across Linguistic, Cultural, and Cognitive Domains

Domains	Considerations
Linguistic	Consider relevant indicators (age at onset, etiology, age at identification, and language[s] used at home and school). Apply caution when using verbal measures and verbally loaded achievement tests, including calculating adaptive measures, as there are many language-loaded items on these. Vocabulary and speech-and-language measures are to be administered in the primary language of the student, using caution when interpreting into American Sign Language.
Cultural	To gain an overall picture of the learner, examiners must assess beyond academics, as one's ethnic background and cultural identity(ies) may influence assessment outcomes.
Cognitive	When reviewing case and educational histories with the student's parents and teachers, it is necessary to investigate developmental and birth history, as many conditions may also manifest themselves as learning issues (Braden, 2005).

2018), when progress is stagnant, and strategies at Tier 1 (core instruction) and Tier 2 (supplemental instruction) appear ineffective, the student is often referred for an evaluation to investigate the cause (Luckner & Pierce, 2013; Guardino & Cannon, 2022, see Chapter 1 for more information about response to intervention [RTI] and MTSS). In the United States, as part of the eligibility guidelines for LDs under IDEA (2017), the law states:

> The child does not achieve adequately for the child's age or to meet State-approved grade-level standards in one or more of the following areas when provided with learning experiences and instruction appropriate for the child's age or State-approved grade-level standards: oral expression, listening comprehension, written expression, basic reading skill, reading fluency skills, reading comprehension, mathematics calculation, or mathematics problem solving. (§ 300.309)

An assessment plan is a critical consideration in evaluating d/Dhh learners who are suspected of having an SLD, given the complexities of this unique population. Assessment plans should be developed by a multidisciplinary or transdisciplinary team and should include family history, preferably through interviews (Plapinger & Sikora, 1990). Several additional factors must be taken into consideration when designing an assessment plan: (a) components of the assessment, (b) the assessment tools, (c) examiners' qualifications, and (d) what critical indicators to look for among the data.

Components of an Assessment

Assessments selected for an evaluation depend on why the learner is referred for testing (e.g., challenges with phonological processing in reading; struggles with mathematics problem-solving skills, insufficient listening comprehension skills; Morgan & Vernon, 1994). The evaluation of a possible LD for a learner who is d/Dhh should contain the following eight components: (1) case history, (2) educational history, (3) two measures of intellectual functioning, (4) a measure of educational achievement, (5) neuropsychological screening, (6) assessment of adaptive or classroom behavior (including teacher input), (7) current audiological and screening evaluation, and (8) information on communication and language skills (Edwards, 2010; Morgan & Vernon, 1994).

Assessment Tools

Assessing this heterogeneous population requires a variety of tools, including a battery of protocols designed to target a suspected SLD (i.e., reading, math), to provide consistency across examiners. For example, if an SLD is suspected in reading, then a standard battery would include tests that measure the following variables: (a) intelligence quotient (IQ), (b) achievement, (c) reading, (d) vocabulary, (e) comprehension, (f) math calculation, (g) working memory, and (h) phonological awareness and processing (rhyming, phonological blending, phoneme and syllable deletion, and pseudoword decoding). Protocols may also be individualized utilizing multiple, similar tests tailored to a specific cognitive function (e.g., sequencing, auditory memory). Assessment batteries may include observations, questionnaires, semistructured interviews, and/or neuropsychological approaches.

The number of assessment tools available for determining whether a student has an LD goes beyond the scope of this chapter, but some guidelines for selection are provided. Evaluators are not required, nor is it suggested to begin assessing the child with a cognitive assessment at the first assessment session (Wood & Dockrell, 2010). When cognitive measures are considered, nonverbal tests are typically used (Braden, 2001, 2005; Miller, 1991; Wood & Dockrell, 2010), as many measures can be inappropriate for d/Dhh students given the auditory-based subtests (Roth, 1991). Nonverbal assessments should be administered before any other assessments to help determine the remaining assessment protocol (Edwards, 2008).

There are very few tests with norms for d/Dhh learners, and determinations from those norms can be challenging given the heterogeneity of the population (Maller, 2003), although verbal aptitude is very important in academic achievement, especially in math and science (Akamatsu et al., 2008). Verbal tests, when given by a knowledgeable, skilled examiner, can have better predictive validity than nonverbal subtests in regards to academic functioning (Wood & Dockrell, 2010). Moreover, subtests that examine abstract reasoning, memory, and visual perception can be helpful when administered by an examiner with knowledge of d/Dhh children (Roth, 1991).

A classroom observation is also critical (Wood & Dockrell, 2010) for multidisciplinary assessment, as well as collecting information related to classroom grades, a consideration in initial eligibility assessment situations (Caemmerer et al., 2016). Tools to evaluate adaptive and classroom behavior can be a very important part of multidisciplinary assessment, especially input from the teacher. Tools that effectively evaluate communication and language skills (e.g., language samples, work samples, observational data) are critical and should be conducted collaboratively with the multidisciplinary, school-based team. Reviewing information from neuropsychological screening tools (e.g., Beery–Buktenica Developmental Test of Visual-Motor Integration; Beery et al., 2010) can provide the school-based team with additional information to consider, given that some screenings have been linked with language skills (Pisoni et al., 2008). Teachers also have vital information to share with the team, especially considering that math calculation skills and classroom grades are indicators of SLD in reading, math, and language (not exclusively math; Caemmerer et al., 2016). Therefore, even if only reading and language SLDs are suspected, evaluators should examine math scores to rule out processing issues rather than a language delay due to the learner's hearing level.

Examiners' Qualifications

Considerations during testing for learners who are d/Dhh include ensuring a communication match between the student and the examiner (Braden, 2005), with interpreters utilized when a match is not available (Sligar et al., 2013). Ideally, the educational psychologist/examiner should be able to communicate directly in the student's primary language (e.g., spoken English, American Sign Language [ASL]; Braden, 2005; Wood & Dockrell, 2010) to foster a rapport and ensure the most optimal assessment environment. The examiner requires specialized training and thorough knowledge of the learner's language and culture (e.g., Deaf culture, hard of hearing culture,

culture related to their ethnicity; Andrews et al., 2003; Cannon & Luckner, 2016). Interpreters for examiners must also know the language needs of the student and be familiar with testing procedures and materials (Morgan & Vernon, 1994; Sligar et al., 2013). Lack of one-to-one communication during testing (i.e., via an interpreter) and how this may impact examiner/examinee rapport should be considered when determining examiner qualifications. School psychologists generally do not have specific training in assessing d/Dhh learners, yet examiner training is vital to avoid misinterpretations that can lead to over- or underidentification of special needs (Roth, 1991). Many schools for the deaf and specialized learning centers have referrals for qualified examiners who have experience assessing learners who are d/Dhh, and these should be consulted by any school-based teams or families seeking support.

Critical Indicators to Look for Among Assessment Data

Examiners should align a battery of tests to areas of concern, in order to determine the learners' strengths and challenges while also considering (a) the reason for referral and (b) the area of academic or social functioning that is of particular interest. Multidisciplinary assessment across professionals (e.g., speech and language pathologist, school psychologist, school counselors) is vital to understand the familial, social, emotional, and educational influences that may impact a learner's performance (Edwards, 2010).

Critical indicators of SLD in reading, math, and language, such as math calculation skills and classroom grades, must be evaluated effectively (Cawthon, & Bond, 2016). Mathematics problem solving must be approached with caution, given the language demands and complications when interpreting English to ASL. For example, it is easy to change the level of difficulty of a problem when translating it into ASL (Ansell & Pagliaro, 2001), and students may also take advantage of visual cues that may inadvertently be provided (Kritzer et al., 2004).

For a suspected reading SLD, tests of reading fluency, basic word reading, and comprehension would need to be selected. For early literacy skills, the test battery could also include phonological processing, depending on the hearing level of the examinee. Examiners should also consider progress monitoring data collected (i.e., mastery of sight words or reading fluency data) and compare students to their own previous assessment data. When addressing language-related LDs, for example, reading comprehension, it is difficult to tease out delays in language and knowledge (Pizzo & Chilvers, 2016), especially given the language delays that are often exhibited by d/Dhh children. Furthermore, children who are d/Dhh are often exposed to multiple modalities and language models, so determining the student's level of functioning may be extremely difficult (Sligar et al., 2013).

RESEARCH WITH LEARNERS WHO ARE D/DHH-LD

A review of the literature regarding learners who are d/Dhh-LD reveals inconsistent results across the past 50 years, with minimal research being conducted within the past decade (see Figure 7.1 and Table 7.3). Before the 21st century, there was a steady increase in publications throughout the decades, with four studies in the pre-1980s, eight from 1980 to 1989, and 10 in 1990–1999 (see Figure 7.1 and Table 7.3). From 2000 to 2009, there was a 50% decrease from the previous decade, with only three publications, and a mere two publications since 2010. Given that students who are d/Dhh-LD constitute the largest group of learners among the potential disabilities (i.e., autism, behavior disorders), it behooves professionals to reconsider the time and attention given to these learners within the literature.

Strategies, Practices, and Accommodations

Strategies and practices that may be effective for students who are d/Dhh-LD have not been thoroughly reported in the literature; however, recommendations include training for teachers to understand what strategies and techniques might be most effective for students who are d/Dhh-LD (Roth, 1991). In order to determine which strategies may be beneficial for students who are d/Dhh-LD, we examine areas identified in the literature by teachers of the d/Deaf and hard of hearing (TDHH; Powers et al., 1988; Samar, 1999; Soukup & Feinstein, 2007).

Dynamic assessment that includes teacher observation data, transdisciplinary collaboration, and use of curriculum-based measures are

Prior to 1980	1980–1989	1990–1999	2000–2009	2010–2018
Auxter (1971)	Powers and Harris (1982)	Plapinger and Sikora (1990)	Berent et al. (2000)	Edwards (2010)
Vockell et al. (1972)	Hill et al. (1985)	Roth (1991)	Stewart and Kluwin (2001)	Caemmerer et al. (2016)
Hagger (1972)	LaSasso (1985)	Mauk and Mauk (1992)	Soukup and Feinstein (2007)	
Hawkins-Shepard (1977)	Powers et al. (1987)	Morgan and Vernon (1994)		
	Powers et al. (1988)	Sikora and Plapinger (1994)		
	Elliott and Powers (1988)	Van Vuuren (1995)		
	Bunch and Melnyk (1989)	Mauk and Mauk (1998)		
	Laughton (1989)	Samar et al. (1998)		
		Calderon (1998)		
		Samar (1999)		

Figure 7.1 A half-century of literature: d/Dhh students with LDs

Note. Go to Table 7.3 for details.

TABLE 7.3 LD Literature Across the Decades

Decade	Literature	Findings/Recommendations

1970–1979	Auxter (1971)	• Significant differences were found between students who are d/Dhh with and without LD
		• Students who are d/Dhh-LD may experience deficits in
		   • muscular strength
		   • motor speed
		   • motor planning
		   • tasks requiring neuromuscular control
		   • Recommended strategies:
		   • progressive resistance training to build neuromuscular strength
		   • sequential activities to develop motor speed
		   • vary movement experiences to build neuromuscular coordination
		   • develop a continuum of academics that moves at a rate that is comfortable for the child

	Vockell et al. (1972)	• Critique of Auxter, 1971 • Not all d/Dhh students learn at rates comparable to those of hearing children, as Auxter stated • Not all children with visual-motor challenges will have LD • Challenged the participants chosen for Auxter's study, not described well, conveniently divided into 2 matching groups of 15 • Auxter used assessment tools not valid or reliable with deaf students • Gender and maturation may have accounted for some of Auxter's findings

(*Continued*)

TABLE 7.3 (*Continued*)

Decade	Literature	Findings/Recommendations

1970–1979	Hagger (1972, April)	• Children with sensory impairments are typically excluded from also being categorized as having an SLD
		• Educators need to know about SLD to be able to adequately serve students who are d/Dhh-LD and thus are likely to need additional training
		• Etiology of deafness may overlap with cause of LD, thus increasing the possibility of the co-occurrence
		• Likely that 25% of children at schools for the deaf have some type of LD, resulting in the need for additional assistance
		• Assessing for an LD in students who are d/Dhh is challenging, yet tests measuring visual perception and coordination are recommended
		• Differentiating between autism, aphasia, and deafness is challenging. Examine these skills as part of the diagnostic procedures:
		  • consistency of response
		  • vocalization
		  • gestures
		  • attention to facial expression and lips
		  • echolalia
		  • motor coordination or lack of

Decade	Literature	Findings/Recommendations
1970–1979	Hawkins-Shepard (1977)	<ul><li>Definition of LD by federal law excludes students who are d/Dhh</li><li>Identification of LD may be appropriate given the significant discrepancy between student performance on the following age-level developmental milestones:<ul><li>gross motor coordination</li><li>sensory motor integration</li><li>visual analysis</li><li>attention and memory</li><li>conceptualizations</li></ul></li></ul>
1980–1989	Powers and Harris (1982)	<ul><li>To help determine whether a child is d/Dhh-LD, compare the learner with the typical child developmental milestones</li><li>Strategies reviewed from the general LD K–12 population</li><li>Suggested strategies for d/Dhh-LD:<ul><li>to plan effective asset-based instruction, know student's strengths, challenges, and developmental levels; when using strategies from the general LD population, apply appropriate modifications for d/Dhh-LD learners, then assess the effectiveness of the strategy objectively</li><li>refer to Table 1, p. 255, for a comprehensive list of studies that include strategies used by the greater LD field</li></ul></li></ul>

(Continued)

TABLE 7.3 (Continued)

Decade	Literature	Findings/Recommendations
1980–1989	Hill et al. (1985)	• Challenges with spelling and math computation proved to be indicators of students who are d/Dhh-LD versus their deaf peers • Visual tasks may prove to be more challenging for students who are d/Dhh-LD • Speculation about the potential for maturation to minimize or make obsolete the characteristics of LD
	LaSasso (1985)	• Professionals need to be careful not to identify d/Dhh students as having an LD • Instruction should be examined prior to diagnosis to be sure curriculum, pacing, and strategies are appropriate for the learner • Learning disabilities in a deaf child may really be the result of a "visual perceptual problem" or "visual memory problem"—focus should be on building language and communication, not on learning deficits
	Powers et al. (1987)	• Survey captured the perspectives of 63 administrators of programs for d/Dhh students • Approximately 6.7% of the total population of d/Dhh students labeled as having an LD • Differentiating between deafness and LD, EBD, and intellectual disability is challenging because some characteristics overlap between the 3 disability areas. • Teacher observation and referral was the greatest method of identifying LD, followed by a diagnostic assessment administered by a qualified professional • The greatest difference between d/Dhh students with LD and those without LD was that there were (1) achievement–potential discrepancy and (2) perceptual problems • No consensus of the best placement for students who are d/Dhh-LD • Teacher preparation programs need to expand learning objectives to include instruction on students who are DWD

Decade	Literature	Findings/Recommendations
1980–1989	Powers et al. (1988)	• Differences in language abilities help determine LDs in learners who are d/Dhh • Teachers report characteristics such as confusion when using sign and spoken language simultaneously • Discrepancy between potential and achievement may indicate an LD • Behavioral and social-emotional challenges may indicate an LD • d/Dhh-LD students struggle to focus on a task, retain information, and maintain organizational skills • Teachers are among the best equipped to identify LD in d/Dhh learners
	Elliott and Powers (1988)	• Survey captured responses from 54 teacher of the d/Dhh preparation programs • Respondents indicated that they did not feel the need for a separate state certification nor a specific teacher preparation program; however, desired coursework to fill the information gap
	Bunch and Melnyk (1989)	• Definition of LD by federal law excludes d/Dhh students • Historical controversy regarding definitions and whether d/Dhh-LD students exist due to the lack of empirical evidence • Calls for agreed-upon assessment procedures if the field wants to be able to identify learners who are d/Dhh-LD • Review of literature from the 1970s

(Continued)

TABLE 7.3 (*Continued*)

Decade	Literature	Findings/Recommendations
1980–1989	Laughton (1989)	• Definition of LD by IDEA, NJCLD, and ACLD; offers a definition for d/Dhh-LD • Discusses the concomitant issues in determining whether learners' difficulties with language development stem from an LD or limited language exposure • Discusses the discrepancy model argument, highlighting the lack of specific criteria as one major concern
1990–1999	Plapinger and Sikora (1990)	Case study of one d/Dhh learner to determine whether they had an LD • Interdisciplinary diagnostic approach recommended. • Highlighted the importance of family histories in diagnostic process
	Roth (1991)	• Definition of LD by federal law excludes d/Dhh students • Collaboration between the teacher of the deaf and an LD specialist is ideal, yet challenging, because each field is experiencing conflict • Need for qualified professionals to administer assessments needed to diagnosis LD in learners who are d/Dhh • Assessment tools available are limited, thus teacher observation and curriculum-based measures are the best tools to identify LD.

Decade	Literature	Findings/Recommendations
1990–1999	Mauk and Mauk (1992)	• Support for examining LD in preschool d/Dhh learners due to etiologies of hereditary, maternal rubella, Rh factors, meningitis, prematurity, cytomegalovirus (CMV) • Discusses controversy over the "definition debate" including pros/cons • Increased incidence of LDs in the d/Dhh population • Challenge to find valid and reliable identification tools including assessments, and procedures for a comprehensive psychoeducational evaluation across domains • Further attention needs to be paid to effective educational programming and training of educators
	Morgan and Vernon (1994)	• A battery of tests must be used to determine if a d/Dhh student has LD, including educational history, IQ tests, behavioral assessment, audiological evaluation, and communication skills • School and neuropsychological standardized assessment tools are recommended to assist with determining LD in d/Dhh learners

(*Continued*)

TABLE 7.3 (Continued)

Decade	Literature	Findings/Recommendations
1990–1999	Sikora and Plapinger (1994)	• Definition of LD by federal law excludes students who are d/Dhh and adoption of the NJCLD definition • Standardized assessments can identify LD in learners who are d/Dhh when previous results are mixed; teacher report is a historical way of identification • Measures across audiology, speech and language, psychological, psychoeducational, and occupational therapy domains. • 16 participants, of whom 2 identified with LD • Little difference in primary students on concrete test items (math, science), but language-based areas (reading, applied math, social studies, humanities) were far more difficult • d/Dhh-LD "acquire information experientially but have difficulty acquiring it didactically. . ." (p. 358) • Recommend inquiry-based learning activities

	Van Vuuren (1995, July)	• Risk factors associated with LD in students who are d/Dhh, which may help identify whether LD is present are as follows:
		  • male
		  • older than classmates
		  • medical conditions
		  • poor mother–child relationship
		  • low academic achievement
		  • low motivation
		  • weak visual perception
		  • weak signing skills
		  • preference for visual communication
		  • low participation and concentration

Decade	Literature	Findings/Recommendations

1990–1999	Mauk and Mauk (1998)	• Considerations:
		  • definition of LD by federal law excludes students who are d/Dhh and adoption of the NJCLD definition
		  • interventions that focus on linguistic theory may be more powerful
		  • cultural and societal importance on academics leads to identification of culturally-valued norms (academics)
		• Conceptualizations:
		  • models for research and to understand patterns of cognitive and academic performance
		  • recommendation for dynamic assessment and multidisciplinary team approach
		• Challenges:
		  • need for more empirical research

	Samar et al. (1998)	• Definition of LD by federal law excludes students who are d/Dhh and adoption of the NJCLD definition • History of debate over the definitions of LD • Discussion of the neurological pathology behind many LD • Research should utilize neuroimaging technology • Phonological awareness training should begin during early intervention and could be used as a possible screener • Interactive multimedia to decrease processing deficits

(Continued)

TABLE 7.3 (*Continued*)

Decade	Literature	Findings/Recommendations
1990–1999	Calderon (1998)	• Definition of LD by federal law excludes students who are d/Dhh • d/Dhh at greater risk for LD • Applying the definition of hearing-LD (2 standard deviations below grade level) to d/Dhh students; majority of all d/Dhh students would be labeled LD by mid-elementary stage; overclassification is a product of poor assessment tools • Cross-discipline collaboration is needed to identify LD
	Samar (1999)	• Definition of LD by federal law excludes students who are d/Dhh • LD stemmed from populations of learners who were susceptible to neural damage, such as students who were deaf. Federal law (PL92–142) later rejected children with sensory impairments as belonging to the same category as children with LD. • Determining dyslexia in students who are d/Dhh proved extremely difficult.

2000–2009	Berent et al. (2000)	• Teachers perceive atypical language development as a potential indicator of LD
		• Teachers also noted other potential indicators that may help identify LD in students who are d/Dhh:
		  • lack of organization and time management
		  • low self-esteem
		  • trouble concentrating
		  • visual processing challenges
		  • retention problems
		  • do not respond to strategies that typically help d/Dhh peers
		  • language processing difficulties
		  • struggle with spelling, reading, and writing
		  • low language skills in English and ASL

Decade	Literature	Findings/Recommendations
2000–2009	Stewart and Kluwin (2001)	• Students may develop at a slower pace than peers • Use modeling, prompting, and shaping • Allow time for students to practice, review, and use information in a variety of settings • Teachers should use positive affirmations and words of encouragement
	Soukup and Feinstein (2007)	• Federal law impedes students from being identified and receiving proper services • Teachers identified 10 common characteristics of students who are d/Dhh-LD through multiple observations and collection of student work • Fifty percent of teachers stated that they feel unprepared to teach students who are d/Dhh-LD • Teacher preparation programs are not preparing teachers to work with students with specialized needs
2010–2018	Edwards (2010)	• Definition of LD by federal law excludes students who are d/Dhh and adoption of the NJCLD and Laughton's (1989) definitions • Explains paucity of research due to complexity of LD and d/Dhh characteristics; role of cultural, cognitive, and linguistics diversity in assessing and the lack of norms; lack of training for practitioners • RTI as a model of evaluation through increasing intensity of the intervention, necessary for d/Dhh-LD learners; delineates poor instruction from LD; implementation varies across educators • Future recommendations: intervention research; norms across tests; increase understanding of LD through neuroimaging

(*Continued*)

TABLE 7.3 (*Continued*)

Decade	Literature	Findings/Recommendations
2010–2018	Caemmerer et al. (2016)	• Definition of LD by federal law excludes students who are d/Dhh • Math calculations and grades can aid in the identification of students who are d/Dhh-LD

Note. ACLD = Association for Children and Adults With Learning Disabilities; LD = learning disability; SLD = specific LD; IDEA = Individuals With Disabilities Education Act; EBD = emotional behavior disorders; IQ = intelligence quotient; NJCLD = National Joint Committee on Learning Disabilities; d/Dhh = d/Deaf or hard of hearing recommended to identify and refer d/Dhh learners who require further support in the classroom to be successful (Calderon, 1998; Roth, 1991). Research with teachers highlights the skill areas in which learners experience difficulty across a hierarchy; those reported with the highest-to-lowest frequency include the following: (a) memory, (b) visual perception, (c) attention, (d) inconsistent performance, (e) poor organizational skills, (f) achievement–potential discrepancy, (g) atypical language development for d/Dhh, (h) behavior, and (i) learning style (Powers et al., 1988).

Strategies and Practices

Determining strategies and practices to address these skill areas with learners who are d/Dhh-LD is a crucial next step, considering the minimal research that has been conducted. Inquiry-based learning under the Universal Design for Learning (UDL; Rose & Gravel, 2010) framework across levels of support may assist learners in processing and synthesizing information via differentiated instruction (Guardino & Cannon, 2022, see Chapters 1 and 10 for further discussion of UDL and educational frameworks to support DWD learners). This call for research is even more crucial considering some researchers report that learners who are d/Dhh-LD do not respond to strategies that typically help support d/Dhh peers (Berent et al., 2000). It may be necessary to conduct research within this unique population to determine the supports they need for success (Edwards, 2010). We challenge all researchers, practitioners, funding agencies, and parents to advocate for research with learners who are d/Dhh-LD utilizing single-case design and other research design methodologies.

Examining the available research (see Table 7.3), we concluded the following recommendations for parents and practitioners: (a) use of modeling, prompting, and shaping; (b) allowing time for students to practice, review, and use information in a variety of settings; (c) use of positive reinforcement and encouragement with learners; (d) conducting phonological awareness training, particularly in conjunction with early intervention services, to reduce future difficulty and serve as a possible screener; (e) using interactive multimedia to decrease processing deficits; and (f) utilizing inquiry-based and experiential learning activities (Samar et al., 1998; Sikora & Plapinger, 1994; Stewart & Kluwin, 2001).

Accommodations

Accommodations may also be provided as supports to learners in order to improve access to the classroom materials and information presented during instruction, as well as to ensure an accurate assessment (Leppo et al., 2013). Learners who are d/Dhh-LD are more likely to use particular accommodations than those without LD and are more likely to use a reader for testing but less likely to use tutors to support instruction (Leppo et al., 2013). It is vital to remember that the learner's hearing level should not be the sole focus for assessments, instead a holistic picture of the learner and their integrated needs is optimal (Leppo et al., 2013).

CONCLUSION

The predicament involving definitions and various terminology associated with LD and those learners who are d/Dhh-LD is critical to understand because it provides a historical context for the current state of the field. Learners who are d/Dhh-LD have the highest incidence rate among d/Dhh learners, yet there still seems to be confusion as to the characteristics that define these learners. This debate may have contributed to the lack of consensus in the literature regarding the use of standardized assessments with students who are d/Dhh until 1994 (Sikora & Plapinger, 1994; see Table 7.3). More recently, frameworks such as RTI and dynamic assessment have been recommended to delineate poor instruction from an actual LD (Edwards, 2010; Wood & Dockrell, 2010). Recommendations also include the use of a transdisciplinary team that supports collaboration among professionals, especially between the TDHH and a specialist in LD (Roth, 1991), while recognizing the logistical challenges that these collaborations may cause. The available literature provides (a) vital skill areas that teachers and parents can monitor, (b) strategies that may improve academic performance, and (c) accommodations to provide access in the evaluation process and in the classroom. Resources to utilize when working with learners who are d/Dhh-LD, their families, and when collaborating with other professionals are provided in the Resources section of this chapter. Finally, we remind the reader of the importance of future research with these heterogeneous learners that investigates individualized assessment, practices, strategies, and accommodations so that they may effectively participate and strive in various learning environments.

Discussion Questions

1. Why are the conflicting definitions and various terminologies associated with learning disability(ies) a potential barrier to adequately serving students who are d/Dhh-LD?
2. What are the challenges of identifying an LD with learners who are d/Dhh?
3. What factors must teachers and other professionals consider when assessing d/Dhh students for a potential LD?
4. Upon examining the review of literature across the decades regarding learners who are d/Dhh-LDs, what are the trends in research findings/recommendations?
5. What are three strategies, practices, and accommodations to utilize with learners who are d/Dhh with an LD?

Resources

- **Council for Learning Disabilities (CLD)**
  - https://council-for-learning-disabilities.org/
  - CLD is an international organization that works to improve the education and quality of life for those with learning disabilities.
- **Learning Disabilities Association (LDA)**
  - https://ldaamerica.org/
  - LDA supports people with learning disabilities, their parents, teachers, and other professionals by providing a wide variety of information on learning disabilities, including strategies, solutions, and a plethora of resources.
- **LD Online**
  - http://www.ldonline.org/
  - This website serves as a resource for educators who teach students with learning disabilities and attention deficit hyperactivity disorder.

- **Learning Disability Today (UK)**
  - https://www.learningdisabilitytoday.co.uk/ldt-blog
  - Learning Disability Today is a resource based out of the United Kingdom. The website contains blogs that discuss common issues, misconceptions, and success stories related to individuals with learning disabilities. In addition, research and resources are provided.
- **National Center for Learning Disabilities (NCLD)**
  - https://www.ncld.org/
  - The NCLD works to improve the lives of those with learning disabilities by educating society and advocating for those with an LD so that every individual has an equal opportunity to succeed.
- **National Center for Learning Disabilities Blog**
  - https://www.ncld.org/blog
  - The NCLD blog provides articles for professionals and families regarding policy, advocacy, and education affecting those with learning disabilities.
- **Raising Deaf Kids**
  - http://www.raisingdeafkids.org/special/ld/
  - This site informs parents on their child's special needs and tells them "How You Can Help Your Child," with specific information regarding students who are deaf with learning disabilities.
- **Smart Kids With LD**
  - https://www.smartkidswithld.org/
  - Smart Kids With LD is a blog run by a nonprofit organization that supports parents of children with learning disabilities by providing informational articles and advice.
- **TeachingLD**
  - https://www.teachingld.org/
  - TeachingLD strives to promote the education, discussion, and research related to individuals with learning disabilities. In addition, TeachingLD aims to inform professionals of effective teaching practices to use with students with LD.
- **Teacher Vision**
  - https://www.teachervision.com/teaching-strategies/special-needs
  - Teacher Vision is a website with information and resources designed for special education teachers working with a variety of students with

varying exceptionalities. The website contains content area, curriculum, and classroom management resources.

- **Understood**
  - https://www.understood.org/en
  - This website provides parents the option to chat with an expert, join a discussion, and experience things "through your child's eye." It provides informational videos and articles on LD-specific topics, such as sensory overload, IEPs, and 504 Plans, as well as screen time management.
- **Understanding DAD**
  - http://understandingdad.net/
  - Understanding Deafness and Diversity (DAD) is a website that provides resources, research, and interviews with experts about students who are deaf with varying disabilities, including learning disabilities.

References

Akamatsu, C. T., Mayer, C., & Hardy-Braz, S. (2008). Why considerations of verbal aptitude are important in educating deaf and hard-of-hearing students. In M. Marschark & P. C. Hauser (Eds.), *Deaf cognition: Foundations and outcomes* (pp. 131–169). Oxford University Press.

Andrews, J. F., Leigh, I. W., & Weiner, M. T. (2003). *Deaf people: Evolving perspectives from psychology, education, and sociology.* Allyn & Bacon.

Ansell, E., & Pagliaro, C. M. (2001). Effects of a signed translation on the types and difficulties of arithmetic story problems. *Focus on Learning Problems in Mathematics, 23*(2 & 3), 41–69.

Association for Children and Adults With Learning Disabilities. (1983). Definition of the condition, specific learning disabilities. *ACLD Newsbrief, 158*, 1 & 3.

Auxter, D. (1971). Learning disabilities among deaf populations. *Exceptional Children, 37*, 573–577.

Berent, G. P., Samar, V. J., & Parasnis, I. (2000). College teachers' perceptions of English language characters that identify English language learning disabled deaf students. *American Annals of the Deaf, 145*(4), 342–357.

Beery, K. E., Buktenica, N. A., & Beery, N. A. (2010). *Beery-Buktenica developmental test of visual motor integration.* Pearson Education.

Braden, J. P. (2001). The clinical assessment of deaf people's cognitive abilities. In M. D. Clark, M. Marschark, & M. Karchmer (Eds.), *Context, cognition, and deafness* (pp. 14–37). Gallaudet University Press.

Braden, J. P. (2005). Hard of hearing and deaf clients: Using the WISC-IV with clients who are hard of hearing or deaf. In A. Priftera, D. H. Saklofske, & L. G. Weiss (Eds.), *WISC-IV: Clinical use and interpretation. Scientist-practitioner perspectives* (pp. 352–381). Elsevier Academic.

Bunch, G. O., & Melnyk, T-L. (1989). A review of the evidence for a learning disabled, hearing impaired sub-group. *American Annals of the Deaf, 134,* 297–300.

Caemmerer, J. M., Cawthon, S. W., & Bond, M. (2016). Comparison of students' achievement: Deaf, learning disabled, and deaf with a learning disability. *School Psychology Review, 45*(3), 362–371.

Calderon, R. (1998). Learning disability, neuropsychology, and deaf youth: Theory, research, and practice. *Journal of Deaf Studies and Deaf Education, 3*(1), 1–3.

Cannon, J. E., & Luckner, J. (2016). Increasing cultural and linguistic diversity in deaf education teacher preparation programs. *American Annals of the Deaf, 161*(1), 89–103.

Cawthon, S. (2015). From the margins to the spotlight: Diverse deaf and hard of hearing student populations and standardized assessment accessibility. *American Annals of the Deaf, 160*(4), 385–394.

Cejas, I., Sarangoulis, C. M., Mestres, A., Nelson, J. A., & Quittner, A. L. (2022). Assessments and strategies for learners who are d/Deaf or hard of hearing with emotional and behavioral challenges. In C. Guardino, J. E. Cannon, & P. V. Paul (Eds.), *Deaf and hard of hearing learners with disabilities: Foundations, strategies, and resources* (pp. 230–261). Routledge.

Edwards, E. (2007). Children with cochlear implants and complex needs: A review of outcome research and psychological practice. *Journal of Deaf Studies and Deaf Education, 12*(3), 258–268. https://doi.org/10.1093/deafed/enm007

Edwards, L. (2010). Learning disabilities in deaf and hard-of-hearing children. In M. Marschark & P. E. Spencer (Eds.), *The Oxford handbook of deaf studies, language, and education* (Vol. 2, pp. 425–438). Oxford University Press.

Edward, L., & Crocker, S. (2008). *Psychological processes in deaf children with complex needs: An evidence-based practical guide.* Jessica Kingsley.

Elliott, R., & Powers, A. (1988). Preparing teachers to serve the learning disabled hearing impaired. *Volta Review, 90*, 13–18.

Gallaudet Research Institute (GRI). (2013). *Regional and national summary report of data from the 2011–2012 Annual Survey of Deaf and Hard of Hearing Children and Youth.* https://www.gallaudet.edu/office-of-international-affairs/demographics

Guardino, C., & Cannon, J. E. (2015). Theory, research, and practice for students who are deaf and hard of hearing with disabilities: Addressing the challenges from birth to postsecondary education. *American Annals of the Deaf, 160*(4), 347–355. https://doi.org/10.1353/aad.2015.0033

Guardino, C., & Cannon, J. E. (2022). Approaches and frameworks that support students who are d/Deaf or hard of hearing with a disabilities. In C. Guardino, J. E. Cannon, & P. V. Paul (Eds.), *Deaf and hard of hearing learners with disabilities: Foundations, strategies, and resources* (pp. 1–24). Routledge.

Guardino, C., & Cannon, J. E. (2022). Cycles of support and tenets of effective practice for learners who are d/Deaf or hard of hearing with disabilities. In C. Guardino, J. E. Cannon, & P. V. Paul (Eds.), *Deaf and hard of hearing learners with disabilities: Foundations, strategies, and resources* (pp. 288–300). Routledge.

Hagger, D. (1972). Specific learning difficulties and deaf children. *Australian Teacher of the Deaf, 13*(1), 13–19.

Hawkins-Shepard, C. (1977). *Educational planning for deaf children with learning disabilities* (ERIC Document Reproduction Service No. ED150 789).

Hill, J. W., Luetke-Stahlman, B., & Kapel, D. E. (1985). *Validating teacher suspected dual diagnosis among select deaf students also thought to be learning disabled* (ERIC Document Reproduction Service No. ED 276 231).

Hoover, J. J., Erickson, J. R., Herron, S. R., & Smith, C. E. (2018). Implementing culturally and linguistically responsive special education eligibility assessment in rural county elementary schools: Pilot project. *Rural Special Education Quarterly, 37*(2), 90–102.

Individuals With Disabilities Education Act (IDEA) of 2004, 20 U.S.C. §§ 1400–1482 (2004 & rev. 2017).

Isaacson, S. L. (1996). Simple ways to assess deaf or hard-of-hearing students' writing skills. *Volta Review, 98*(1), 183–199.

Jackson, R. L. W., Ammerman, S. B., & Trautwein, B. A. (2015). Deafness and diversity: Early intervention. *American Annals of the Deaf, 160*(4), 356–367.

Kritzer, K., Pagliaro, C., & Ansell, E. (2004). Deaf/hard of hearing students' use of language cues to solve signed story problems. *EdPitt, 1*(1). http://www.pitt.edu/~edpitt/currentissueKRITZER.html

LaSasso, C. (1985). Learning disabilities: Let's be careful before labeling deaf children. *Perspectives, 3*(5), 2–4.

Laughton, J. (1989). The learning disabled, hearing impaired student: Reality, myth, or overextension? *Topics in Language Disorders, 9*(4), 70–79.

Leppo, R. H. T., Cawthon, S. W., & Bond, M. P. (2013). Including deaf and hard of hearing students with co-occurring disabilities in the accommodations discussion. *Journal of Deaf Studies and Deaf Education, 19*(2), 189–202.

Luckner, J., & Pierce, C. (2013). Response to intervention and students who are deaf or hard of hearing. *Deafness and Education International, 15*(4), 222–240. https://doi.org/10.1179/1557069X 13Y.0000000027

Maller, S. J. (2003). Intellectual assessment of deaf people: A critical review of core concepts and issues. In M. Marschark & P. E. Spencer (Eds.), *Oxford handbook of deaf studies, language, and education* (Vol. 1, pp. 451–463). Oxford University Press.

Mauk, G. W., & Mauk, P. P. (1992). Somewhere, out there: Preschool children with hearing impairment and learning disabilities. *Topics in Early Childhood Special Education: Hearing Impaired Preschoolers, 12*(2), 174–195.

Mauk, G. W., & Mauk, P. P. (1998). Considerations, conceptualizations, and challenges in the study of concomitant learning disabilities among children and adolescents who are deaf or hard of hearing. *Journal of Deaf Studies and Deaf Education, 3*(1), 15–34.

McCracken, W., Ravichandran, A., & Laoide-Kemp, S. (2008). Audiological certainty in deaf children with learning disabilities: An imperative for inter-agency working. *Deafness and Education International, 10*(1), 4–21. https://doi.org/10.1002/dei.231

Miller, M. S. (1991). Experimental use of signed presentations of the verbal scale of the WISC-R with profoundly deaf children: A preliminary report. In D. S. Martin (Ed.), *Cognition, education, and deafness: Directions for research and instruction* (pp. 134–136). Gallaudet University Press.

Mitchell, R. E., & Karchmer, M. A. (2010). Demographic and achievement characteristics of deaf and hard of hearing students. In M. Marschark & P. E. Spencer (Eds.), *Oxford handbook of deaf studies, language, and education* (Vol. 2, pp. 18–31). Oxford University Press.

Morgan, A., & Vernon, M. (1994). A guide to the diagnosis of learning disabilities in deaf and hard of hearing children and adults. *American Annals of the Deaf, 139*, 358–370.

National Joint Committee on Learning Disabilities (NJCLD). (2016). *Definition of learning disabilities.* https://njcld.files.wordpress.com/2018/10/ld-definition.pdf

Nelson, N. W., & Crumpton, T. (2015). Reading, writing, and spoken language assessment profiles for students who are deaf and hard of hearing compared with students with language learning disabilities. *Topics in Language Disorders, 35*(2), 157–179.

Pisoni, D. B., Conway, C. M., Kronengerger, W. G., Horn, D. L., Karpicke, J., & Henning, S. C. (2008). Efficacy and effectiveness of cochlear implants in deaf children. In M. Marschark & P. C. Hauser (Eds.), *Deaf cognition: Foundations and outcomes* (pp. 52–101). Oxford University Press.

Pizzo, L., & Chilvers, A. (2016). Assessment and d/Deaf and hard of hearing multilingual learners: Considerations and promising practice. *American Annals of the Deaf, 161*(1), 56–66.

Plapinger, D., & Sikora, D. (1990). Diagnosing a learning disability in a hearing-impaired child. *American Annals of the Deaf, 135*, 285–292.

Powers, A., Elliott, R., Fairbank, D., & Monaghan, C. (1988). The dilemma of identifying learning disabled hearing impaired students. *Volta Review, 90*, 209–218.

Powers, A., Elliott, R., & Funderburg, R. (1987). Learning disabled hearing-impaired students: Are they being identified? *Volta Review, 89,* 99–105.

Powers, A. R., & Harris, A. R. (1982). Strategies for teaching language-and/or learning-disabled hearing-impaired children. In D. Tweedie & E. H. Shroyer (Eds.), *The multihandicapped hearing impaired: Identification and instruction* (pp. 249–263). Gallaudet College.

Rose, D. H., & Gravel, J. W. (2010). Universal design for learning. In E. Baker, P. Peterson, & B. McGaw (Eds.), *International encyclopedia of education* (3rd ed., pp. 119–124). Elsevier. http://www.udlcenter.org/resource_library/articles/udl

Roth, V. (1991). Students with learning disabilities and hearing impairment: Issues for the secondary and postsecondary teacher. *Journal of Learning Disabilities, 24*(7), 391–397.

Samar, V. J., Paranis, I., & Berent, G. P. (1998). Learning disabilities, attention deficit disorders, and deafness. In M. Marschark & M. D. Clark (Eds.), *Psychological perspectives on deafness* (Vol. 2, pp. 199–242). Erlbaum.

Samar, V. (1999). Identifying learning disabilities in the deaf population: The leap from Gibraltar. *NTID Research Bulletin, 4*(1), 1–4.

Sikora, M. D., & Plapinger, S. D. (1994). Using standardized psychometric tests to identify learning disabilities in students with sensorineural hearing impairments. *Journal of Learning Disabilities, 27*(6), 352–359.

Sligar, S. R., Cawthon, S., Morere, D., & Moxley, A. (2013). Equity in assessment for individuals who are deaf or hard of hearing. *Journal of the American Deafness & Rehabilitation Association (JADARA), 47*(1), 110–127.

Soukup, M., & Feinstein, S. (2007). Identification, assessment, and intervention strategies for deaf and hard of hearing students with learning disabilities. *American Annals of the Deaf, 152*(1), 56–62.

Stewart, D. A., & Kluwin, T. N. (2001). Classroom management and learning disabilities. In D. A. Stewart & T. N. Kluwin (Eds.), *Teaching deaf and hard of hearing students: Content, strategies, and curriculum* (pp. 289–313). Allyn & Bacon.

Van Vuuren, E. (1995, July 16–20). *The deaf pupil with learning disabilities* [Paper presentation]. International Congress on Education of the Deaf, Tel Aviv, Israel.

Vockell, E. L., Hirshoren, A., & Vockell, K. (1972). A critique of Auxter's "Learning disabilities among deaf populations." *Exceptional Children, 38*, 647–650.

Wiley, S. (2014). Children who are deaf or hard of hearing with additional learning needs. *Perspectives on Hearing Disorders in Childhood, 22*(2), 57–67. http://doi.org/10.1044/hhdc22.2.57

Wood, N., & Dockrell, J. (2010). Psychological assessment procedures for assessing deaf or hard-of-hearing children. *Educational & Child Psychology, 27*(2), 11–22.

8

Assessment and Strategies for Learners Who Are d/Deaf or Hard of Hearing With Emotional and Behavioral Challenges

Ivette Cejas, Christina M. Sarangoulis, Alex Mestres, Jenna A. Nelson, and Alexandra L. Quittner

LEARNING OBJECTIVES

Readers will:

- Identify common externalizing and internalizing challenges in d/Deaf and hard of hearing (d/Dhh) children.
- Discuss screening measures and tools that can identify children at-risk for emotional and behavioral disorders.
- Describe evidence-based interventions for externalizing and internalizing behaviors.
- Provide additional resources regarding assessment and instructional strategies to use with d/Dhh learners with emotional and behavioral challenges.

Deaf and hard of hearing (d/Dhh) children may face a number of challenges across their life span that affect their developmental, social, and educational outcomes. Although the focus is often on providing access to communication and language, children's behavioral and emotional development is often not addressed. Children with varying

DOI: 10.4324/9781003252054-8

hearing levels are at greater risk for both externalizing and internalizing behavioral challenges, and these difficulties are often linked to significant language and communication delays (Barker et al., 2009; Stevenson et al., 2015; Theunissen et al., 2015).

This chapter focuses on discussing behavior challenges in this population, including assessments and instructional strategies. Readers are encouraged to think about the impact of language deprivation in individuals who are d/Dhh and how that influences the higher rates of behavior problems reported in the literature. Auditory deprivation or lack of an accessible language may cause delays that impact behavior. The window for developing language does not change for visual versus spoken communication, and it is important that d/Dhh children have access to language, regardless of modality (Hall, 2017). The bulk of the research that exists on students who are d/Dhh with emotional behavioral challenges is focused on students who receive cochlear implants (CIs) or use hearing aids. Additional research across all students who are deaf with emotional behavioral challenges, regardless of use or absence of assistive technology, is imperative for better understanding this population of learners.

Defining Emotional Behavioral Disorder

The Individuals With Disabilities Education Act (IDEA, 2004) of the United States defines emotional disturbance as follows:

> The term emotional disturbance means a condition exhibiting one or more of the following characteristics over a long period of time and to a marked degree that adversely affects a student's educational performance:
>
> (A) An inability to learn which cannot be explained by intellectual, sensory, or health factors
> (B) An inability to build or maintain satisfactory interpersonal relationships with peers and teachers
> (C) Inappropriate types of behavior or feelings under normal circumstances

(D) A general pervasive mood of unhappiness or depression
(E) A tendency to develop physical symptoms or fears associated with person or school problems.

The term includes children who are schizophrenic. The term does not include students who are socially maladjusted, unless it is determined that they have an emotional disturbance. (§ 300.8 [c] [4] [i])

The terms "emotional" or "behavioral disorder" mean a disability that is characterized by the following: (1) behavioral or emotional responses in school programs, which are different from the responses of a typical child of appropriate age, cultural, or ethnic norms and which adversely affect educational performance, including academic, social, vocational, or professional skills; (2) more than a temporary, expected response to stressful events in the environment; (3) consistently exhibited in two different settings, at least one of which is school-related; and (4) unresponsive to direct intervention applied in general education, or the condition of a child is such that general education interventions would be insufficient (Weller-Clarke, 2011).

Externalizing Versus Internalizing Behaviors

As previously mentioned, children who are d/Dhh are at greater risk of struggling with externalizing and internalizing behavior challenges. Externalized behaviors are observable and reflect the child's interactions with the environment (e.g., inattentive, disruptive, hyperactive, or aggressive). These difficulties in young children are fairly common and are often characterized as a typical developmental phase (e.g., terrible twos). However, early behavior problems are considered risk factors for future behavior challenges, poor academic performance, and peer rejection. Children manifesting problematic externalizing behaviors in early childhood are likely to continue having behavior difficulties during school age, adolescence, and adulthood (Campbell et al., 2000; Moffitt & Caspi, 2001; Pierce et al., 1999). In its more severe form, these behaviors can be associated with disorders, such as attention deficit hyperactivity disorder (ADHD), oppositional defiant disorder (ODD), and conduct disorder (CD).

Internalizing behaviors affect the child's internal environment and reflect his/her emotional adjustment (e.g., anxiety, excessive worrying, depression, withdrawal; see Table 8.1). Similarly, they have been linked to children's future mood, learning, academic, and conduct challenges (Bornstein et al., 2010; Kovacs & Devlin, 1998; Kremer et al., 2016). Importantly, internalizing behaviors are often overlooked because they cause little disruption in social contexts.

Although we will discuss several common disorders found in childhood, our intention is not to label or diagnose these children but to help professionals and teachers identify these behaviors to intervene early and to prevent long-term negative consequences. Furthermore, although children who are d/Dhh are at higher risk for these disorders, little is known about the actual rate of clinical diagnoses in this population. Moreover,

TABLE 8.1 Types of Behaviors and Corresponding Disorders

Externalizing Behaviors	Internalizing Behaviors
Difficulty paying attention/distractibility	Frequent sadness, tearfulness, and crying
Physical or verbal aggression	Decreased interest in activities
Difficulty in organizing tasks	Persistent boredom, low energy
Anger	Sensitivity to rejection or failure
Impulsivity	Poor concentration
Disruptive	Increased irritability
Externalizing Disorders	Internalizing Disorders
Attention deficit hyperactivity disorder	Anxiety
Oppositional defiant disorder/conduct disorder	Depression

there is little-to-no literature disentangling how these rates differ by degree of hearing loss, type of hearing device used, or communication method (spoken versus visual). Research is needed to help identify children who are at a greater risk for emotional behavior challenges and the evidence-based interventions that are most effective for these learners. This chapter will focus on current available literature and clinical recommendations for management of emotional and behavioral disorders.

EXTERNALIZING BEHAVIOR CHALLENGES

The prevalence of externalizing behavior difficulties in typically developing children is 3%–18% (Hinshaw & Lee, 2003); in children with varying hearing levels, the prevalence is much higher, at 30%–38% (Cejas et al., 2015; Van Eldik et al., 2004; Vostanis et al., 1997). A large-scale national study of externalizing behavior challenges in d/Dhh toddlers and preschoolers (ages 1.5–5 years) awaiting CI surgery found higher rates of difficulties compared to children with typical hearing across a variety of measures (e.g., video observations, parent rating scales; Barker et al., 2009). Participants were identified with severe language delays and used spoken English, American Sign Language (ASL), and a combination of spoken and manual communication. Barker et al. (2009) describe that the increased behavioral challenges may be a cause of their inability to express needs and wants, as well as understand societal rules. Significant differences in attention were found between hearing children and d/Dhh children on a parent rating scale and in observations of child negativity during structured and unstructured play tasks (e.g., pushing, irritability, frustration).

A study of attention and hyperactivity in school-age children with CIs reported a higher percentage of behavior challenges and attentional diffi-culties (11%), such as impulsive responding and distractibility, using both a parent rating scale and a continuous performance task (CPT; Hoffman et al., 2018). Notably, parents' reports of behavior challenges correlated with the child's performance on the CPT. These findings illustrate the challenges d/Dhh children have in dividing their attention between auditory and visual stimuli. These children often "look" distracted because they need to monitor their environment visually in the absence of clear auditory information from their hearing aids or CIs and, thus, have trouble focusing on the task at hand (Quittner et al., 2007).

Attention Deficit Hyperactivity Disorder

Children with ADHD are often described as learners who have trouble paying attention, are easily distractible and fidgety, have difficulty staying seated, and struggle with peer relationships. A number of these behaviors must be present across multiple contexts (e.g., home, school) for a diagnosis of ADHD to be considered. ADHD is more commonly diagnosed in men than in women (2.28:1), with 50% of diagnoses occurring before age 7, 95% before age 12, and 99% before age 16 (Kieling et al., 2010; Norman et al., 2022, see Chapter 9; Ramtekkar et al., 2010).

The research on ADHD in the d/Dhh population is limited; however, it is estimated that between 5.4% and 11.8% of d/Dhh children have ADHD compared to about 3%–5% of hearing children (Sibley, 2015). Despite limited research on clinical diagnoses of ADHD, these children are at a higher risk for attention problems and are often identified later (Cejas et al., 2015). Researchers have found that children with CIs tend to improve or "catch up" to their hearing peers in their visual attention skills (Hoffman et al., 2018; Quittner et al., 2007).

Oppositional Defiant Disorder/Conduct Disorder

The symptoms of ODD include impatience, being easily annoyed and argumentative, purposely annoying and bothering others, and blaming others for mistakes. These behaviors must be present for a substantial amount of time (e.g., 6 months) and occur frequently (American Psychiatric Association, 2013). ODD is typically diagnosed in younger children and is more common among men than women (3.2% vs 1.8%; Boylan et al., 2007).

Conduct disorder is characterized as "a repetitive and persistent pattern of behavior in which the basic rights of others or major age-appropriate societal norms or rules are violated" (American Psychiatric Association, 2013, p. 469). Symptoms include, but are not limited to, bullying, threatening or intimidating others, initiating physical fights, deliberately setting fires, breaking into someone's house, and truancy, with onset before 13 years. To be diagnosed with CD, several symptoms must be present and those behaviors must have been observed or measured over a 12-month period. Furthermore, these symptoms must cause significant impairment in functioning (American Psychiatric Association, 2013). Symptoms of CD typically start in middle childhood or adolescence and are more common among men (Substance Abuse and Mental Health Services Administration, 2011).

Currently, the rates of ODD/CD in the d/Dhh population are unknown; however, d/Dhh children are at higher risk for these disorders (Barker et al., 2009; Mitchell & Quittner, 1996). Fiorillo et al. (2017) found that 48% of children aged 2–5 years who were d/Dhh met the diagnostic criteria for ODD. This was true for both children with hearing aids and children with CIs. As Fiorillo and her colleagues discuss, reasons for this increase in ODD symptoms may be caused by additional comorbidities, language delays, poor communication skills, and the quality and dynamics of the parent–child relationship (Fiorillo et al., 2017).

INTERNALIZING BEHAVIOR

Internalizing behaviors are characterized by sad or worried affect, social withdrawal, negative emotions, and negative self-image. The prevalence of internalizing behavior challenges in typically developing children is 2%–17% (Albano et al., 2003; Hammen & Rudolph, 2003), compared to 25%–38% in children who are d/Dhh (Barker et al., 2009; Theunissen et al., 2012; van Eldik et al., 2004). Two common internalizing disorders are anxiety and depression.

Anxiety

Anxiety disorders affect 17%–24% of all children, with several specific subcategories. The most common and broad diagnosis is generalized anxiety disorder (GAD). To have a diagnosis of GAD, one must have excessive anxiety and worry most of the time over a period of 6 months. In addition, the worry must be difficult to control. Children must also experience one additional symptom, such as irritability, sleep disturbance, or difficulty in concentrating. These symptoms must impact the child's functioning at home and at school (American Psychiatric Association, 2013). Additional subcategories of anxiety include separation anxiety, phobias, social anxiety, and panic disorder. For children, the type of anxiety diagnosed differs by age. Children younger than 12 years of age are commonly diagnosed with separation anxiety or specific phobias, while social phobias occur more often in adolescence. GAD is often identified in later adolescence and into adulthood (Beesdo et al., 2009).

The majority of research has shown that school-age and adolescent learners who are d/Dhh have higher levels of anxiety, as confirmed via self-report forms, compared to learners with typical hearing levels (Li & Prevatt, 2010; Theunissen et al., 2012; Van Eldik, 2005). These studies also report that children who are d/Dhh with anxiety describe the world as more fearful and intimidating. However, some researchers have reported that there is no difference in anxiety between hearing children and those who are d/Dhh (Remine & Brown, 2010). Theunissen et al. (2012) reported that learners using CIs might not have higher rates of general and social anxiety; thus, the difference was attributed to those learners who used hearing aids, of ages 9–15 years, who reported more social anxiety. In addition, they noted that the age at which the learners received their CIs, along with longer CI usage, was related to lower levels of anxiety. Similarly, parents of hearing aid users also reported that their child was more prone to develop symptoms consistent with generalized anxiety.

Depression

Depression is characterized by persistent feelings of sadness, diminished interest in activities, fatigue or loss of energy, feelings of worthlessness or excessive guilt, and changes in eating and sleeping patterns. Childhood depression is rare, but it increases in adolescence and is more common in women. Estimates of depression range from 0.4% to 2.5% for children and from 0.4% to 8.3% for adolescents (Albert, 2015; Birmaher et al., 1997; Costello et al., 2006). To be diagnosed with depression, several of the symptoms listed above must be present for 2 weeks almost every day (American Psychiatric Association, 2013).

Several studies have reported a higher prevalence of depression in d/Dhh learners compared to learners with typical hearing levels (Konuk et al.,

2006; Van Eldik, 2005; Van Eldik et al., 2004). However, one study examining depression in adolescents who used CIs did not find any differences (Sahli et al., 2009). Specifically, incidence of depression in the d/Dhh population has been estimated to be about 7%, whereas lifetime prevalence of depression is far greater, approximately 26% (Fellinger et al., 2009; Kim et al., 2017). Studies have reported that children who are d/Dhh who have been teased, isolated, or maltreated are more likely to have depression (Fellinger et al., 2009; Mick et al., 2014). Moreover, learners who are d/Dhh with disabilities (e.g., visual impairment, neurological disorders, and cognitive delays) are at higher risk for depression (Huber & Kipman, 2011). Theunissen et al. (2011) examined the depressive symptoms of 83 children with CIs or conventional hearing aids compared with 117 children with typical hearing. Participants who were d/Dhh, those who attended mainstream settings, or those who used only speech to communicate had fewer depressive symptoms. The results also showed that participants who were deaf reported more depressive symptoms than the hearing participants. This is important for educators and caregivers to keep in mind so that preventative and treatment measures can be initiated to help support the emotional and behavioral well-being of students who are d/Dhh.

MEASURES AND SCREENING TOOLS

There are several age-appropriate measures of externalizing and internalizing behavior that can be used with d/Dhh children to identify those with significant challenges (see Table 8.2). This information can be used to identify learners in need of assistance and those who need intervention. Standardized measures allow for a comparison between that individual and an age- and gender-normed group, facilitating the identification and referral process. There are challenges in using standardized measures that are not normed on d/Dhh children. It is important to consider the child's reading ability and preferred mode of communication if the measure is self-reported.

When administering any of these measures, accommodations (similar to academic testing accommodations) should be used for d/Dhh learners. These accommodations may include extra time, interpretation of test content, and alternate test forms. Cawthon (2008) reported that the most common accommodations used by teachers for their d/Dhh students were as follows: (a) administering the test content in a small group or separate room; (b) allowing for extra time; and (c) interpreting test directions. Other accommodations included interpreting the test items into ASL, reading the questions out loud to the student, and allowing the students to sign their answers with a scribe writing it (Cawthon, 2008, 2010).

Applications to Collect Behavioral Data

Electronic applications ("apps") can be used to track a learner's behavior to analyze behavioral trends that can lead to the diagnosis of a behaviorial or emotional challenge. These apps make the process of collecting behavioral data much quicker and more seamless without the need for storage of paper forms, hand scoring, and manual data entry. Apps are efficient at organizing and presenting the information in an interpretable format. There are several behavioral tracking apps available (see Table 8.3).

INSTRUCTIONAL APPROACHES AND STRATEGIES

Positive Behavioral Supports

When a child's behavior interferes with their learning or overall functioning, it is important for professionals to take a proactive stance in turning negative behaviors into positive ones. Positive behavioral support (PBS; Carr et al., 2002) is one mechanism that addresses a learner's behavior in conjunction with their differing communication levels, needs, and abilities. PBS requires professionals to analyze what the student is communicating through their behavior and assists them with identifying more appropriate behaviors to replace the negative ones. Given that information, classroom personnel can develop strategies to help the student maintain positive outcomes. Some strategies may include routines, sitting near the teacher, and/or a prearranged signal that the teacher or learner can give to communicate without having to single out the child. For example, if a student is constantly throwing their pencil, PBS will identify why this is happening. If it is because the student does not understand the lesson and

TABLE 8.2 Measures and Screening Tools

Test Title	Test Description	Age Range	Language(s)
Child Behavior Checklist (CBCL; Achenbach, 1983)	• Measures behavior and emotional challenges • Self, parent, and teacher forms	• Parents of children 1.5–5 years • 6–18 years	• Several languages
Behavior Assessment System for Children (BASC; Reynolds & Kamphaus, 2015)	• Assesses behavior and self-perceptions of children and young adults • Self, parent, and teacher forms	• 2–25 years	• Several languages
Parents' Evaluation of Developmental Status (PEDS; Glascoe, 2013)	• Evaluates parental concerns, such as language, motor, self-help, early academic skills, behavior, and social-emotional/mental health in children • Can be completed in 2 minutes	• Birth–8 years	• 35+ languages
Vineland Adaptive Behavior Scales (VABS; Sparrow et al., 2016)	• Measures of adaptive behavior that assess intellectual, developmental, and other disabilities • Interview, as well as self and teacher forms	• Birth to adulthood	• English and Spanish

Test Title	Test Description	Age Range	Language(s)
Meadow/Kendall Social-Emotional Assessment Inventory for Deaf Students (SEAI; Meadow, 1980)	• Preschool version: sociable and communicative behaviors; impulsive and dominating behaviors • School-age version: social adjustment, self-image, and emotional assessment • Completed by teachers in close contact with students who are d/Dhh • Developed prior to newborn hearing screening and access to cochlear implants for children	• Preschool version: 3–7 years • School-age version: 7–21 years	• English
Task-based measures of attention (Gordon Diagnostic System and Conners' CPT 3; Gordon, 1986; Conners, 2014)	• Measures sustained and selective attention, impulsivity, and distractibility • Connors: Can be self-administered • Gordon: Good test for children who are d/Dhh because there is no verbal or auditory component, computerized	• Gordon: 4–16 years • Connors: 8 years to adulthood	• N/A

(*Continued*)

TABLE 8.2 (*Continued*)

Test Title	Test Description	Age Range	Language(s)
Revised Children's Manifest Anxiety Scale: Second Edition (RCMAS-2; Reynolds, 2008)	• Identifies source and level of anxiety in children	• 6–19 years	• English, Italian, and Spanish
Screen for Child Anxiety Related Emotional Disorders (SCARED; Birmaher et al., 1997)	• Evaluates symptoms of anxiety disorders in four domains (panic/somatic, separation anxiety, generalized anxiety, and school phobia) • Takes 10 minutes to administer • Parent and child version	• 8–18 years	• Many world languages
Generalized Anxiety Disorder (GAD-7; Spitzer et al., 2006)	• Identifies symptoms of anxiety • Takes <5 minutes to complete	• 12 years to adulthood	• All major world languages

Test Title	Test Description	Age Range	Language(s)
Children's Depression Inventory (CDI; Kovacs, 2011)	• Assesses cognitive, affective, and behavioral signs of depression in children • CDI 2 takes approx.15 to 20 minutes to complete • CDI Short Form takes approx.5 minutes to complete • Teacher and parent forms	• 7–17 years	• English and Spanish
Patient Health Questionnaire-9 (PHQ-9; Kroenke et al., 2001)	• Identifies depressive symptoms • Takes <5 minutes to complete	• 12 years to adulthood	• All major world languages
Health-Related Quality of Life (HRQoL; Hoffman et al., 2018)	• Evaluates health-related quality of life in children with cochlear implants • Electronic administration using multimodal format (see Figure 8.1)	• 6–12 years	• English

TABLE 8.3 Behavior-Tracking Apps

App Icon	App Name	App Capabilities
	BehaviorSnap	• Tracks multiple behaviors simultaneously • Visually represents behaviors with graphs • Created by school psychologists
	Best Behavior	• Tracks behaviors to identify possible triggers and potential treatments
	Easy Behavior Tracker	• Allows users to log behavior data and comments • Directly contacts parents through app

feels embarrassed raising their hand, classroom personnel may develop a card system for the student. If the student understands, they will keep their card flipped on the green side. If they do not understand, they can flip it to the red side. This will allow the teacher to elaborate further on a certain point without the student feeling embarrassed and frustrated to the point that they throw the pencil.

Functional Behavioral Assessment

Functional Behavioral Assessment (FBA) is another comprehensive and individualized tool that can be used to assist school personnel in assessing concerning behaviors, including the frequency and antecedents of the behavior. Data are collected in a variety of settings and consider the variables that may lead to occurrences over an established period of time. Direct assessment during this process tracks the behavior (time of day and frequency) using an antecedent–behavior–consequence chart, allowing the whole cycle of disruption to be analyzed. During this process, indirect assessments (e.g., teacher and parent interviews) can be used to ensure an accurate representation of the behaviors. The FBA team then meets to analyze the information, creating a hypothesis of why the behaviors are occurring and to brainstorm potential solutions with the student or within the learning environment to support positive behavioral changes.

The data from the FBA is then used to develop a behavioral intervention plan (BIP), which includes parent input, to determine the best way to support the learner experiencing behavioral challenges. The FBA team can use the BIP to target behaviors and use strategies to support behavioral change. For students who are eligible for special education services, such as those who are d/Dhh, these tools should be implemented in conjunction with the individualized education plan (IEP).

If the behaviors are persistent or are part of a medical/clinical diagnosis and meet the eligibility criteria for emotional disturbance (ED), the IEP team should consider whether an additional eligibility is beneficial. By including ED as an eligibility on the IEP, using PBS, conducting an FBA, and developing a BIP, the team understands the comprehensive needs of the learner, including the impacts on their education and the possible goals, strategies, interventions, and accommodations that would promote positive academic and emotional growth.

Strategies for Externalizing Behaviors

Learners with additional disabilities, such as ADHD or ODD/CD, may also benefit from accommodations and PBS. Learners with externalizing disorders may have trouble following directions, sitting still, and paying attention. Strategies that teachers can use include (a) seating the child close to the front of the room and close to the teacher, (b) providing assignments in writing, and (c) splitting students into smaller groups for certain activities. Furthermore, these students may benefit from frequent breaks and refocusing through nonverbal cues. Learners with attention challenges can also benefit from exercise and movement in the classroom. Teachers can encourage movement by incorporating music and dance into lessons and having students get up and place their assignments in designated spots, rather than the teacher picking them up. Teachers can also take time for small breaks and encourage students to stand and stretch (Murine et al., 2008). Visual strategies, such as the use of a behavior chart and/or a picture chart illustrating what is expected of the child, can also be used to help students who are d/Dhh with behavior challenges.

Strategies for Internalizing Behaviors

For internalizing disorders, strategies may include teaching the learner mindfulness, deep breathing, and relaxation techniques. One way to teach young children deep breathing is to tell them to pretend to smell a flower (inhale) and then blow out a candle (exhale). This makes the concept of deep breaths easier for young children to understand. Teachers can also put up visual cues, such as a poster or sticky note, in areas that the learner associates with stress to remind them to use the relaxation techniques. For learners who are anxious, teachers can allow them to preview the upcoming lessons to know what to expect. There are also helpful books, such as Huebner's (2005) *What to Do When You Worry Too Much*. It is important that teachers use a collaborative approach and utilize resources such as school psychologists when needed.

Learners with varying hearing levels have also been shown to have delays in social functioning and may struggle to feel socially accepted by their peers due to language delays (Hoffman et al., 2015, 2016). In addition, learners who are d/Dhh with emotional or behavior disorders may have difficulties with pragmatics, including understanding sarcasm and humor (Jeanes et al., 2000). Social stories can be used to help role-play and model how to respond appropriately in social situations. Teachers can also facilitate activities in the classroom that help learners make friends, such as practicing turn-taking, student presentations, and small group activities.

Strategies to Improve Attention

There are many different strategies that can be used to improve an individual's overall attention (American Academy of Pediatrics [AAP], 2011), depending on the learner's needs. For preschool-aged children (4–5 years), the AAP recommends evidence-based parent and/or teacher-administered behavior therapy as the first line of treatment, as well as stimulant medication when needed. For school-aged and adolescent children, the AAP recommends a combination of stimulant medication and behavioral intervention.

Strategies that can be used to improve attention in school include the following: (a) breaking longer assignments into smaller steps; (b) repeating instructions in a clear manner; (c) using reminders such as alarm clocks, kitchen timers, and visual schedules; (d) focusing on areas of great interest to the learner; (e) seating the learner closer to the teacher to decrease distractibility; (f) giving positive feedback; (g) refocusing their attention through physical proximity; and (h) using visual and verbal cues to present information (Hoffman et al., 2018; Wender, 2001)

Cognitive Behavioral Interventions

Evidence supports therapeutic interventions that aim to enhance emotional and behavioral regulation (Disorder & Management, 2011). Cognitive behavioral therapy (CBT) is a form of psychotherapy that aims to change cognitive and behavioral patterns that interfere with everyday activities. Scheeringa et al. (2007) report that CBT can be utilized with children as young as 4 years old to address different issues, such as anxiety, depression, sleeping difficulties, posttraumatic stress disorder, ADHD, and other challenging behaviors. CBT has been used with learners with varying hearing levels. In a study of 30 d/Dhh children, ages 7–11 years, the subgroup receiving CBT had a significant reduction in anxiety and depression compared to a control group (Gharashi & Moheb, 2018).

Strategies for Families

Intervening at the family level is critically important for young learners given that parents spend a lot of time with their children and exert a major influence on their behavior. A recent study of maternal sensitivity in young children with CIs indicated that parents demonstrated less warmth and praise and greater intrusiveness (e.g., controlling their child's play or interactions) in videotaped parent–child interactions compared to parents of hearing children (Quittner et al., 2013). The quality of parent–child interactions was also predictive of later oral language development (Cruz et al., 2013; Niparko et al., 2010; Quittner et al., 2013).

Parent–Child Interaction Therapy

Children who experience emotional and behavioral disorders may benefit from parent–child interaction therapy (PCIT; Eyberg et al., 1995). PCIT is an evidence-based therapy that teaches parents to interact in a warmer and more effective way with their child to increase positive behaviors and decrease negative ones (Eyberg et al., 1995). PCIT uses a family-centered model, with the therapist coaching the parent during live sessions (using "bug-in-the ear" technology) that include the parent, the child, and the interventionist. The skills parents are taught are referred to as "PRIDE" skills: praise, reflection, imitation, describing, and enjoying. Parents are encouraged to use praise when their child demonstrates a positive behavior. They are also taught to reflect on what the child is saying and imitate what they are doing. For example, if a child picks up a doll, says or signs "doll," and starts playing with the doll, the parent can respond by saying or signing, "yes, that is a doll," and join in the play. Further, parents are taught to describe what the child is doing; so, if the child is rocking the doll, the parent can say, "you're rocking the baby to sleep." Lastly, parents are told to enjoy their time with their child (McNeil & Hembree-Kigin, 2010) using any language skills (e.g., ASL, gestures, nonverbal cues, listening and speaking, drawing, and writing) they possess to facilitate communication.

Given that d/Dhh children have higher rates of externalizing disorders, PCIT can be extremely beneficial for this population. In fact, PCIT has been adapted for several different populations, including Deaf individuals who use ASL (Day et al., 2018). Day et al. (2018) recommend that, if possible, the therapist should communicate through the same language modality as the parent and the child. If that is not possible, the therapist should use an interpreter and make an effort to understand any cultural differences.

Teacher–Child Interaction Therapy

Teacher–Child Interaction Therapy (TCIT) is a program designed to provide teachers with classroom behavior management skills and to enhance positive teacher–student relationships. Additionally, TCIT aims to improve student behavior and create a more constructive academic environment with more positive teacher–student interactions (Filcheck et al., 2004). TCIT is somewhat different from other classroom strategies in that teachers receive live coaching during their classroom instruction through a bug-in-the-ear device. Through TCIT, teachers learn how to improve students' behaviors by modeling positive behaviors and providing students with specific positive social attention whenever they are engaged in appropriate behaviors. TCIT also allows for the use of addition or removal of privileges/reinforcers when needed.

As in PCIT, TCIT begins with the child-directed interaction phase, during which teachers learn to apply and withdraw their attention to improve student behavior. Specifically, teachers learn to use the PRIDE skills for appropriate behaviors and to actively ignore minor inappropriate behaviors. In the second phase, referred to as the teacher-directed interaction (TDI; McIntosh et al., 2000), teachers learn to present direct and clear instructions and give positive or negative consequences in a consistent manner. Students have been shown to increase on-task behavior and decrease disruptive behaviors when teachers increase praise and decrease critical speech (Jennings & Greenberg, 2009; Leflot, van Lier et al., 2010). Therefore, TCIT appears to be an ideal strategy given its specific focus on increasing teachers' skills and fostering more positive student-teacher relationships. In a recent randomized trial, TCIT was compared across classrooms where teachers received TCIT with those who did not. Classrooms with teachers that received TCIT demonstrated large student effects in reducing existing behavior challenges (Fernandez et al., 2015). Further, TCIT teachers reported significantly less distress than control group teachers, which is a significant predictor of teacher attrition.

Parent–Child Early Approaches to Increasing Language Skills

Researchers developed a parent intervention specifically designed for children using CIs who are learning spoken language, to increase parental sensitivity and their use of higher-level language strategies. An individual's intervention, Parent-Child Early Approaches to Raising Language Skills (PEARLS; Department of Otolaryngology, 2016), has a manual and consists of 10 sessions with homework assigned after each. The PEARLS program was designed to be implemented by speech–language pathologists who have regular appointments with the parent and the child. PEARLS focuses on coaching parents to follow their child's lead during the session while demonstrating warmth, sensitivity, and positive regard. Families are encouraged to practice what they learn in the PEARLS sessions at home by completing the homework given by the therapist. Parental sensitivity techniques taught in PEARLS include stepping forward, stepping back, and staying warm and positive. The program also coaches parents on language techniques such as (a) asking open-ended questions, (b) expansion, (c) expatiation, (d) recast, and (e) parallel talk, all crucial for language development.

Application-Based Approaches

Similar to behavior tracking applications ("apps"), there are also digital, application-based interventions (see Table 8.4). Although these apps may be used by professionals and parents of d/Dhh children to help reduce emotional difficulties, they are not a substitute for professional assistance. Digital technology may be an avenue to motivate young learners to self-regulate their emotions and behaviors, especially considering their everyday use of these accessible platforms.

TABLE 8.4 App-Based Interventions

App Icon	App Name	App Capabilities
	Moodnotes	• Designed for ages ≥12 years • User indicates their mood and is provided examples of how to reframe thought (e.g. "Although I did not get an 'A' on this test, I put in my very best effort")
	Pacifica for Stress and Anxiety	• Designed for ages ≥12 years • Teaches meditation • Uses CBT strategies • Tracks mood
	Mindshift	• Designed for teens and young adults to cope with anxiety • Aims to shift negative thinking to a more positive frame

Note. CBT = cognitive behavioral therapy.

Conclusion

Learners with varying hearing levels experience higher rates of behavioral and emotional challenges and disorders in childhood and beyond, including higher rates of depression and anxiety. Educators and health-care professionals must be able to identify these concerns early in order to provide appropriate and effective instruction. Several screening measures for internalizing and externalizing behaviors are available to assess d/Dhh learners who need further evaluation or behavioral strategies. Research has shown early intervention prevents minor issues from becoming major problems. Families also need guidance in understanding how varying hearing levels may affect the child's development, and when emotional or behavioral issues warrant further evaluation. Additional research is needed to accurately determine the effects of language delays as a potential catalyst of these challenges, and characteristics of the participants should be reported by researchers to more clearly understand the impact of these delays on internalizing and externalizing behaviors.

Although rates of emotional and behavioral disorders are higher in d/Dhh learners, they often do not meet the criteria for a diagnosis—or "label"—of emotional behavior disorder but still need support and accommodations. These behavior challenges are often linked to language and communication delays. Educators should not focus on the label (e.g., ADHD, OCD, ED), yet be aware of early signs and symptoms that a child is struggling with attention, anxiety, or sadness. When these early signs are observed, guidance and input should be sought from school counselors or psychologists who specialize in understanding children's emotional and behavioral health. Optimally, providers who are familiar with deafness should be utilized. Interventions that can be used include PBS, CBT, and TCIT, as well as family approaches such as PCIT and PEARLS.

Discussion Questions

1. Describe the characteristics of a child who is d/Dhh and experiencing internalizing versus externalizing behavioral difficulties.
2. How can professionals design their work environments to be less distractible and potentially increase academic engagement?

3. What are some strategies that professionals can utilize to help students who are d/Dhh develop social skills?
4. What are some strategies that could assist parents in teaching their child who is d/Dhh to cope with emotional and behavioral issues?
5. List the PRIDE skills and a real-life example of how they would be used.

Resources

Books

- Jent, J., Weinstein, A., Srivatsa, N., Simpson, G., Gisbert, P., & Simmons, S. (2014). *Pocket PCIT: Child-directed interaction: A parent-child interaction therapy resource for parents.* University of Miami.
  o Interactive ebook available from Apple Books and Amazon Kindle
- Phifer, L. W., Crowder, A., Elsenraat, T,, & Hull, R. (2017). CBT Toolbox for Children and Adolescents: Over 200 worksheets & exercises for trauma, ADHD, autism, anxiety, depression & conduct disorders. PESI Publishing.
- Pierangelo, R., & Giuliani, G. (2015). *Classroom management techniques for students with ADHD: A step-by-step guide for educators.* Skyhorse.
- Reilly, N. (2015) *Anxiety and depression in the classroom: A teacher's guide to fostering self-regulation in young students.* Norton.
- Stewart, D., & Kluwin, T. 2001. *Teaching deaf and hard of hearing students: Content, strategies, and curriculum.* Pearson.
- Storey, K., & Post, M. *Positive behavior supports in classrooms and schools: Effective and practical strategies for teachers and other service providers* (2nd ed.). Charles C. Thomas Publishing.

Support Organizations

- **AG Bell**
  o https://www.agbell.org/
- **American Society for Deaf Children**
  o http://www.deafchildren.org/

- **Beginnings**
  - https://ncbegin.org/
- **Hands & Voices**
  - http://www.handsandvoices.org/
- **Hearing Loss Association of America**
  - https://www.hearingloss.org/
- **International Federation of Hard of Hearing People**
  - https://www.ifhoh.org/
- **Raising Deaf Kids**
  - http://www.raisingdeafkids.org/special/index.php
- **Rochester Institute of Technology—Educating Deaf Children**
  - https://www.rit.edu/ntid/educatingdeafchildren/?cat=14

Websites

- **American Psychiatric Association**
  - https://www.psychiatry.org/patients-families
- **American Psychological Association**
  - https://www.apa.org/education-career#k12
- **Centers for Disease Control–Children's Mental Health**
  - https://www.cdc.gov/childrensmentalhealth/index.html
- **Centers for Disease Control and Prevention–ADHD**
  - https://www.cdc.gov/ncbddd/adhd/index.html
- **PACER-Children's Mental Health and Emotional or Behavioral Disorders Project**
  - https://www.pacer.org/cmh/

References

Achenbach, T. (1983). *Manual for the child: Behavior checklist and revised child behavior profile.* Department of Psychiatry, University of Vermont.

Albano, A. M., Chorpita, B. F., & Barlow, D. H. (2003). Childhood anxiety disorders. In E. J. Mash & R. A. Barkley (Eds.), *Child psychopathology* (2nd ed., pp. 279–329). Guilford.

Albert, P. R. (2015). Why is depression more prevalent in women? *Journal of Psychiatry and Neuroscience, 40*(4), 219–221.

American Academy of Pediatrics. (2011). ADHD: Clinical practice guideline for the diagnosis, evaluation, and treatment of attention-deficit/ hyperactivity disorder in children and adolescents. *Pediatrics, 128*(5), 1007–1022. https://doi.org/10.1542/peds.2011-2654

American Psychiatric Association. (2013). *Diagnostic and statistical manual of mental disorders* (5th ed., DSM-5). https://doi.org/10.1176/ appi.books.9780890425596

Barker, D. H., Quittner, A. L., Fink, N. E., Eisenberg, L. S., Tobey, E. A., Niparko, J. K., & the CDaCI Investigative Team. (2009). Predicting behavior problems in deaf and hearing children: The influences of language, attention, and parent-child communication. *Developmental Psychopathology, 21*(2), 373–392.

Beesdo, K., Knappe, S., & Pine, D. S. (2009). Anxiety and anxiety disorders in children and adolescents: Developmental issues and implications for DSM-V. *Psychiatric Clinics of North America, 32*(3), 483–524.

Birmaher, B., Khetarpal, S., Brent, D., Cully, M., Balach, L., Kaufman, J., & Neer, S. M. (1997). The Screen for Child Anxiety Related Emotional Disorders (SCARED): Scale construction and psychometric characteristics. *Journal of the American Academy of Child & Adolescent Psychiatry, 36*(4), 545–553. https://doi.org/10.1097/00004583–199704000–00018

Bornstein, M. H., Hahn, C.-S., & Haynes, O. M. (2010). Social competence, externalizing, and internalizing behavioral adjustment from early childhood through early adolescence: Developmental cascades. *Development and Psychopathology, 22*(4), 717–735. https://doi.org/10.1017/S0954579410000416

Boylan, K., Vaillancourt, T., Boyle, M., & Szatmari, P. (2007). Comorbidity of internalizing disorders in children with oppositional defiant disorder. *European Child and Adolescent Psychiatry, 16*(8), 484–494.

Campbell, S. B., Shaw, D. S., & Gillion, M. (2000). Early externalizing behavior problems: toddlers and preschoolers at risk for later maladjustment. *Development and Psychopathology, 12*(3), 467–488.

Carr, E. G., Dunlap, G., Hornet, R. H., Koegel, R. L., Sailor, W., Turnbull, A. P., Anderson, J. L., Albin, R. W., Koegel, L. K., & Fox, L. (2002). Positive behavior support: Evolution of an applied science. *Journal of Positive Behavior Interventions, 4*(1), 4–16, 20.

Cawthon, S. W. (2008). Accommodations use for statewide standardized assessments: Prevalence and recommendations for Students who are deaf or hard of hearing. *Journal of Deaf Studies and Deaf Education, 13*(1), 55–76.

Cawthon, S. W. (2010). Science and evidence of success: Two emerging issues in assessment accommodations for students who are deaf or hard of hearing. *Journal of Deaf Studies and Deaf Education, 15*(2), 185–203.

Cejas, I., Hoffman, M. F., & Quittner, A. L. (2015). Outcomes and benefits of pediatric cochlear implants in children with additional disabilities: A review and report of family influences on outcomes. *Pediatric Health, Medicine and Therapeutics, 6,* 45–63.

Conners, C. (2014). *Conners' Continuous Performance Test user's manual.* Multi-Health Systems.

Costello, J., Erkanli, A., & Angold, A. (2006). Is there an epidemic of child or adolescent depression? *Journal of Child Psychology and Psychiatry and Allied Disciplines, 47*(12), 1263–1271.

Cruz, I., Quittner, A. L., Marker, C., DesJardin, J. L., & the CDaCI Investigative Team. (2013). Identification of effective strategies to promote language in deaf children with cochlear implants. *Child Development, 84*(2), 543–559.

Day, L. A., Costa, E. A., Previ, D., & Caverly, C. (2018). Adapting parent-child interaction therapy for deaf families that communicate via American sign language: A formal adaptation approach. *Cognitive and Behavioral Practices, 25,* 7–21.

Department of Otolaryngology. (2016). *PEARLS manual.* University of Miami.

Eyberg, S., Boggs, S., & Algina, J. (1995). Parent-child interaction therapy: A psychosocial model for the treatment of young children with conduct problem behavior and their families. *Psychopharmacology Bulletin, 31,* 83–91.

Fellinger, J., Holzinger, D., Sattel, H., Lauchr, M., & Goldberg, D. (2009). Correlates of mental health disorders among children with hearing impairments. *Developmental Medicine and Child Neurology, 51*(8), 635–641. https://doi.org/10.1111/j.1469-8749.2008.03218.x

Fernandez, M. A., Adelstein, J. S., Miller, S. P., Areizaga, M. J., Gold, D. C., Sanchez, A. L., Rothschild, S. A., Hirsch, E., & Gudiño, O. G.

(2015). Teacher-child interaction training: A pilot study with random assignment. *Behavior Therapy, 46*(4), 463–477.

Filcheck, H. A., McNeil, C. B., Greco, L. A., & Bernard, R. S. (2004). Using a whole-class token economy and coaching of teacher skills in a preschool classroom to manage disruptive behavior. *Psychology in the Schools, 41*(3), 351–361.

Fiorillo, C. E., Rashidi, V., Westgate, P. M., Jacobs, J. A., Bush, M. L., & Studts, C. R. (2017). Assessment of behavioral problems in children with hearing loss. *Otology & Neurotology, 38*(10), 1456–1462.

Gharashi, K., & Moheb, N. (2018). The effect of cognitive-behavioral therapy on reducing the anxiety and depression of children with hearing loss. *Auditory and Vestibular Research, 27*(1), 31–37.

Glascoe, F. (2013). *Parents' Evaluation of Developmental Status* (PEDS). https://www.pedstest.com

Gordon, M. (1986). Microprocessor-based assessment of attention deficit disorders, *Psychopharmacology Bulletin, 22*(1), 288–290.

Hall, W. C. (2017). What you don't know can hurt you: The risk of language deprivation by impairing sign language development in deaf children. *Maternal Child Health, 21*, 961–965.

Hammen, C., & Rudolph, K. D. (2003). Childhood mood disorders. In E. J. Mash & R. A. Barkley (Eds.), *Child psychopathology* (2nd ed., pp. 238–278). Guilford.

Hinshaw, S. P., & Lee, S. S. (2003).Conduct and oppositional defiant disorders. In E. J. Mash & R. A. Barkley (Eds.), *Child psychopathology* (2nd ed., pp. 144–198). Guilford.

Hoffman, M. F., Cejas, I., Quittner, A. L., & the CDaCI Investigative Team. (2016). Comparisons of longitudinal trajectories of social competence: Parent ratings of children with cochlear implants. *Otology and Neurotology, 37*(2), 152–159.

Hoffman, M. F., Quittner, A. L., & Cejas, I. (2015). Comparisons of social competence in young children with and without hearing loss: A dynamic systems framework. *Journal of Deaf Studies and Deaf Education, 20*(2), 115–123.

Hoffman, M. F., Tiddens, E., Quittner, A. L., & the CDaCI Investigative Team. (2018). Comparisons of visual attention in school-age children with cochlear implants versus hearing peers and normative data.

Hearing Research, 359, 91–100. https://doi.org/10.1016/j.heares.2018.01.002

Huber, M., & Kipman, U. (2011). The mental health of deaf adolescents with cochlear implants compared to their hearing peers. *International Journal of Audiology, 50*(3), 146–154.

Huebner, D. (2005). *What to do when you worry too much: A kid's guide to overcoming anxiety.* Magination.

Individuals With Disabilities Education Act (IDEA) of 2004, 20 U.S.C. §§ 1400–1482 (2004 & rev. 2015).

Jeanes, R. C., Nienhuys, T. G. W. M., & Rickards, F. W. (2000). The pragmatic skills of profoundly deaf children. *Journal of Deaf Studies and Deaf Education, 5*(3), 237–247. https://doi.org/10.1093/deafed/5.3.237

Jennings, P. A., & Greenberg, M. T. (2009). The prosocial classroom: Teacher social and emotional competence in relation to student and classroom outcomes. *Review of Educational Research, 79*(1), 491–525.

Kieling, C., Kieling, R. R., Augusto Rhode, L., Frick, P. J., Moffitt, T., Nigg, J. T., Tannock, R., & Xavier Catellanos, F. (2010). The age at onset of attention deficit hyperactivity disorder. *American Journal of Psychiatry, 167*(1), 14–16.

Kim, S. Y., Kim, H. J., Park, E. K., Joe, J., Sim, S., & Choi, H. G. (2017). Severe hearing impairment and risk of depression: A national cohort study. *PLoS One, 12*(6), e0179973.

Konuk, N., Erdogan, A., Atik, L., Ugur, M. B., & Simsekyilmaz, O. (2006). Evaluation of behavioral and emotional problems in deaf children by using the child behavior checklist. *Neurology Psychiatry and Brain Research, 13*(2), 59–64.

Kovacs, M. (2011). *Children's Depression Inventory (CDI2): Technical manual.* Multi-Health Systems.

Kovacs, M., & Devlin, B. (1998). Internalizing disorders in childhood. *Journal of Child Psychology and Psychiatry, and Allied Disciplines, 39*(1), 47–63.

Kremer, K. P., Flower, A., Huang, J., & Vaughn, M. G. (2016). Behavior problems and children's academic achievement: A test of growth-curve models with gender and racial differences. *Children and Youth Services Review, 67*, 95–104. https://doi.org/10.1016/j.childyouth.2016.06.003

Kroenke, K., Spitzer, R. L., & Williams, J. B. W. (2001). The PHQ-9. *Journal of General Internal Medicine, 16*(9), 606–613. https://doi.org/10.1046/j.1525-1497.2001.016009606.x

Leflot, G., van Lier, P. A., Onghena, P., & Colpin, H. (2010). The role of teacher behavior management in the development of disruptive behaviors: An intervention study with the good behavior game. *Journal of Abnormal Child Psychology, 38*(6), 869–882.

Li, H., & Prevatt, F. (2010). Deaf and hard of hearing children and adolescents in China: Their fears and anxieties. *American Annals of the Deaf, 155*(4), 458–466.

McIntosh, D. E., Rizza, M. G., & Bliss, L. (2000). Implementing empirically supported interventions: Teacher-child interaction therapy. *Psychology in the Schools, 37*(5), 453–462.

McNeil, C. B., & Hembree-Kigin, T. L. (2010). *Parent-child interaction therapy* (2nd ed.). Springer Science & Business.

Meadow, K. (1980). *Meadow/Kendall Social-Emotional Assessment Inventory for Deaf Students: Manual.* Gallaudet College.

Mick, P., Kawachi, I., & Lin, F. R. (2014). The association between hearing loss and social isolation in older adults. *Otolaryngology—Head and Neck Surgery, 150*(3), 378–384.

Mitchell, T. V., & Quittner, A. L. (1996). Multimethod study of attention and behavior problems in hearing-impaired children. *Journal of Clinical Child Psychology, 25*(1), 83–96.

Moffitt, T. E., & Caspi, A. (2001). Childhood predictors differentiate life-course persistent and adolescence-limited antisocial pathways among males and females. *Development and Psychopathology, 13*(2), 355–375.

Murine, C. F., Prater, M. A., & Jenkins, A. (2008). The active classroom: Supporting students with attention deficit hyperactivity disorder through exercise. *Teaching Exceptional Children, 40*(5), 16–22.

Niparko, J. K., Tobey, E .A., Thal, D. J., Eisenberg, L. S., Wang, N. Y., Quittner, A. L., Fink, N. E., & the CDaCI Investigative Team. (2010). Spoken language development in children following cochlear implantation. *JAMA, 303*(15), 1498–1506.

Norman, N., Rohatyn-Martin, N., & Luckner, J. (2022). Supporting students who are Deaf and hard of hearing and have attention deficit hyperactivity disorder: Strategies for success. In C. Guardino, J. E.

Cannon, & P. V. Paul (Eds.), *Deaf and hard of hearing learners with disabilities: Foundations, strategies, and resources* (pp. 262–287). Routledge.

Pierce, E. W., Ewing, L. J., & Campbell, S. B. (1999). Diagnostic status and symptomatic behavior of hard-to-manage preschool children in middle childhood and early adolescence. *Journal of Clinical Child Psychology, 28*(1), 44–57.

Quittner, A. L., Barker, D. H., Snell, C., Cruz, I., McDonald, L.-G., Grimley, M. E., & the CDaCI Investigative Team. (2007). Improvements in visual attention in deaf infants and toddlers after cochlear implantation. *Audiological Medicine, 5*(4), 242–249. https://doi.org/10.1080/16513860701745401

Quittner, A. L., Cruz, I., Barker, D. H., Tobey, E., Eisenbery, L. S., Niparko, J. K., & the CDaCI Investigative Team. (2013). Effects of maternal sensitivity and cognitive and linguistic stimulation on cochlear implant users' language development over four years. *Journal of Pediatrics, 162*(2), 343–348.e.3.

Ramtekkar, U. P., Reiersen, A. M., Todorov, A. A., & Todd, R. D. (2010). Sex and age difference in attention-deficit/hyperactivity disorder symptoms and diagnoses: Implications for DSM-V and ICD-11. *Journal of the American Academy of Child and Adolescent Psychiatry, 49*(3), 217–228.e1-3.

Remine, M. D., & Brown, P. M. (2010). Comparison of the prevalence of mental health problems in deaf and hearing children and adolescents in Australia. *Australian and New Zealand Journal of Psychiatry, 44*(4), 351–357.

Reynolds, C. R. (2008). *Revised Children's Manifest Anxiety Scale (RCMAS-2): Manual.* Western Psychological Services.

Reynolds, C., & Kamphaus, R. W. (2015). *BASC-3 Behavioral and Emotional Screening System Manual.* Pearson Education.

Sahli, S., Arslan, U., & Belgin, E. (2009). Depressive emotioning in adolescents with cochlear implant and normal hearing. *International Journal of Pediatric Otorhinolaryngology, 73*(12), 1774–1779.

Scheeringa, M. S., Salloum, A., Arnberger, R. A., Weems, C. F., Amaya-Jackson, L., & Cohen, J. A. (2007). Feasibility and effectiveness of cognitive-behavioral therapy for posttraumatic stress disorder in preschool children: Two case reports. *Journal of Traumatic Stress, 20*(4), 631–636. https://doi.org/10.1002/jts.20232

Sibley, J. A. (2015). *ADHD and hearing loss: A study examining the co-occurrence of the two disorders* [Master's thesis, The University of Texas at Arlington]. UTA Research Commons. https://rc.library.uta.edu/uta-ir/bitstream/handle/10106/25019/Sibley_uta_2502M_13045.pdf?isAllowed=y&sequence=1

Sparrow, S., Cicchetti, D., & Saulnier, C. (2016). *Vineland Adaptive Behavior Scales* (3rd ed., Vineland-3). Pearson Education.

Spitzer, R. L., Kroenke, K., Williams, J. B. W., & Löwe, B. (2006). A brief measure for assessing generalized anxiety disorder: The GAD-7. *Archives of Internal Medicine, 166*(10), 1092–1097. https://doi.org/10.1001/archinte.166.10.1092

Stevenson, J., Kreppner, J., Pimperton, H., Worsfold, S., & Kennedy, C. (2015). Emotional and behavioural difficulties in children and adolescents with hearing impairment: A systematic review and meta-analysis. *European Child & Adolescent Psychiatry, 24*(5), 477–496. https://doi.org/10.1007/s00787-015-0697-1

Substance Abuse and Mental Health Services Administration. (2011). *Interventions for disruptive behavior disorders: Characteristics and needs of children with disruptive behavior disorders and their families.* https://store.samhsa.gov/sites/default/files/d7/priv/sma11-4634-characteristicsandneeds-idbd.pdf

Theunissen, S. C. P. M., Rieffe, C., Kouwenberg, M., De Raeve, L., Scoede, W., Briaire, J. J., & Frijns, J. H. M. (2012). Anxiety in children with hearing aids or cochlear implants compared to normally hearing controls. *Laryngoscope, 122*(3), 654–659.

Theunissen, S. C. P. M., Rieffe, C., Kouwenberg, M., Scoede, W., Briaire, J. J., & Frijns, J. H. (2011). Depression in hearing-impaired children. *International Journal of Pediatric Otorhinolaryngology, 75*(10), 1313–1317.

Theunissen, S. C. P. M., Rieffe, C., Soede, W., Briaire, J. J., Ketelaar, L., Kouwenberg, M., & Frijns, J. H. M. (2015). Symptoms of psychopathology in hearing-impaired children. *Ear and Hearing, 36*(4), e190–e198. https://doi.org/10.1097/AUD.0000000000000147

Van Eldik, T. (2005). Mental health problems of Dutch youth with hearing loss as shown on the Youth Self-Report. *American Annals of the Deaf, 150*(1), 11–16.

Van Eldik, T., Treffers, P. D., Veerman, J. W., & Verhulst, F. C. (2004). Mental health problems of deaf Dutch children as indicated by parents' responses to the Child Behavior Checklist. *American Annals of the Deaf, 148*(5), 390–395.

Vostanis, P., Hayes, M., Du Feu, M., & Warren, J. (1997). Detection of behavioral and emotional problems in deaf children and adolescents: Comparison of two rating scales. *Child: Care, Health and Development, 23*(3), 233–246.

Weller-Clarke, A. (2011). Behavior disorders. In S. Goldstein & J. A. Naglieri (Eds.), *Encyclopedia of child behavior and development* (pp. 223–225). Springer.

Wender, P. H. (2001). *ADHD: Attention-deficit hyperactivity disorder in children and adults*. Oxford University Press.

9

Supporting Students Who Are Deaf and Hard of Hearing and Have Attention Deficit Hyperactivity Disorder: Strategies for Success

Nancy Norman, Natalia Rohatyn-Martin, and John Luckner

LEARNING OBJECTIVES

Readers will:

- Examine the current literature related to attention deficit hyperactivity disorder (ADHD) as related to d/Deaf and hard of hearing (d/Dhh) learners.
- Determine the implications of ADHD on learning, as well as social and emotional development and well-being.
- Describe the theoretical frameworks of Universal Design for Learning (UDL) and Differentiated Instruction (DI) to support d/Dhh learners who have ADHD.
- Discuss evidence-based strategies and classroom supports for students who are d/Dhh-ADHD.
- Identify resources for d/Dhh students with ADHD.

DOI: 10.4324/9781003252054-9

Attention deficit hyperactivity disorder (ADHD) is diagnosed in childhood and characterized by developmentally atypical levels of inattention, impulsivity, and hyperactivity, which affect behavioral, emotional, cognitive, academic, and social functions (American Psychiatric Association, 2013). ADHD is the most common neurodevelopmental disorder (i.e., originating in the brain) of children (Leung & Hon, 2016). A meta-analysis of 175 research studies on ADHD prevalence in children under the age of 18 years reported that approximately 7.2% of the school-age population has been diagnosed with ADHD (Thomas et al., 2015). Although it used to be believed that ADHD gradually disappeared in adulthood, it is currently understood that this is not the case. More than 75% of children with ADHD continue to experience significant symptoms in adulthood. The National Institute of Mental Health (2017) reports that the overall prevalence of adults with ADHD is 4.4%.

IDENTIFICATION

The primary purposes of conducting an evaluation for ADHD is to (a) determine the presence or absence of the disorder; (b) ascertain if there are co-occurring conditions (i.e., anxiety, defiant behavior, aggressiveness); (c) determine eligibility for special education services if eligible disabilities are present (i.e., deaf, hard of hearing, intellectual disability); and (d) identify potential strategies to address the effects of ADHD and any accompanying academic, social and/or behavioral issues (Barkley, 2015).

The diagnosis of ADHD is a complex process. A comprehensive evaluation conducted by a pediatrician, psychologist, social worker, nurse practitioner, neurologist, or psychiatrist, using the *Diagnostic and Statistical Manual of Mental Disorders* (5th ed.; DSM–5; American Psychiatric Association, 2013) diagnostic criteria for ADHD, is necessary. ADHD cannot be reliably diagnosed in children younger than 4 years of age (Leung & Hon, 2016). Behaviors must persist for at least 6 months to a degree that is inconsistent with their developmental age, and the behaviors must negatively impact directly on social and academic activities. In addition, the behaviors need to be present in two or more settings (e.g., home, school, community).

The diagnostic process incorporates multiple assessment methods that rely on the perceptions of the parents/caregivers, teachers, and other important adults in a learners' life regarding the nature of their difficulties and strengths across multiple situations. Interviews with parents/caregivers, teachers, and the child should be conducted, and parent/caregiver and teacher rating scales of child behavior or surveys of child adaptive functioning should be obtained and reviewed (Barkley, 2015). Concurrently, a thorough review of information about a child's academic performance, attention span, distractibility, activity level, behavioral problems, and peer relationships from multiple observers across home, school, and community settings should be undertaken. As stated by the American Psychiatric Association (2013), "confirmation of substantial symptoms across settings typically cannot be done accurately without consulting informants who have seen the individual in those settings" (pp. 37–38).

Many standardized parent–teacher questionnaires are available, such as the Child Behavior Checklist (CBCL; Achenbach, 2001), Behavior Assessment System for Children (BASC-2; Reynolds & Kamphaus, 2004), the ADHD Rating Scale–IV (DuPaul et al., 1998), and the Barkley Functional Impairment Scale–Children and Adolescents (BFIS-CA; Barkley, 2012a). Most scales are based on the 18 symptoms listed in the DSM-5 and include a Likert scale scoring system for a frequency of symptoms ranging from 0 to 3 (0 = *never*, 1= *occasionally*, 2 = *often*, and 3 = *very often*). See the section on resources for a link to the DSM-5 diagnostic criteria.

CHARACTERISTICS

ADHD is not a disability directly addressed by the Individuals With Disabilities Education Act (IDEA, 2004). Many students with ADHD in the United States are served through Section 504 of the Vocational Act of 1973. Alternatively, if ADHD severely impacts the student's ability to function in the educational setting, they may qualify for special education services under the eligibility category of "other health impairment" (OHI), as defined by the IDEA (2004). The diagnosis of ADHD is based on the DSM-5, which includes an extensive list of behaviors that are often organized into three presentations: (a) inattention;

(b) hyperactivity and impulsivity; and (c) combined inattention, hyperactivity, and impulsivity (see Table 9.1).

IMPACT ON EXECUTIVE FUNCTIONS AND SELF-REGULATION

Individuals with ADHD often demonstrate difficulty with self-management, which includes behaviors such as organizing, planning, completing tasks in a timely manner, self-monitoring, and self-inhibition. Collectively, these behaviors are often referred to as executive functions (EFs). EFs have been defined as "those self-directed actions needed to choose goals and to create, enact, and sustain actions toward those goals" (Barkley, 2012b, p. 60). EFs enable us to: (a) sustain effort in the absence of immediate reward, (b) voluntarily focus or shift attention, (c) regulate strong emotions, and (d) inhibit behaviors when appropriate—all these skills are needed to succeed in school (Hoffman et al., 2012).

Executive functions help to promote self-regulation, which is the ability to monitor and control one's behavior, emotions, or thoughts, altering

TABLE 9.1 DSM-5 ADHD Presentations

Presentations	Behaviors	DSM-5 Diagnosis
Inattention	Students make careless mistakes, have difficulty organizing tasks and activities, are easily distracted, and seem forgetful	ADHD—predominantly inattentive type
Hyperactivity and impulsivity	Students demonstrate high amounts of movement and an inability to think before acting	ADHD—predominantly hyper-active–impulsive type
Inattention and hyperactivity–impulsivity	Students demonstrate both inattention and hyperactivity–impulsivity	ADHD—combined type

them per the demands of the situation. Self-regulation includes the abilities to inhibit first responses, to resist interference from irrelevant stimulation, and to persist on relevant tasks even when one does not enjoy them (Heatherton & Wagner, 2011). The ability to sustain attention and self-regulate is critical for succeeding in school as well as for being able to live cooperatively, achieve goals, and maintain health throughout one's life span. "Self-regulation enables people to make plans, choose from alternatives, control impulses, inhibit unwanted thoughts, and regulate social behavior" (Heatherton & Wagner, 2011, p. 132). In addition, EFs are associated with working memory, which regulates attention information, facilitates information processing, and sustains attention (McCabe et al., 2010).

For students with ADHD, difficulties with EFs, behavioral inhibition, sustained attention, internalization of speech, and working memory, interfere with learning (Barkley, 1997). In classroom settings, students with ADHD are frequently reported to have challenging behaviors, which include: (a) fidgeting and squirming, (b) leaving their desks and leaving the classroom, (c) running and climbing at inappropriate times, (d) talking excessively, (e) interrupting conversations, (f) blurting out answers and comments, (g) not being able to follow classroom rules, and (h) having a difficult time playing or working quietly (Nass & Leventhal, 2011; Winzer, 2008).

Impact on Learning and Challenges at School

Given the characteristics of individuals with ADHD, it is not surprising that the majority of youth with ADHD experience difficulty with academics and the demands of school (Feldman & Reiff, 2014). Yet, because ADHD is not related to intellectual ability, the academic performance of students with ADHD can vary significantly. Some students are gifted and talented (Assouline & Whiteman, 2011), while others consistently achieve below the expected age norms (DuPaul & Langberg, 2015). The variability of performance is related to the severity of the symptoms and the effectiveness of the strategies that are put into place.

Although variability of school performance exists, research indicates that students with ADHD tend to show significant deficits in reading, mathematics, and spelling (Czamara et al., 2013). Inattention caused by ADHD may manifest as high rates of off-task behavior, careless work, and the inability to sustain effort to complete assignments (DuPaul & Langberg, 2015). Further, difficulties with emotional self-regulation hinder social functioning, social connection, and emotional well-being (Mrug et al., 2012).

Impact on Social and Emotional Development and Well-Being

The impacts of ADHD extend beyond the classroom. Research indicates that students with ADHD are four times more likely than neurotypically developing peers to have difficulties making and maintaining friendships (Normand et al., 2013). Specifically, students with ADHD are at risk for unstable peer relationships (e.g., lack of a consistent friendship group) and significant peer rejection (e.g., isolation and loneliness; Normand et al., 2013). In a study by Hoza et al. (2005), approximately 56% of the students with ADHD in their sample (n = 165; ages 6–13 years) had no meaningful reciprocal friendships with peers and were less likely to be selected as friends by peers. DuPaul and Weyandt (2006) noted that classroom observations of social interactions involving students with ADHD were marked by low levels of cooperation, turn-taking, and reciprocity in conversation. Further, Mrug et al. (2001) connected the symptoms of ADHD to maladaptive social functioning, with interpersonal styles being bossy or unfriendly, aggressive, and impulsive—leading to students with ADHD being identified as socially immature compared to typically developing peers. Mikami (2010) and Ros and Graziano (2018) suggest that the characteristics of ADHD (inappropriate social behaviors and social understanding, dysregulated emotions, social-cognitive and social-perceptual deficits) impact the student's ability to navigate social relationships successfully.

Given that students with ADHD often struggle in social interactions and relationships, and because these relationships are central to healthy social and emotional development during childhood and adolescence, it is likely that students with ADHD have difficulties with their emotional well-being—most notably, heightened anxiety (Mikami et al., 2011), low self-esteem (Travell & Visser, 2006), and poor psychosocial health (Klassen et al., 2006), all of which have a pervasive impact on their overall quality of life (Danckaerts et al., 2010).

Deaf and Hard of Hearing Learners With ADHD

Much of the limited research that has investigated students who are d/Dhh with ADHD (d/Dhh-ADHD) has largely focused on assessment and identification practices. As previously stated, the diagnosis of ADHD is a complex process that requires an interdisciplinary team approach. When evaluating students who are d/Dhh, teams should include multiple perspectives from teachers, parents, and counselors, each providing a detailed and in-depth view of the student's history, academic evaluations, psychoeducational assessments, and medical evaluations (Kelly et al., 1993a; Kelly et al., 1993). Similar to students with typical hearing levels, assessment data and evaluation of d/Dhh students should include a variety of measures, including interviews, observational reports, and standardized measurements of attention (Parasnis et al., 2001). However, caution should be taken during the assessment and evaluation process, as previous research indicates that d/Dhh students are vulnerable to overdiagnosis of ADHD (Kelly et al., 1993b). In part, overdiagnoses are due to the lack of sensitivity across assessment measures to recognize the characteristics of learners who are d/Dhh, as well as having ADHD, on learners' behavior and academic achievement (Parasnis et al., 2001). As noted by Kelly et al. (1993b), standard measures may not differentiate between the common characteristics of ADHD (e.g., aggression, anxiety, depression, hyperactivity, inattention, impulsivity) and the common characteristics of other disabilities (e.g., learning disabilities, emotional and behavior disorders); thus, there is the potential for d/Dhh students to be misdiagnosed with ADHD.

Attention-related challenges in students who are d/Dhh have been examined to determine whether the cause of such behavior is due to the lack of language exposure and social communication during early childhood development (Dye & Bavelier, 2013; Dye & Hauser, 2014). Dye and Hauser (2014) examined the sustained attention and cognitive control of 37 Deaf children of Deaf parents compared with 60 hearing children of hearing parents. All participants were between the ages of 6 and 13 years. Their findings suggest that younger Deaf children struggle with sustained attention when presented with distractors. However, there was less of a difference between older (ages 9–13 years) Deaf children and their hearing counterparts when comparing sustained attention on varying tasks. Cognitive control tests showed that Deaf participants performed lower than the hearing participants. The researchers explained that this difference may be due to deaf children having increased attention to peripheral vision. This coincides with other research that demonstrates that deaf individuals have increased peripheral attention (Chen, Ming, & Xiaolin, 2006), which may be a struggle for young deaf children but an asset as the children grow older and learn how to manage acute awareness of peripheral vision (Buckley et al., 2010; Codina et al., 2011). More research is needed to determine the causes of attention and hyperactivity characteristics in deaf children.

Educational placement and classroom settings have also been investigated for students who are d/Dhh-ADHD. Kelly et al. (1993a) suggest that traditional classrooms in which students who are d/Dhh-ADHD can be seated in a quiet area of the room with minimal distractions (e.g., at the front, near the teacher, away from windows and doors to minimize visual distractions) work well. These researchers suggest strategies that include structured lessons (e.g., outlines, examples, or graphic organizers to coordinate thoughts), provide alternate lesson materials (e.g., provide larger print or less text on the page, limit the number of questions on a page/test), and directly teach organizational techniques and skills needed to complete assignments. The next section expands on the aforementioned suggestions and strategies useful for students who are d/Dhh-ADHD.

STRATEGIES FOR SUCCESS

Two prominent theoretical frameworks, Universal Design for Learning (UDL) and Differentiated Instruction (DI), are used by educators to plan and implement effective supports for diverse learners within school settings. Evidence-based strategies that have been demonstrated to be effective with students with typical hearing levels are provided for consideration when planning instruction for students who are d/Dhh-ADHD.

Universal Design for Learning

UDL is a theoretical framework of learning and instruction used to guide the development of curricula so that learning opportunities are maximized for all learners (Rose et al., 2014a). The objective of UDL is to remove the barriers to learning through explicit, thoughtful, and flexible instructional design of methods, materials, and assessments. Edyburn (2011) describes UDL as an inclusive framework within which educators systematically plan, design, and teach lessons to support different learner needs. The goal of UDL for educators is to proactively vary classroom supports so that all students have access to the curriculum in a way that best suits their diverse learning needs (Tomlinson, 2014).

UDL has three essential guiding principles, multiple means of (a) engagement, (b) representation, and (c) action and expression (Rose & Meyer, 2002; Rose et al., 2014b). Each of the three principles guides instructional planning (Centre for Applied Special Technology [CAST], 2011).

- *Multiple means of engagement.* Encourages teachers to incorporate student interest to increase motivation. This includes pedagogical approaches that provide students with choice and self-directed tasks. For example, allow learners to choose a topic of interest to motivate them and feel a sense of ownership of their learning. In addition, implement the use of a self-monitoring checklist to encourage the student to stay focused and attend to the topic.
- *Multiple means of representation.* Aims to ensure a variety of ways for students to access curricular information. This includes providing students with options such as the use of multimedia formats, text-to-speech tools, and graphic organizers. For example, it allows learners to benefit from closed captioning while watching videos in class, as well as pre-teaching opportunities for new vocabulary and concepts within a unit.
- *Multiple means of action and expression.* Addresses the need for flexibility in how students display understanding and learning of curricular content. This includes providing options for presentations, creating projects, and assessment strategies. For example, it allows presentations in the students' preferred communication mode and autonomy by providing choices in how they will demonstrate their understanding.

Differentiated Instruction

Within the overarching framework of UDL, DI is a useful lens for educators to plan and adjust curriculum to meet the varying learning needs in the classroom. While UDL emphasizes planning and curricular design, DI centers on the "how-to" of teaching and learning. Tomlinson and Moon (2013) explain that through DI, educators consider individual student's interests, learning styles, and readiness to learn before linking curriculum to day-to-day lesson plans.

> It means teachers proactively plan varied approaches to what students need to learn, how they will learn it, and/or how they will show what they have learned in order to increase the likelihood that each student will learn as much as [they] can, as efficiently as possible. (p. 10)

The fundamental principles of DI emphasize flexibility in instruction and engagement in learning tasks, whereby assessment is ongoing and focused on the formative "process" of learning, rather than on the summative outcomes of learning. A key component of DI is for educators to embed choice throughout the learning process—that is, choice of curriculum (content), choice in modes of instruction (process), choice in ways to demonstrate learning (product), and choice in learning environments, each with consideration of individual student interests, learning styles, and readiness needs.

Student Engagement and Student Understanding

Strategies and adaptations that support the learning needs of all students, particularly students who are d/Dhh-ADHD, tend to fall under two general categories: (a) student engagement and (b) student understanding. Student engagement relates to feeling an attraction to an idea/task or a connection between what is being taught and their own lives, therefore resulting in a connection to the curriculum (Tomlinson & Moon, 2013). Student understanding relates to being able to learn, understand, and then use the curriculum (Tomlinson & Moon, 2013), which first requires having access to the curriculum through strategies and adaptations that meet their learning needs. Tomlinson and Moon (2013) suggest the following strategies to enhance student engagement and student understanding for all students, which can be applied to students who are d/Dhh-ADHD:

- *Structure lessons for clarity.* Carefully structure lessons to ensure that students understand the content and give an outline of what is to occur for a specified time period. This can be done by listing the steps on the board, giving a handout to students, or explaining each step. Placing the knowledge and skills in the context of previously taught lessons is essential for students who are d/Dhh (Cannon & Guardino, 2012) and can be applied to those who have ADHD. The teacher provides clarity by highlighting key points and guiding students to where they should focus their attention.
- *Provide graphic organizers.* Use of graphic organizers assists students with planning and organizing their thoughts. The teacher utilizes graphic organizers to support the construction of ideas and to serve as a "powerful way to improve comprehension by helping the students see how concepts connect to each other" (Busch, 2012, p. 7).
- *Diversify learning materials.* Diversify teaching materials to cater to multiple learner needs and styles; thus, allowing students to work in/ with a modality that best suits their needs. Some strategies may include students working on a computer instead of using a paper/pencil format, using peers as models/mentors, and/or receiving work divided into smaller units (Tomlinson, 2017).
- *Perform ongoing evaluation.* Embed multiple opportunities for ongoing assessment of student understanding of lessons/units throughout the school year by incorporating formative assessments (e.g., checklists, handing in work for review, and regular discussions with students about their learning) into lessons and unit plans (Algozzine & Anderson, 2007; McTighe & O'Connor, 2009).
- *Monitor noise levels in the classroom.* Create strategies with d/Dhh students to monitor classroom noise (i.e., how will the students let teachers know when the sound levels in the classroom are getting too loud?). These strategies may include flashing the lights, holding up a sign, or doing a repetitive action, such as stomping feet. For students who are d/Dhh, high levels of noise in the classroom can be distracting. This distraction

might be amplified for students who are d/Dhh-ADHD. Noise levels can be suppressed through material goods (e.g., curtains on windows, tennis balls on the legs of chairs, keeping windows closed; Guardino & Antia, 2012). These strategies support the adaptation of classroom environments to meet the need for d/Dhh learners with ADHD.

- *Provide a quieter setting.* Classroom settings can be noisy and distracting and students may benefit from having a quiet area to work, especially during exams and other activities that require prolonged attention and engagement. These environments could be a quiet area within the classroom or an alternative room in the school (e.g., Kelly et al., 1993a). In terms of supporting inclusive practices and UDL in schools, the separate setting could be available for all students to use as needed.

Challenging Behaviors and Social Engagement

Strategies for addressing challenging behavior and supporting social engagement for students who are d/Dhh-ADHD are most successful when integrated throughout the curriculum and focused on providing individualized, student-centered supports (U.S. Department of Education, 2006). These strategies include a focus on (a) directing student attention and facilitating concentrated effort, (b) providing opportunities for self-monitoring and self-reflection, (c) directly teaching organizational skills, and (d) providing ongoing evaluation of the individualized behavior strategies (see Table 9.2).

Research has highlighted the following strategies as being helpful in addressing challenging student behaviors in a school environment:

- *Set behavioral expectations and be consistent.* Educators need to communicate clear expectations to students and enforce the consequences if/when boundaries are crossed—consistency is key. By having students create classroom rules and consequences, this strategy assists with clear expectations and assists with buy-in when applying consequences (Owens et al., 2018).
- *Define appropriate behavior while giving praise.* Praise students when they are staying on task or following directions by reinforcing appropriate and expected behavior in the classroom (Pfiffner et al., 2006).

TABLE 9.2 Strategies to Support Challenging Student Behavior

Strategy	Definition	Modifications for Students Who Are d/Dhh-ADHD
Directing student attention (Moore, 2009)	Varying behaviors or learning activities so that students receive new stimuli to keep their attention directed toward the lesson or task at hand (e.g., gestures, varied teaching styles, shifts in sensory stimuli, movement)	It may be necessary to allow down-time or provide auditory/visual breaks to allow the student time to refocus due to cognitive fatigue (Rohatyn-Martin & Hayward, 2016)
Provide opportunities for self-monitoring and self-reflection (Dunlap et al., 1995; Rafferty, 2010; Webber et al., 1993)	Student self-monitoring and reflection allows students to examine their behavior by recording their behavior and comparing it to a pre-determined standard (e.g., rating one's focus at the end of a class period, or describing social behaviors when approached by a teacher over the school day)	Developing self-awareness (a precursor to self-regulation) is a gradual process that often requires direct instruction and structured opportunities over time and across contexts (Calderon & Greenberg, 2003)

Strategy	Definition	Modifications for Students Who Are d/Dhh-ADHD
Teach organizational skills (Gureasko-Moore et al., 2006; Langberg et al., 2012)	Students need organizational skills to effectively manage time, energy, and resources, especially in a school setting, including the ability to manage materials and belongings (e.g., transfer of homework assignments to and from school) and time (e.g., planning ahead to ensure adequate time is spent studying)	Organizational skill development takes time and for d/Dhh students with ADHD, repeated direct instruction may be needed (Norman & Jamieson, 2015)
Ongoing evaluation of behavior intervention (DuPaul & Stoner, 2014; Pfiffner et al., 2006)	Behavioral programs and interventions usually require modification over time, so continued monitoring and adjusting of programming over time for maximal effectiveness	No modification needed for students who are d/Dhh-ADHD

- *Provide calming manipulatives.* Some students may need sensory input to be able to manage challenging behavior. There are two types of manipulatives that educators can utilize: tactile and visual. Some students who are d/Dhh-ADHD need tactile input to calm themselves. Examples include squeezing a stress ball, rubbing a piece of cloth, or fidgeting with malleable objects. These tactile objects may help with a student's need to move or fidget, making it easier to stay on task (Rief, 2015). The use of manipulatives is one method of differentiating instruction for student readiness to learn. Other students may prefer visuals to focus their attention elsewhere before completing a long or challenging task. Colorful or motion-based manipulatives, such as lava lamps or black lights, also work well (Hallowell & Ratey, 2017).
- *Allow for learning breaks to refocus attention.* Students may need short learning breaks to be able to mitigate feelings of fatigue or distraction (Rohatyn-Martin & Hayward, 2016). Having a quiet corner for students to visit, allowing students to put their heads down on their desk for a few minutes, or allowing them to take a short walk may aid in attempts to refocus attention.

Rief (2015) noted four additional strategies to further assist students who have ADHD, which may also be helpful for students who are d/Dhh-ADHD in terms of developing social and emotional competence.

- *Connect with peers.* Educators can provide opportunities and support for students who are d/Dhh-ADHD to interact with peers. Educators should directly teach appropriate social behaviors and provide corrective feedback.
- *Support self-awareness.* Educators can promote students' self-awareness skills by modeling appropriate skills, giving positive attention, and reinforcing students' displays of prosocial behaviors.
- *Use peers as models.* Educators can include students who are positive role models and supportive peers in cooperative groups to help facilitate social connections.
- *Increase mindfulness.* Educators can provide opportunities to include mindfulness practices throughout the day, with the goals of (a) reducing stress, (b) promoting self-management and self-regulation,

(c) promoting overall emotional well-being, and (e) building relationship skills. Mindfulness and stress reduction practices, such as yoga or mindful minutes, incorporate the following: deep breathing, focused attention, mindful awareness, body and emotional awareness, and impulse control.

CONCLUSION

Providing appropriate service for students who are d/Dhh-ADHD is complex and challenging. When not supported, the presence of ADHD in students who are d/Dhh may create long-lasting impacts on development, learning, and social and emotional well-being. Educators of students who are d/Dhh-ADHD need to be uniquely positioned to implement various strategies that address students' needs across curricular areas and developmental domains. A variety of practical strategies are presented herein, and implementation of the principles of UDL and DI can provide d/Dhh students with ADHD both access to learning the curriculum and social connections with peers. Planning and delivery of lessons should be individualized to meet the specific learning needs of each student, and strategies should be monitored through ongoing formative assessment. It is important to note that limited research exists about how best to provide appropriate services for students who are d/Dhh-ADHD. As a result, it would be beneficial to conduct and publish case studies and single-case design research to increase the knowledge of evidence-based practices that positively impact students' behavior, as well as academic and/or social and emotional development. In addition, it would be valuable to have a better understanding of how teams of professionals and families collaborate together to determine effective service delivery models that lead to positive outcomes for this unique population.

DISCUSSION QUESTIONS

1. Describe the characteristics associated with ADHD and discuss how these characteristics may impact learning.
2. What are the three presentations of ADHD behaviors?

3. Students with ADHD often have difficulty navigating social interactions and relationships. What strategies can be used to address these challenges?
4. Describe UDL and give an example of how it could be used with students who are d/Dhh-ADHD.
5. How are UDL and DI related and how can these frameworks impact students who are d/Dhh-ADHD?
6. Identify three strategies that can be used to enhance student engagement and understanding and then describe how these strategies might be used for a student who is d/Dhh-ADHD.

Resources

Books

- Dawson, P., & Guare, R. (2009). *Smart but scattered: The revolutionary "executive skills" approach to helping kids reach their potential.* Guilford.
  - This book provides a hands-on approach to understanding and assessing executive functioning in children and youth, and it is filled with useful strategies for educators and parents.
- Hallowell, E. M., & Ratey, J. J. (2017). *Delivered from distraction: Getting the most out of life with attention deficit disorder.* Random House Digital.
  - This book provides an in-depth discussion of ADHD, as well as many strategies for educators, parents, and students.
- Rief, S. F. (2015). *The ADHD book of lists: A practical guide for helping children and teens with attention deficit disorders.* Jossey-Bass.
  - This book provides many educational strategies across developmental domains and age ranges.
- U.S. Department of Education, Office of Special Education and Rehabilitative Services, Office of Special Education Programs, *Teaching Children with Attention Deficit Hyperactivity Disorder: Instructional Strategies and Practices.* Washington, D.C., 2008.
  - https://www2.ed.gov/rschstat/research/pubs/adhd/adhd-teaching-2008.pdf

Websites

- **ADDitude**
  - https://www.additudemag.com/
  - *ADDitude* magazine provides information for parents of those with ADHD, as well as for individuals with ADHD themselves. The website also houses forums and articles for professional educators.
- **American Academy of Child and Adolescent Psychiatry**
  - https://www.aacap.org/aacap/families_and_youth/resource_centers/adhd_resource_center/Home.aspx
  - This website provides research on ADHD and answers frequently asked questions for parents.
- **Attention Deficit Disorder Association**
  - https://add.org/
  - This website provides recent news related to ADD, provides an outlet for those with ADD/ADHD to share their stories, and houses a directory of resources.
- **CHADD National Resource Center on ADHD**
  - http://www.chadd.org
  - This website provides a foundation for the presentations of ADHD, the signs, symptoms, and treatments. This resource also provides suggestions for educational resources, support groups, and advocacy to parents on how to help their child with ADHD.
- **The Children's Attention Project**
  - https://www.mcri.edu.au/
  - https://www.education.vic.gov.au/Documents/school/principals/participation/tipsmanagingadhdinclass.pdf
  - This website provides a list of useful strategies for educators to support a student with ADHD in terms of behavior support and management.
- **DSM-5 (Attention Deficit Hyperactivity Disorder) Diagnostic Criteria**
  - https://images.pearsonclinical.com/images/assets/basc-3/basc3resources/DSM5_DiagnosticCriteria_ADHD.pdf
  - This website outlines the DSM-5 diagnostic criteria for each of the three presentations of ADHD.
- **Misunderstood Minds: Attention**
  - http://www.pbs.org/wgbh/misunderstoodminds/attention.html

- o This website provides experiential learning opportunities through ADHD simulation activities, as well as an overview of the characteristics of ADHD, with suggested strategies for home and school.
- **National Institute of Mental Health**
  - o https://www.nimh.nih.gov/health/topics/attention-deficit-hyperactivity-disorder-adhd/index.shtml
  - o This website provides medical information on ADHD as well as organization and management techniques for those with ADHD.
- **Teach ADHD**
  - o https://www.teachspeced.ca/adhd
  - o This website provides education professionals with resources and materials that have been developed specifically to bridge the substantial gap between current neuroscientific understanding of ADHD and classroom practice.

REFERENCES

Achenbach, T. M. (2001). *Child Behavior Checklist–Cross-Informant Version*. Author.

Algozzine, B., & Anderson, K. M. (2007). Tips for teaching: Differentiating instruction to include all students. *Preventing School Failure: Alternative Education for Children and Youth, 51*(3), 49–54.

American Psychiatric Association. (2013). *Diagnostic and statistical manual of mental disorders* (5th ed., (DSM-5)). https://doi.org/10.1176/appi.books.9780890425596

Assouline, S. G., & Whiteman, C. S. (2011). Twice-exceptionality: Implications for school psychologists in the post-IDEA era. *Journal of Applied School Psychology, 27*, 380–402.

Barkley, R. A. (1997). Behavioral inhibition, sustained attention, and executive functions: Constructing a unifying theory of ADHD. *Psychological Bulletin, 121*(1), 65.

Barkley, R. A. (2012a). *Barkley Functional Impairment Scale-Children and Adolescents* (BFIS-CA). Guilford.

Barkley, R. A. (2012b). *Executive functions: What they are, how they work, and why they evolved*. Guilford.

Barkley, R. A. (Ed.). (2015). *Attention-deficit hyperactivity disorder: A handbook for diagnosis and treatment* (4th ed.). Guilford.

Buckley, D., Codina, C., Bhardwaj, P., & Pascalis, O. (2010). Action video game players and deaf observers have larger Goldmann visual fields. *Vision Research, 50*(5), 548–556. https://doi.org/10.1016/j.visres.2009.11.018

Busch, S. (2012). *Students who are deaf/hard of hearing with learning challenges: Strategies for classroom instruction.* https://digitalcommons.wustl.edu/cgi/viewcontent.cgi?article=1637&context=pacs_capstones

Calderon, R., & Greenberg, M. T. (2003). Social and emotional development of deaf children: Family, school and program effects. In M. Marschark & P. Spencer (Eds.), *Oxford handbook of deaf studies, language, and education* (Vol. 1, pp. 177–189). Oxford University Press.

Cannon, J. E., & Guardino, C. (2012). Literacy strategies for deaf/hard-of-hearing English language learners: Where do we begin? *Deafness & Education International, 14*(2), 78–99. https://doi.org/10.1179/1557069X12Y.0000000006

Centre for Applied Special Technology (CAST). (2011). http://www.cast.org

Chen, Q., Zhang, M., & Zhou, X. (2006). Effects of spatial distribution of attention during inhibition of return (IOR) on flanker interference in hearing and congenitally deaf people. *Brain Research, 1109*(1), 117–127. https://doi.org/10.1016/j.visres.2009.11.018

Codina, C., Buckley, D., Port, M., & Pascalis, O. (2011). Deaf and hearing children: A comparison of peripheral vision development. *Developmental Science, 14*(4), 725–737. https://doi.org/10.1111/j.1467-7687.2010.01017.x.

Czamara, D., Tiesler, C. M., Kohlböck, G., Berdel, D., Hoffmann, B., Bauer, C. P., Koletzko, S., Schaaf, B., Lehmann, I., Herbarth, O., von Berg, A., Müller-Myhsok, B., Schulte-Körne, G., & Heinrich, J. (2013). Children with ADHD symptoms have a higher risk for reading, spelling and math difficulties in the GINIplus and LISAplus cohort studies. *PLoS One, 8*(5), e63859. https://doi.org/10.1371/journal.pone.0063859

Danckaerts, M., Sonuga-Barke, E. J., Banaschewski, T., Buitelaar, J., Döpfner, M., Hollis, C., Santosh, P., Rothenberger, A., Sergeant, J., Steinhausen, H.-C., Taylor, E, Zuddas, A., & Coghill, D. (2010). The quality of life of children with attention deficit/hyperactivity disorder: A systematic review. *European Child & Adolescent Psychiatry, 19*, 83–105. https://doi.org/10.1007/s00787-009-0046-3

Dunlap, G., Clarke, S., Jackson, M., Ramos, E., & Brinson, S. (1995). Self-monitoring of classroom behaviors with students exhibiting emotional and behavioral challenges. *School Psychology Quarterly, 10*, 165–177.

DuPaul, G. J., & Langberg, J. M. (2015). Educational impairments in children with ADHD. In R. Barkley (Ed.), *Attention-deficit hyperactivity disorder: A handbook for diagnosis and treatment* (4th ed., pp. 169–190). Guilford.

DuPaul, G. J., & Weyandt, L. L. (2006). School-based intervention for children with attention deficit hyperactivity disorder: Effects on academic, social, and behavioural functioning. *International Journal of Disability, Development and Education, 53*(2), 161–176.

DuPaul, G. J., Power, T. J., Anastopoulos, A. D., & Reid, R. (1998). *The ADHD Rating Scale—IV: Checklists, norms, and clinical interpretation.* Guilford.

Dye, M. W. G., & Bavelier, D. (2013). Visual attention in deaf humans: A neuroplasticity perspective. In A. Kral, R. R. Fay, & A. N. Popper (Eds.), *Springer handbook of auditory research: Deafness.* Springer.

Dye, M. W. G., & Hauser, P. C. (2014). Sustained attention, selective attention and cognitive control in deaf and hearing children. *Hearing Research, 309*, 94–102.

Edyburn, D. (2011). Harnessing the potential of technology to support the academic success of diverse students. *New Directions for Higher Education, 154*, 37–44. https://doi.org/10.1002/he.432

Feldman, H. M., & Reiff, M. I. (2014). Attention deficit-hyperactivity disorder in children & adolescents. *New England Journal of Medicine, 370*, 838–846.

Gallaudet Research Institute (GRI). (2013). *Regional and national summary report of data from the 2011–2012 Annual Survey of Deaf and*

Hard of Hearing Children and Youth. http://research.gallaudet.edu/Demographics/2012_National_Summary.pdf

Guardino, C., & Antia, S. (2012). Modifying the classroom environment to increase engagement and decrease disruption with students who are deaf or hard of hearing. *Journal of Deaf Studies and Deaf Education, 17*(3), 518–533.

Gureasko-Moore, S., DuPaul, G., & White, G. (2006). The effects of self-management in general education classrooms on the organizational skills of adolescents with ADHD. *Behavior Modification, 30*(2), 159–183.

Hallowell, E. M., & Ratey, J. J. (2017). *Delivered from distraction: Getting the most out of life with attention deficit disorder*. Random House.

Heatherton, T. F., & Wagner, D. D. (2011). Cognitive neuroscience of self-regulation failure. *Trends in Cognitive Sciences, 15*, 132–139. https://doi.org/10.1016/j.tics.2010.12.005

Hoffman, W., Schmeichel, B. J., & Baddeley, A. D. (2012). Executive functions and self-regulation. *Trends in Cognitive Sciences, 16*, 174–180. https://doi.org/10.1016/j.tics2012.01.006

Hoza, B., Mrug, S., Gerdes, A. C., Bukowski, W. M., Kraemer, H. S., Wigal, T., & Arnold, L. E. (2005). What aspects of peer relationships are impaired in children with attention deficit/hyperactivity disorder? *Journal of Consulting and Clinical Psychology, 73*, 411–423.

Individuals With Disabilities Education Improvement Act of 2004, 20 U.S.C 1400 *et seq.* (2004).

Kelly, D. P., Forney, G. P., Parker-Fisher, S. J., & Jones, M. L. (1993a). Evaluating and managing attention deficit disorder in children who are deaf or hard of hearing. *American Annals of the Deaf, 138*(4), 349–357.

Kelly, D. P., Forney, G. P., Parker-Fisher, S. J., & Jones, M. L. (1993b). The challenge of attention deficit disorder in children who are deaf or hard of hearing. *American Annals of the Deaf, 138*(4), 343–348.

Kelly, D. P., Jones, M., Moulton, N., Verhulst, S., & Bell, S. (1993). Attention deficits in children and adolescents with hearing loss: A survey. *American Annals of the Deaf, 147*(4), 737–741.

Klassen, A. F., Miller, A., & Fine, S. (2006). Agreement between parent and child report of quality of life in children with attention-deficit/

hyperactivity disorder. *Child Care Health Development, 32*, 397–406. https://doi.org/10.1111/j.1365-2214.2006.00609.x

Langberg, J. M., Epstein, J. N., Becker, S. P., Girio-Herrera, E., & Vaughn, A. J. (2012). Evaluation of the Homework, Organization, and Planning Skills (HOPS) Intervention for Middle School Students with ADHD as implemented by school mental health providers. *School Psychology Review, 41*(3), 342–364.

Leung, A. K. C., & Hon, K. L. (2016). Attention-deficit/hyperactivity disorder. *Advances in Pediatrics, 63*, 255–280.

McCabe, D. P., Roediger, H. L. III, McDaniel, M. A., Balota, D. A., & Hambrick, D. Z. (2010). The relationship between working memory capacity and executive functioning: Evidence for a common executive attention construct. *Neuropsychology, 24*(2), 222–243. doi: 10.1037/a0017619

McTighe, J., & O'Connor, K. (2009). Seven practices for effective learning. In K. Ryan and J. M. Cooper (Eds.), *Kaleidoscope: Contemporary and classic readings in education*, (pp. 174–180). Wadsworth Cengage Learning.

Mikami, A. Y. (2010). The importance of friendship for youth with attention-deficit/hyperactivity disorder. *Clinical Child and Family Psychology Review, 13*(2), 181–198. https://doi.org/10.1007/s10567-010-0067-y

Mikami, A., Ransone, M., & Calhoun, C. (2011). Influence of anxiety on the social functioning of children with and without ADHD. *Journal of Attention Disorders, 15*, 473–484. https://doi.org/10.1177/1087054710369066

Moore, K. (2009). *Effective instructional strategies: From theory to practice.* Sage.

Mrug, S., Hoza, B., & Gerdes, A. C. (2001). Children with attention-deficit/hyperactivity disorder: Peer relationships and peer-oriented interventions. In D. W. Nangle & C. A. Erdley (Eds.), *The role of friendship in psychological adjustment* (pp. 51–77). Jossey-Bass.

Mrug, S., Molina, B. G., Hoza, B., Gerdes, A. C., Hinshaw, S. P., Hechtman, L., & Arnold, L. (2012). Peer rejection and friendships in children with attention-deficit/hyperactivity disorder: Contributions to long-term outcomes. *Journal of Abnormal Child Psychology, 40,* 1013–1026.

Nass, R., & Leventhal, F. (2011). *100 Questions and answers about your child's ADHD; From pre-school to college.* Jones & Bartlett Learning.

National Institute of Mental Health. (2017). *Attention-deficit/hyperactivity disorder (ADHD).* https://www.nimh.nih.gov/health/statistics/attention-deficit-hyperactivity-disorder-adhd.shtml

Norman, N., & Jamieson, J. R. (2015). Social and emotional learning and the work of itinerant teachers of the deaf and hard of hearing. *American Annals of the Deaf, 160,* 273–288. https://doi.org/10.1353/aad.2015.0024

Normand, S., Schneider, B. H., Lee, M. D., Maisonneuve, M.-F., Chupetlovska-Anastasova, A., Kuehn, S. M., & Robaey, P. (2013). Continuities and changes in the friendships of children with and without ADHD: A longitudinal, observational study. *Journal of Abnormal Child Psychology, 41,* 1161–1175. https://doi.org/10.1007/s10802-013-9753-9

Ohan, J. L., Visser, T. A. W., Strain, M. C., & Allen, L. (2011). Teachers' and education students' perceptions of and reactions to children with and without the diagnostic label "ADHD." *Journal of School Psychology, 49*(1), 81–105. https://doi.org/10.1016/j.jsp.2010.10.001

Owens, J. S., Holdaway, A. S., Smith, J., Evans, S. W., Himawan, L. K., Coles, E. K., Girio-Herrera, E., Mixon, C. S., Egan, T. E., & Dawson, A. E. (2018). Rates of common classroom behavior management strategies and their associations with challenging student behavior in elementary school. *Journal of Emotional and Behavioral Disorders, 26*(3), 156–169.

Parasnis, I., Samar, J. V., & Berent, G. P. (2001). Evaluating ADHD in the deaf population: Challenges to validity. *NTID Research Bulletin, 6*(1), 1–5.

Pfiffner, L., Barkley, R., & DuPaul, G. (2006). Treatment of ADHD in school settings. In R. A. Barkley (Ed.), *Attention deficit hyperactivity disorder: A handbook for diagnosis and treatment,* (3rd ed., pp. 547–589). Guilford.

Rafferty, L. (2010). Step-by-step: Teaching students to self-monitor. *Teaching Exceptional Children, 43*(2), 50–58.

Reynolds, C., & Kamphaus, R. (2004). *Behavior Assessment System for Children* (2nd ed., BASC-2). American Guidance Service.

Rief, S. F. (2015). *The ADHD book of lists: A practical guide for helping children and teens with attention deficit disorders.* Jossey-Bass.

Rohatyn-Martin, N., & Hayward, D. (2016). The challenge of fatigue for students who are deaf or hard of hearing in inclusive classrooms. *International Journal of Learner Diversity and Identities, 23,* 23–31.

Ros, R., & Graziano, P. (2018). Social functioning in children with or at-risk for attention deficit/hyperactivity disorder: A meta-analytic review. *Journal of Clinical Child and Adolescent Psychology, 47,* 213–235. https://doi.org/10.1080/15374416.2016.1266644

Rose, D. H., Gravel, J. W., & Gordon, D. (2014a). Universal design for learning. In L. Florian (Ed.), *SAGE handbook of special education,* (2nd ed., pp. 475–491). SAGE. https://doi.org/10.4135/9781446282236.n30

Rose, D. H., Meyer, A., & Gordon, D. (2014b). Reflections: Universal design for learning and the common core. *The Special EDge, 27*(2), 3–5.

Rose, D. H., & Meyer, A. (2002). *Teaching every student in the digital age: Universal design for learning.* Association for Supervision and Curriculum Development.

Thomas, R., Sanders, S., Doust, J., Beller, E., & Glasziou, P. (2015). Prevalence of attention-deficit/hyperactivity disorder: A systematic review and meta-analysis. *Pediatrics, 135,* e994–e1001. https://doi.org/10.1542/peds.2014-3482

Tomlinson, C. (2014). *The differentiated classroom: Responding to the needs of all learners* (2nd ed.). ASCD.

Tomlinson, C. A. (2017). *How to differentiate instruction in academically diverse classrooms.* ASCD.

Tomlinson, C., & Moon, T. (2013). *Assessment and student success in a differentiated classroom.* ASCD.

Travell, C., & Visser, J. (2006). "ADHD does bad stuff to you": Young people's and parents' experiences and perceptions of attention deficit hyperactivity disorder (ADHD). *Emotional and Behavioural Difficulties, 11,* 205–216. https://doi.org/10.1080/13632750600833924

U.S. Department of Education, Office of Special Education and Rehabilitative Services. (2006). *Teaching with attention deficit hyperactivity disorder: Instructional strategies and practices.* http://www2. ed.gov/rschstat/research/pubs/adhd/adhd-teaching-2006.pdf

Webber, J., Scheuermann, B., McCall, C., & Coleman, M. (1993). Research on self monitoring as a behavior management technique in special education classrooms: A descriptive review. *Remedial & Special Education, 14*(2), 38–56.

Winzer, M. (2008). *Children with exceptionalities in Canadian schools.* Pearson Education Canada.

10

Cycles of Support and *Tenets of Effective Practice for Learners Who Are d/Deaf or Hard of Hearing With Disabilities*

Caroline Guardino and Joanna E. Cannon

LEARNING OBJECTIVES

Readers will:

- Recall the demographics of learners who are d/Deaf or hard of hearing (d/Dhh) with disabilities (DWD) in relation to the overall population of d/Dhh learners.
- Review a synthesis of publications and chapters that highlight the importance of collaboration among professionals and families with an open-minded, asset-based approach.
- Synthesize information at the macro- and microlevels in the *Nested Cycle of Support*, including assessment, identification, planning and placement, and instruction.
- Summarize the levels of support for learners with complex needs and how they can be nested within a cycle of best practices.
- Describe the Tenets of Effective Practice for Learners who are DWD, including Universal Design for Learning (UDL), tiered systems of supports, The Radical Middle (TRM), Vygotsky's sociocultural theory and zone of proximal development (ZPD), and collaboration.
- Review future recommendations for parents, teachers, and researchers.

DOI: 10.4324/9781003252054-10

In this era in which information is often seconds from our fingertips, professionals and families teaming with learners who are d/Deaf and hard of hearing (d/Dhh) with disabilities (DWD) need not dig for resources. Rather, this text illustrates that through collaborative efforts, information can be readily shared, providing us considerably more knowledge than in the past. The 24 authors of this text share common themes that often pose challenges for families and professionals working with students who are DWD. These inherent challenges are associated with the systematic discordance of (a) identifying appropriate standardized assessment to assist in the diagnosis of a disability, (b) federal definitions used to identify students with twice exceptionalities, and (c) determining educational placement.

Although there are numerous systematic challenges, the authors provide recommendations to overcome these struggles by suggesting strategies of effective support and instruction, through an asset-based approach. An asset-based approach focuses on the strengths of the learner, to help develop new and refined skills. Learners who are DWD are capable of growth across all developmental domains, especially when an asset-based approach is used for learning. The complex needs of learners who are DWD are not barriers but opportunities to find supports that are beneficial to "all" students, with careful attention paid to those who are DWD.

After reviewing and analyzing the nine preceding chapters, the authors synthesized the common themes and recommendations to create a *Nested Cycle of Support*. The nested cycle offers professionals a process of pedagogical best practice: (a) assessment, (b) identification, (c) planning and placement, and (d) instruction. We propose that professionals and families use the *Nested Cycle of Support* as a reminder of best practices and the levels of support necessary for many learners who are DWD to participate in their own learning. We also propose a framework, *Tenets of Effective Practice for Learners Who Are d/Deaf or Hard of Hearing With Disabilities*, which we believe should guide our work with learners who are DWD. Ultimately, through the use of these practices and beliefs, we are confident that professionals and families can be partners in advancing knowledge in the field and improving the learning outcomes for students who are DWD.

Nested Cycle of Support

Synthesizing the content across the nine chapters presented by the 23 authors in this text, along with the available literature, we discovered common themes of effective support and instruction for learners who are DWD. These themes were evident at both the macro- and microlevels of (a) assessment, (b) identification, (c), planning and placement, and (d) instruction. We contextualize these themes by presenting a *Nested Cycle of Support* (see Figure 10.1). Visually, the figure depicts support as an ongoing and leveled process, based on individualized needs. The cycle illustrates the need for continuous examination of practices at a varied level of intensity, given the complexity of the learner's disability(ies). In the following section, we discuss the macro- and microlevels of the *Nested Cycle of Support* that professionals should apply as they work with learners who are DWD and their families.

Assessment

Assessment is dynamic, perpetual, individualized, and essential. Assessment serves four major purposes for students with disabilities: (a) determining eligibility, (b) informing the development of the Individualized Education Program (IEP), (c) guiding instructional planning and implementation, and (d) evaluating the effectiveness of instruction (Nelson et al., 2022, see Chapter 6; Riggio & McLetchie, 2008; Rowland, 2009). The purposes of assessment range from the macro- to the microlevels in the *Nested Cycle of Support* (see Figure 10.1) to meet distinctive learning and achievement profiles. Across the chapters in this text, the authors recommend dynamic assessment of complex learners in multiple environments with input from a transdisciplinary team of professionals to meet the heterogeneous needs of learners who are DWD.

Assessment—Macrolevel

On a macrolevel, we assess learners to determine the presence of disabilities (e.g., specific learning disabilities [SLD], emotional–behavioral disorders [EBD], autism spectrum disorder [ASD]) in order to identify specialists

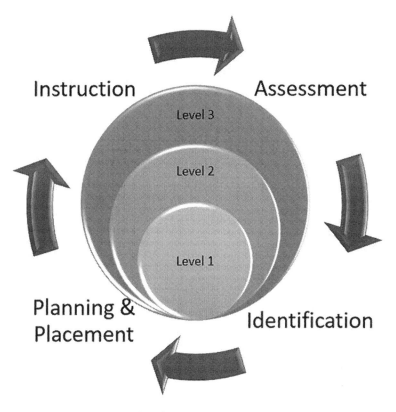

FIGURE 10.1 Nested Cycle of Support

who can meet their needs. Cognitive or educational psychologists with experience across a range of ages, languages, learning challenges, and communication modalities should administer standardized measures to examine cognitive ability and facilitate the identification and referral process for learners who are DWD (Luft, 2022, see Chapter 5; Miller et al., 2015). Standardized measures do not have norms for children who are DWD and should be used with accommodations to provide equal access to the assessment. Luft (2022, see Chapter 5) also reminds families and professionals that accommodations are not sufficient to fill linguistic or experiential gaps in completing assessment tasks. Finding professionals who are able to assess a learner with complex needs while simultaneously upholding the validity of the examination is challenging (Cawthon, 2015). One can face these challenges by utilizing regional or national resource centers, seeking expertise from members of the transdisciplinary team (which optimally includes an adult who is d/Dhh), and by accessing the resources provided throughout this text. However, results of assessment measures should be interpreted with caution because they may not differentiate between common characteristics of learners who are d/Dhh and those with other disabilities (Norman et al., 2022, see Chapter 9). The goal of assessment at the macrolevel is accurate identification to reduce overrepresentation and/or misdiagnosis of d/Dhh learners.

Assessment—Microlevel

On a microlevel, we continually use formative assessment of learners to monitor progress across developmental domains (e.g., academic, social, behavioral) to drive instruction. Assessment tools across these domains should form the basis for an IEP to document learner needs and supports, determine accommodations, as well as guide planning and placement decisions. Some of the tools and resources provided in this text include (a) developmental and ecological scales (Nelson et al., 2022, see Chapter 6); (b) functional assessments of hearing, vision, and behavior (Nelson et al., 2022, see Chapter 6); (c) arena or play-based assessments (Jackson et al., 2022, see Chapter 2); (d) dynamic assessments (Cejas et al., 2022, see Chapter 8); and (e) Functional Behavioral Assessment and Behavioral Intervention Plan (Cejas et al., 2022, see Chapter 8). Formative assessment tools should be used regularly to monitor progress. Formative assessment includes curriculum-based measures, teacher-made tests, student work samples, observations, and/or technology-based programs.

Students who are DWD are unique by virtue of their deafness (i.e., age at identification, communication modality/ies; hearing level, hearing technology), and their disability(ies). Selection of assessments and the procedures to administer them must align with the learners' style and level. Dynamic and varied assessments should be conducted at the micro- and macrolevels by a variety of professionals in collaboration with family and community service providers to achieve optimal data to guide the identification of needs and supports.

Identification

As discussed in Chapter 1 (Guardino & Cannon, 2022) and subsequent chapters through the text, determining prevalence rates is challenging across all disability areas. Consensus regarding definitions of learning disabilities (LD; Cannon et al., 2022, see Chapter 7) and attention deficit hyperactivity disorder (ADHD; Norman et al., 2022, see Chapter 9) exacerbate the lack of demographic information. Agreeing on definitions has been especially challenging among disabilities that appear to be language delays experienced by some children who are d/Dhh (e.g., ASD, LD, developmental delays [DDs]). This differential diagnosis will help determine eligibility for special education services (Borders et al., 2022, see Chapter 3) and identify potential best/evidence-based practices and instruction to support their needs.

Identification—Macrolevel

At the macrolevel, identification of hearing loss and disabilities is guided by assessment. Significant gains in technology and research have led to learners receiving supports (e.g., hearing technology, early intervention services, mobility assistance) at younger ages than ever before. However, because hearing loss in the United States and Canada is typically identified at birth, a differential diagnosis (Borders et al., 2022, see Chapter 3 for further discussion of differential diagnosis) of a disability may not be detected for a significant period of time. This is especially problematic for those children with disabilities that are more difficult to diagnose because of their overlapping characteristics with language delays (e.g., ASD, LD, DD). Assessment teams and family members must identify the domains (communication, physical, social-emotional, cognitive, and adaptive) where learners need support, and use this information to develop and update the IEP. The IEP can then be used to assist in educational planning and placement decisions for learners who are DWD.

Identification—Microlevel

At the microlevel, identification of needed supports must be utilized in the planning process to determine IEP goals, objectives, and accommodations/modifications. IEP teams must also identify the least restrictive environment

(LRE) for an individual learner. Identification of learner needs also informs the type of accommodations and modifications necessary to support the student in and outside the classroom. Progress-monitoring techniques assist in determining needs and provide the IEP team with data-driven instructional recommendations.

Planning and Placement

Planning and the subsequent educational placement of a learner who is DWD should always be approached with a child-centered and asset-based perspective, keeping a learner's strengths in mind. To combat historical challenges, placement options should be rigorously explored and challenged as necessary to ensure that an appropriate learning environment is chosen that best meets the varied needs of students who are DWD. The importance of finding an appropriate placement is echoed by Borders et al. (2017), who describe the "zipper trajectory," whereby students who are d/Dhh-ASD receive inconsistent programming and thus do not have the same academic, language, and behavioral trajectories as their peers who are d/Dhh. Luft (2022) also shares that placements for students who are d/Dhh-ID have historically underestimated the potential of these individuals. However, when professionals focus on the assets of the individual who is DWD, as well as what is best for that particular student (child-centered), placement options can be fine-tuned in order to select the environment that is most advantageous for that child.

Planning—Macrolevel

Planning at the macrolevel focuses on using comprehensive assessment techniques to identify needs and guide placement and instructional decisions. Communication plans are now mandated in many states for students who are d/Dhh and should be developed and reviewed in advance of or concurrently with the IEP to provide a systematic review of a learners' language and communication levels (Luft, 2022, see Chapter 5). Planning who will support the communication plan is crucial for students who are DWD with multiple challenges in expressive or receptive communication. Access to communication is the foundation upon which all assessment, identification, planning, and instruction take place. Utilizing the expertise of the transdisciplinary team, along with the assessment data, to develop a communication plan for all learners who are DWD is highly recommended. Ongoing planning and implementation of the student's IEP based on assessment data will lead to effective instruction.

Planning—Microlevel

Planning at the microlevel involves using the principles of Universal Design for Learning (UDL) to provide multiple means of representation, engagement, action, and expression to all learners in every unit and lesson plan (CAST, 2011; Guardino & Cannon, 2022, see Chapter 1, Table 1; Rose & Gravel, 2010). Planning with a UDL perspective provides access to information across learning styles and skill levels with an inclusive, asset-based lens. This flexible planning of instructional methods, materials, and assessments provides students with greater access to learning and professionals with more choices when evaluating learners' knowledge and skills. This type of planning addresses the learning needs of each student and can be monitored through ongoing formative assessment (Norman et al., 2022, see Chapter 9). Planning to effectively meet learners' needs includes providing learning environments and strategies that offer (a) choice, (b) quiet areas with minimal distractions, (c) structured lessons, (d) alternative lesson materials, (e) assistance with organizing materials and concepts, and (d) technology-based avenues to accessibility (Norman et al., 2022, see Chapter 9). As students progress through school, teams must also be mindful of the importance of transition planning, which should be an ongoing, person-centered process with family involvement and consideration of the individual's abilities, strengths, and preferences (Luft, 2022, see Chapter 5; Nelson et al., 2022, see Chapter 6).

Instruction

Effective assessment, identification, and planning all lead to evidence-based instruction, which is then guided by formative assessment data, thus the *Nested Cycle of Support* continues (see Figure 10.1). At the macrolevel, instruction is driven by the educational and team approaches utilized to meet students' needs. A variety of approaches have been described throughout the chapters of this text, including transdisciplinary and interdisciplinary.

Instruction—Macrolevel

At the macrolevel of instruction, the transdisciplinary approach is an indirect evidence-based service model that involves professionals sharing roles and knowledge across disciplines (Jackson et al., 2022, see Chapter 2). This approach has many advantages including (a) high levels of collaboration and interaction among the team members, (b) reduced fragmentation and duplication of services, (c) increased communication and service efficiency, (d) use of "planned role release" to exchange knowledge and skills across disciplines and team members in complementary ways, and (e) maximizing the familiarity of professionals working with both the child and the family (Carpenter, 2005; Cole et al., 2011; Giangreco et al., 2000; Jackson et al., 2021, see Chapter 2; King et al., 2009; Moeller et al., 2013; Pletcher, 2012; Pletcher & Younggren, 2013).

In contrast, the interdisciplinary approach consists of professionals making decisions by consensus, with individual service providers interacting directly with the child and the family (Borders et al., 2022, see Chapter 3; Cloninger, 2004). This approach may be necessary in certain districts, particularly in rural areas with minimal allocation of resources and services. Use of video conferencing and other technology can be used to assist in collaboration, and may provide the most accessible approach possible for families with learners who are DWD.

Instruction—Microlevel

At the microlevel, the use of a UDL perspective when planning instruction increases learners' engagement and aids in the uptake of concepts during a lesson. In a general education classroom, inclusive practices should be utilized to ensure that the student is meaningfully participating in all activities across the curriculum, as well as social opportunities throughout the school. Aligned with UDL and formative assessment techniques, differentiated instruction focuses on flexibility and engagement in all lessons. The principles of the differentiated instruction approach are based on choice in context, process, product, and learning environment (Norman et al., 2022, see Chapter 9). These techniques, as well as explicit evidence-based instruction, should be used with all learners, yet are essential for students who are DWD. The level to which we implement these techniques in order to maximize time and capacity depends on the learner.

Nested Levels of Support

The cycle of assessment, identification, planning and placement, and instruction provides a model of effective practice for all learners, especially those who are DWD. Learners who are DWD may need the *Nested Cycle of Support* across social, emotional, behavioral, and cognitive domains. Figure 10.1 provides a visual depiction of a systemic cycle of best practices for effective instruction at both macro- and microlevels. The nested levels of support housed within the center of the cycle are based on the tiered levels of the Response to Intervention (RTI) and Multitiered System of Supports (MTSS) frameworks, offering less support at the "core" (i.e., Level 1), more support at Level 2, and the most support at Level 3 (Guardino & Cannon, 2022, see Chapter 1). The level of intensity is in grayscale, which can also be seen within the framework presented in the next section. Children and adolescents may move back and forth among the levels as they require more— or less—support across domains and stages of development. The *Nested Cycle of Support* should be utilized within the framework of the *Tenets of Effective Practice for Learners who are d/Deaf or Hard of Hearing With Disabilities*, as it encompasses the complexity of learners who are DWD and provides a visual representation of the theory and practices necessary to meet their needs.

A Framework for Working With Learners Who Are DWD

After a careful analysis of the literature on deafness and diversity, across several decades, in addition to an intense year of processing, synthesizing, and reviewing these chapters, we propose a framework to support the practice of professionals and families working with learners who are DWD. The framework of the *Tenets of Effective Practice for Learners Who Are d/Deaf or Hard of Hearing With Disabilities* is illustrated in Figure 10.2.

This framework is based on the underpinnings of Vygotsky's sociocultural theory in relation to UDL and the leveled tiers of support that professionals and families provide (Vygotsky, 1978). The pillars of the framework include: (a) methods of collaboration, (b) an asset-based approach, (c) scaffolding instruction using the zone of proximal development (ZPD),

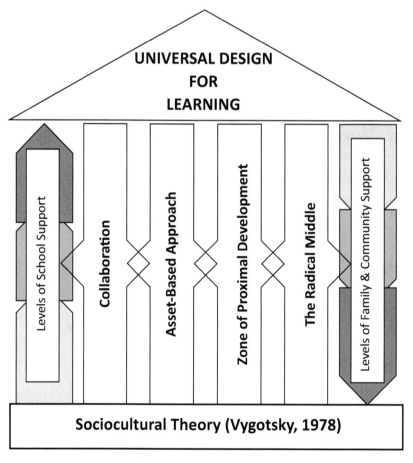

Figure 10.2   *Tenets of Effective Practice for Learners Who Are d/Deaf or Hard of Hearing With Disabilities*

and (d) The Radical Middle (TRM) perspective. The walls of the framework are represented by grayscale levels. These walls are the family, school, and community implementing the *Nested Cycle of Support* based upon the individual's needs. The framework is symbolic of a house, illustrating the importance of a strong foundation grounded in the sociocultural theory and protected by the "roof" or principles of UDL.

The Foundation

The sociocultural theory lays the foundation that learners who are DWD benefit from natural social interaction and the experiences of a more knowledgeable other to learn social and behavioral cultural norms. Professionals, families, and peers influence learners' cognitive growth as they engage in events and activities that help build the learners' background knowledge in conjunction with cultural beliefs and practices. Jackson et al. (2022, see Chapter 2) emphasize the importance of professionals developing cultural competence in order to understand the family and the learner from their native and natural perspective. The authors suggest the importance of d/Dhh role models and cultural brokers as team members to bridge cultural gaps and aid in communication. Nelson et al. (2022, see Chapter 6) reassert the need for culturally responsive assessment and practice when working with learners who are deafblind. The framework illustrates the need to ground practice on the principles of the sociocultural theory in order to provide learners who are DWD with opportunities to increase social interaction and, therefore, their view of the world.

The Roof

UDL is the roof that ensures that "all" individuals are provided the opportunity to thrive in environments that are accessible and equipped to meet diverse learning needs. Guardino and Cannon (2022, see Chapter 1) describe how UDL promotes instruction that accounts for diverse learning styles and levels, essential when working with learners who are DWD. Implementation of UDL concepts result in a supportive, accessible environment that encourages participation and engagement through differentiated instruction. Norman et al. (2022, see Chapter 9) describe the importance of UDL for learners who are d/Dhh-ADHD. These learners, like many learners who are DWD, need explicit, thoughtful, and flexible instruction with multiple opportunities for engagement, representation, and expression (Rose & Gravel, 2010). Professionals who use UDL principles in their practice, proactively provide safety supports needed for learners who are DWD to thrive across settings.

The Pillars

Within the framework, UDL and the sociocultural theory are upheld by The *Tenets of Effective Practice*: (a) collaboration, (b) asset-based approach, (c) ZPD, and (d) TRM. The level at which collaboration and ZPD are applied depends on the learners and their families, as previously described through the *Nested Cycle of Support*. Finally, the framework illustrates how the family, school, and community collaboratively work together to support the learner; they are the protective walls ensuring that the tenets are upheld through a leveled support system.

THE TENETS OF EFFECTIVE PRACTICE

The framework, namely, *Tenets of Effective Practice for Learners Who Are d/ Deaf or Hard of Hearing With Disabilities*, houses four pillars (collaboration, asset-based approach, ZPD, and TRM) that serve as tenets for effective practice when working with learners who are DWD and their families. The strongest and most effective practice occurs when these four tenets are simultaneously enacted, supporting one another and equally distributing the increased responsibilities that these complex learners may bring to the home, school, and community environments. The following section synthesizes how these tenets are discussed by various authors throughout the nine chapters, thus serving as recommendations for families, teachers, and researchers.

Collaboration

Of utmost importance is the need for collaboration, to every extent possible, among members from the school, home, and community. Collaboration is critical across professionals and disciplines in education, speech and language pathology, audiology, occupational therapy, social work, school counseling, psychology, orientation and mobility therapy, adaptive physical education, assistive technology, as well as others serving students who are DWD. In this text, every author discusses the need for at least one type of collaboration, either face to face or virtual: telepractice (Jackson et al., 2022, Chapter 2), transdisciplinary (Jackson et al., 2022, Chapter 2; Borders et al., 2022, Chapter 3), multidisciplinary (Luft, 2022, Chapter 5), interdisciplinary (Borders et al., 2022, Chapter 3), interprofessional teams (Bruce et al., 2022, Chapter 4; Nelson et al., 2022, Chapter 6), online forums (Norman et al., 2022, Chapter 9), and active membership in organizations (Cejas et al., 2022, Chapter 8).

Collaboration is critical because it provides a platform for professionals and parents to share their expertise with one another, in the best interests of the learner who is DWD. Although collaboration takes place in many forms, it is most successful when professionals are open minded and respect the differences among team members, including family members and the DWD learner. This open-minded perspective is well defined by TRM and asset-based approaches.

The Radical Middle and Asset-Based Approach

While TRM and an asset-based approach are the pillars of effective practice, they may also be considered a lens through which to view and implement our collaborative work with families and learners who are DWD. TRM perspective respects the spectrum of beliefs and practices shared across professionals with varying expertise and families from diverse backgrounds. Professionals that practice TRM approach are willing to try anything that may help the learner grow academically, social-emotionally, and behaviorally. TRM supports a balanced perspective whereby professionals and parents can discuss the spectrum of options without the fear of criticism or failure. The goal of TRM is as follows:

> To encourage scholars who are representative of a wide range of educational, cultural, and linguistic philosophies to learn and work together through research and collaborative scholarship, holding a common goal of doing what is best educationally, culturally, and linguistically for each deaf and hard of hearing child and his or her family. (TRM, http://radicalmiddledhh.org/mission-and-goals/)

Therefore, once the tenets of collaboration through TRM perspective are achieved, professionals and parents can agree upon strategies that focus on the learner's strengths, as realized through an asset-based approach.

An asset-based approach offers parents and professionals the opportunity to focus on what a child is able to do, in order to develop and build new skills and knowledge. By using the learner's assets to guide practice, we are able to maximize their learning potential through scaffolded instruction, as described by Vygotsky's ZPD. ZPD helps professionals identify the learner's developmental level in comparison to their level of potential. Professionals use the learner's ZPD to increase academic, social, cognitive, and behavioral outcomes. In Chapter 1, Guardino and Cannon (2022) discuss how professionals and parents can utilize an asset-based approach and ZPD to scaffold learning to foster positive and continual growth (Vygotsky, 1978).

The *Tenets of Effective Practice for Learners Who Are d/Deaf or Hard of Hearing With Disabilities* framework contains the four critical components of collaboration, asset-based approach, ZPD, and TRM. When working in unison, these tenets serve as structural pillars that support learners and their families. These tenets work in tandem with the *Nested Cycle of Support*, offering the learner and the family flexibility in how needs are met across domains. Most importantly, these tenets must be rooted in the sociocultural theory to ensure that the learners are presented with authentic experiences within their environment to increase knowledge and skills, mindful of culture and diversity. The authors encourage professionals and caregivers to use the framework in understanding the macrolevel of theory, research, and practice and how it relates to learners who are DWD. In addition, we suggest considering the framework as a guide to the following recommendations for practice and research.

Recommendations for Practitioners and Parents

Recommendations for parents and practitioners include: (a) engaging in continuous communication and collaboration with one another (e.g., practitioners, parent peers, community service providers); (b) understanding how regulations and policy may differ across states and countries; (c) realizing that learners who are DWD are not d/Dhh "plus" a disability; (d) participating in ongoing training and participation in information-sharing venues; and (e) using technology as a tool to propel our field forward when working with students who are DWD. Because collaboration has been discussed in detail above, the latter four recommendations are presented in detail below.

Parents and practitioners need to be aware that policies differ across states, complicating the assessment, identification, placement, and graduation processes. In Chapter 2, the authors discuss how the Individuals With Disabilities Education Act (IDEA) allows states to determine whether or not to offer early intervention and special education services to infants and toddlers who exhibit characteristics of a DD (IDEA, 2015; Jackson et al., 2022). Because states are not required to provide these services, children who are at risk of a DD may miss the services necessary to mitigate the risk factors associated with DD. Luft (2022, see Chapter 5) also describes inconsistencies with graduation requirements, as defined by varying state laws. For example, only 19 states have alternative assessments that replace the traditional standardized test required to graduate. Cannon et al. (2022, see Chapter 7) describe the challenges of identifying a student who is d/Dhh with an LD. Identification cannot occur without a consensus on the definition, since learners with sensory disabilities are excluded from the IDEA criteria. Parents and professionals must be aware of these legal nuances when making educational decisions and planning future trajectories for children and students who are DWD.

Students who are DWD are not merely d/Dhh or their disability eligibility category. Rather, their combined identities create a unique learner with the possible need for specialized assessment, identification, planning, and instruction. Nelson et al. (2022, see Chapter 6) assert that "deafblindness" is a singular term because the conditions of hearing loss and blindness constitute a new eligibility category, not merely a merger of two conditions that can be addressed separately. The *Nested Cycle of Support* allows professionals and parents to evaluate the needs of the learner and build instructional practices based upon those needs. The evaluation process should include multiple perspectives from professionals who specialize in the combined eligibility areas, or at a minimum, representation from professionals who specialize in each area. By doing so, the team can ensure a holistic approach to planning well-rounded services.

Professionals and parents need to participate in training and information-sharing venues essential to personal and professional growth. The authors of each chapter provide a list of resources to explore and further one's education. These resources include professional organizations, forums, webinars, and online training modules in which parents and practitioners can engage in discourse with experts who specialize in varying disability areas. While there are few professionals who specialize in learners who are DWD, collaboration among professionals offers greater insight than if we stand on our own respective islands of knowledge.

The final recommendation is to use technology, as it is a powerful tool that can help unite us when working with students who are DWD. Technology has shaped our ability to implement UDL and RTI/MTSS, in addition to reaching families in remote areas through telepractice. Guardino and Cannon (2022, see Chapter 1) suggest the use of technology to make learning environments more accessible. For example, students who are deafblind may benefit from braille watches, braillewriters, refreshable braille display, braille printers, and notetakers (Nelson et al., 2022, see Chapter 6). Practitioners and parents working with students who are d/Dhh with emotional behavior challenges may benefit from using applications that help track behaviors and emotions. These applications can be used to monitor behavior trends on a daily, weekly, or a longer time period (Cejas et al., 2022, see Chapter 8). Technology can help professionals reach families in remote areas who ordinarily would not have access to services because of the potential barriers of distance, time, and money. Jackson et al. (2022, see Chapter 2) describe how telepractice can be implemented with families who have young children who are at risk of a DD. Telepractice allows the professional to mentor and guide parents using a webcam, alleviating the time and money typically needed for travel to a family's home or professionals' office. Although technology can be intimidating, teaming with those familiar with different platforms and software programs is essential to knowledge mobilization and sharing.

Recommendations for Researchers/Scholars

As a field, in order to propel our understanding of learners who are DWD, researchers must collectively contribute to the body of research. To date, the research on the DWD population is scarce, making it difficult to bridge the existing gap between research and practice. Researchers typically have concerns about including students who are DWD in their study because they are considered outliers and can skew the research results. Researchers may also be concerned that they are not informing the field of what the general population of d/Dhh learners are capable of accomplishing if they include learners who are DWD as participants in their studies. We suggest including these learners in every study possible and analyzing the data to learn how a strategy can impact d/Dhh learners with and without disabilities.

Additional research is needed across the diverse spectrum of students who are DWD to close the gaps in the existing literature base. Scholars should begin by examining the recommended strategies set forth by the authors of this text. Researchers can test these strategies across learners with the same disability, as well as those with disabilities that share similar characteristics (e.g., ID and LD; ADHD and EBD). Research methodologies that most easily support studies of students who are DWD include case studies and single-case design (Guardino & Cannon, 2016). Both of these research methods allow scholars to examine the whole learner from multiple perspectives, including those who are DWD themselves, across long or short periods of time.

Over the past two decades, only three publications exist that focus on students who are d/Dhh with giftedness (Belcastro, 2004; Coyne, et al., under review; Lupart and Toy, 2009). Little can be understood about learners who are d/Dhh and gifted given the lack of current evidence and information to guide recommendations. Essentially, this is an unexplored area. Researchers should study these learners to better understand their demographics (e.g., gender, communication modality, amplification used), assessment, identification, placement, planning, and instruction practices currently being implemented with these learners.

CONCLUSION

As a community of professionals and parents, we now have resources and tools needed to better work with learners who are DWD. In the past, collective bodies of information were scarce, as well as far and few between. We understood these learners on a surface level. This is no longer the case. The editors and authors of this text have provided the field with a framework, the *Tenets of Effective Practice for Learners Who Are d/Deaf or Hard of Hearing With Disabilities*, to guide our work. The *Nested Cycle of Support* defines a leveled systematic method for addressing the complexities of assessment, identification, planning, and instruction. We encourage the use of this framework and cycle of support when addressing the ongoing challenges that professionals and families encounter when working with these learners. The academic, social-emotional, and behavioral outlook for learners who are DWD is positive. This text provides the field with resources and recommendations that can only serve to advance our learning and their developmental outcomes. We are now armed to be proactive and make informed decisions that can impact the potential and future for learners who are DWD.

DISCUSSION QUESTIONS

1. What is the goal of assessment at the macrolevel? How does this differ from the microlevel?
2. Identify the five domains that assessment teams should utilize when drafting and updating IEPs for students who are DWD. Explain why these domains are important.
3. What are the consequences associated with not placing a student in their least restrictive environment (LRE)?
4. Describe the advantages of using a transdisciplinary approach with students who are DWD.
5. Why should professionals use the *Nested Cycle of Support* in their practice with students who are DWD?
6. Describe each of the *Tenets of Effective Practice for Learners Who Are d/ Deaf or Hard of Hearing With Disabilities* and provide an example of how and why it should be implemented when working with learners who are DWD and their families?

RESOURCES

- **Positive Behavioral Interventions & Supports MTSS**
  o https://www.pbis.org/pbis/tiered-framework

- **Simple Psychology and Vygotsky**
  - https://www.simplypsychology.org/vygotsky.html
- **The Radical Middle Project**
  - https://radicalmiddledhh.org/
- **Universal Design for Learning Guidelines**
  - http://www.cast.org/
- **WestEd's Zone of Proximal Development Research and Resources**
  - https://www.wested.org/resources/zone-of-proximal-development/#

References

Belcastro, F. P. (2004). Rural gifted students who are deaf or hard of hearing: How electronic technology can help. *American Annals of the Deaf, 149*(4), 309–313. https://doi.org/10.1353/aad.2005.0001

Borders, C. M., Bock, S. J., Probst, K., & Kroesch, A. (2017). Deaf/hard of hearing students with disabilities. In S. Lenihan (Ed.), *Preparing to teach, committing to learn: An introduction to educating children who are deaf/hard of hearing.* National Center for Hearing Assessment and Management, Utah State University. http://www.infanthearing.org/ebook-educating-children-dhh/index.html

Borders, C. M., Probst, K. M., & Bock, S. J. (2022). Learners who are Deaf or hard of hearing with autism spectrum disorders. In C. Guardino, J.E. Cannon, & P.V. Paul (Eds.), *Deaf and hard of hearing learners with disabilities: Foundations, strategies, and resources* (pp. 63–95). Routledge.

Bruce, S. M., Nelson, C., & Stutzman, B. (2022). Understanding the needs of children who are d/Deaf or hard of hearing with disabilities due to genetic causes. In C. Guardino, J. E. Cannon, & P. V. Paul (Eds.), *Deaf and hard of hearing learners with disabilities: Foundations, strategies, and resources* (pp. 96–132). Routledge.

Cannon, J. E., Guardino, C., Clements, A., & Cawthon, S. W. (2022). Learners who are d/Deaf or hard of hearing with a learning disability. In C. Guardino, J. E. Cannon, & P. V. Paul (Eds.), *Deaf and hard of hearing learners with disabilities: Foundations, strategies, and resources* (pp. 193–229). Routledge.

Carpenter, B. (2005). Early childhood intervention: Possibilities and prospects for professionals, families, and children. *British Journal of Special Education, 32*(4), 176–183.

Cawthon, S. W. (2015). From the margins to the spotlight: Diverse deaf and hard of hearing student populations and standardized assessment accessibility. *American Annals of the Deaf, 160,* 385–394.

Cejas, I., Sarangoulis, C. M., Mestres, A., Nelson, J. A., & Quittner, A. L. (2022). Assessment and intervention for learners who are d/Deaf or hard of hearing with emotional and behavioral challenges. In C. Guardino, J. E. Cannon, & P. V. Paul (Eds.), *Deaf and hard of hearing learners with disabilities: Foundations, strategies, and resources* (pp. 230–261). Routledge.

Center for Applied Special Technology (CAST). (2011). *Universal design for learning (UDL) guidelines: Version 2.0.* CAST.

Cloninger, C. J. (2004). Designing collaborative educational services. In F. P. Orelove, D. Sobsey, & R. K. Silberman (Eds.), *Educating children with multiple disabilities: A collaborative approach* (4th ed., pp. 1–29). Brookes.

Cole, P., Oser, C., & Walsh, S. (2011). Building on the foundations of Part C legislation: Beginning the conversation for reauthorization. *Zero to Three, 31*(4), 52–60.

Coyne, J., Catalano, J., & Guardino, C. (under review). Learners who are deaf and hard of hearing and gifted: A review of the literature.

Giangreco, M. F., Prelock, P. A., Reid, R. R., Dennis, R. E., & Edleman, S. W. (2000). Role of related service personnel in inclusive schools. In R. A. Villa & J. S. Thousand (Eds.), *Restructuring for caring and effective education: Piecing the puzzle together* (2nd ed., pp. 360–388). Brookes.

Guardino, C., & Cannon, J. E. (Eds.). (2016). Deafness and diversity: Reflections and directions [Special issue]. *American Annals of the Deaf, 161*(1), 104–112.

Guardino, C., & Cannon, J. E. (2022). Approaches and frameworks that support students who are d/Deaf or hard of hearing with a disabilities. In C. Guardino, J. E. Cannon, & P. V. Paul (Eds.), *Deaf and hard of hearing learners with disabilities: Foundations, strategies, and resources* (pp. 1–24). Routledge.

Individuals With Disabilities Education Act (IDEA) of 2004, 20 U.S.C. §§ 1400–1482 (2004 & rev. 2015).

Jackson, R. L. W., Ammerman, S. B., & Trautwein, B. A. (2022). Infants and toddlers who are d/Deaf or hard of hearing with a developmental delay or are at risk for developmental delays. In C. Guardino, J. E. Cannon, & P. V. Paul (Eds.), *Deaf and hard of hearing learners with disabilities: Foundations, strategies, and resources* (pp. 25–62). Routledge.

King, G., Strachan, D., Tucker, M., Duwyn, B., Desserud, S., & Shillington, M. (2009). The application of a transdisciplinary model for early intervention services. *Infants & Young Children, 22*(3), 211–223.

Luft, P. (2022). Deaf and hard of hearing learners with intellectual disabilities: Current understandings and remaining challenges. In C. Guardino, J. E. Cannon, & P. V. Paul (Eds.), *Deaf and hard of hearing learners with disabilities: Foundations, strategies, and resources* (pp. 133–161). Routledge.

Lupart, J. L., & Toy, R. E. (2009). Twice exceptional: Multiple pathways to success. In Shavinina, L. V. (Ed.), *International handbook on giftedness* (pp. 507–525). Springer, Dordrecht. https://doi.org/10.1007/978-1-4020-6162-2_23

Miller, M. S., Thomas-Presswood, T. N., Metz, K., & Lukomski, J. (2015). *Psychological and psychoeducational assessment of deaf and hard of hearing children and adolescents*. Gallaudet University Press.

Moeller, M. P., Carr, G., Seaver, L., Stredler-Brown, A., & Holzinger, D. (2013). Best practices in family-centered early intervention for children who are deaf or hard of hearing: An international consensus statement. *Journal of Deaf Studies and Deaf Education, 18*(4), 429–445. https://doi.org/10.1093/deafed/ent034

Nelson, C., Bruce, S. M., & Barnhill, B. A. (2022). Future directions in the field of deafblindness. In C. Guardino, J. E. Cannon, & P. V. Paul (Eds.), *Deaf and hard of hearing learners with disabilities: Foundations, strategies, and resources* (pp. 162–192). Routledge.

Norman, N., Rohatyn-Martin, N., & Luckner, J. (2022). Supporting students who are Deaf and hard of hearing and have attention deficit hyperactivity disorder: Strategies for success. In C. Guardino, J. E. Cannon, & P. V. Paul (Eds.), *Deaf and hard of hearing learners with disabilities: Foundations, strategies, and resources* (pp. 262–287). Routledge.

Pletcher, L. (2012). *The transdisciplinary team approach* [Presentation]. Family Infants Toddler (FIT) Program annual meeting. University of New Mexico's Center for Development and Disability, Albuquerque, NM.

Pletcher, L., & Younggren, N. (2013). *The early intervention workbook: Essential practices for quality services.* Brookes.

Riggio, M., & McLetchie, B. (2008). Assessment. In M. Riggio & B. McLetchie (Eds.), *Deafblindness: Educational service guidelines.* (pp. 35–45). Perkins School for the Blind.

Rose, D. H., & Gravel, J. W. (2010). Universal design for learning. In E. Baker, P. Peterson, & B. McGaw (Eds.), *International encyclopedia of education* (3rd ed., pp. 119–124). Elsevier. http://www.udlcenter.org/resource_library/articles/udl

Rowland, C. (2009). *Assessing communication and learning in young children who are deafblind or have multiple disabilities.* http://www.design-tolearn.com/uploaded/pdf/DeafBlindAssessmentGuide.pdf

Vygotsky, L. S. (1978). *Mind in society: The development of higher psychological processes.* Harvard University Press.

Index

Note: Page numbers in *italics* indicates figures and page numbers in **bold** indicates tables.

behavioral intervention plans (BIPs) 245
Behavior Assessment System for
     Children (BASC-2) 264
*Best Practices in Family-Centered Early
     Intervention for Children Who Are
     Deaf or Hard of Hearing* (Moeller
     et al.) 42
biases and asset-based approaches 7–8, 19
Blackorby, J. 4
blindness *see* deafblindness (DB); vision
     issues
Bock, Stacey Jones 63
Borders, Christy M. 63, 68, 82, 294
Bowen, S. K. 17
braille 118, 180, 304
breathing exercises 246, 277
Brown, D. 110
Bruce, Susan 96, 112, 162

Callier Azusa G Scale 171
Cannon, Joanna E. 1, 5, 64, 193, 288,
     299, 302–304
CARS (Childhood Autism Rating Scale)
     66–67
Carter, K. 43
causes of deafblindness 163–164
causes of deafness 136–137
Cawthon, Stephanie W. 193, 239
CBT (cognitive behavioral therapy) 247
CD (conduct disorder) 235–236, 245
CEEDAR (Collaboration for Effective
     Educator, Development,
     Accountability, and Reform
     Center) 180
Cejas, Ivette 230
cell phones 148, 180
Centers for Disease Control and
     Prevention (CDC) 64
CHARGE syndrome: and deafblindness
     163; educational implications
     of 112–113; overview 108–109;

physical and medical implications
     of 110–111; resources for
     122–123; sensory implications
     of 109–110; social-emotional
     implications of 111–112
Charting the LifeCourse™ 83
Child Behavior Checklist (CBCL) 264
child-centered perspectives 142, 294
child-guided approaches 175
Childhood Autism Rating Scale (CARS)
     66, 67
classroom observation assessments 203
classroom placements *see* placement
     considerations
Clements, Amanda 193
CLS (Cornelia de Lange syndrome)
     100, 119
CMV (cytomegalovirus) 136, 164
cochlear implants (CI) 109, 114, 231,
     234–235, 237
cognitive behavioral interventions **72**,
     247
cognitive behavioral therapy (CBT) 247
collaboration 301; *see also* teams of
     professionals
Collaboration for Effective Educator,
     Development, Accountability, and
     Reform Center (CEEDAR) 180
Commission for the Blind 118
communication: and autism 67–71;
     and CHARGE syndrome 109,
     112; and deafblindness 164, 166,
     168, 170–171, 175–179; and
     developmental delays 32, **33–34**;
     and Down syndrome 106; and
     intellectual disabilities 134–141,
     135, 144, *146–147*; promotion of
     42; and role models and mentors
     in d/Dhh community 46, 299; and
     Usher syndrome 115–118
Communication Matrix 171

premature infants 30, 163
prevalence, defined 97
Prickett, H. T. 5
primary provider model 43–44
privacy 49
Probst, Kristi M. 63
prompting **77**, 176
protactile ASL 178–179
PRT (Pivotal Response Training) **76**
psychosocial health 267–268

Quittner, Alexandra L. 230

Radical Middle (TRM) approach, The
    7–8, 301–302
recommendations: for practitioners
    and parents 219, 302–304; for
    researchers/scholars 304–305
*Recommended Practices in Early
    Intervention/Early Childhood Special
    Education* (Division for Early
    Childhood) 43
redirection **77**
rehabilitation counselors for the deaf 143
reinforcement **72**, **77**, 177
research recommendations 304–305
residential schools 142, 172
response/interruption redirection **77**
response to intervention (RTI) 16–18,
    297
Rh incompatibility 136
Rief, S. F. 276
Rohatyn-Martin, Natalia 262
role models 46, 118, 299
role release 43, 296
Ros, R. 267
RTI (response to intervention) 16–18,
    297

Sarangoulis, Christina 230
Sauerburger, D. 115
scaffolding learning 8, 12, 15–16, 302

Scheeringa, M. S. 247
screen readers 180
scripting **77**
SLDs (specific learning disabilities)
    194–195, **197**, 202–205
seating arrangements 179–180, 245,
    247
secondary disabilities 3–4, 198–199
SEELS (Special Education Elementary
    Longitudinal Study) 3
self-awareness **274**, 276
self-determination 140, 181
self-esteem 267–268
self-management **78**
self-regulation 265–266
service delivery options and settings
    47–49
Shield, A. 68
Shroyer, E. H. 5
sign language: and assessment strategies
    203–204, 239; tactile 116,
    178–179; and vision limitations
    115–116
Silberman, R. 164
Simpson, K. L. 114
smartphones 148, 180
social connectedness 164–165, 298–299
social-emotional implications: and
    ADHD 267–268, 273–277,
    274–275; and autism 70; and
    CHARGE syndrome 111–112;
    and deafblindness 168; and
    developmental delays 37; and
    Down syndrome 106; and
    intellectual disabilities 139; and
    Usher syndrome 116–117
social narratives **78**
social skills training **79**
sociocultural theory (Vygotsky) 8,
    298–299, 302
Special Education Elementary
    Longitudinal Study (SEELS) 3

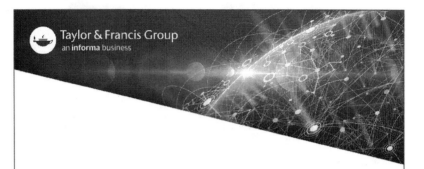